P9-AOP-341

THE FIVE MYTHS

OF TELEVISION

POWER

OR

WHY THE MEDIUM
IS NOT THE MESSAGE

DOUGLAS DAVIS

SIMON & SCHUSTER

New York London Toronto Sydney Tokyo Singapore

SIMON & SCHUSTER
Simon & Schuster Building
Rockefeller Center
1230 Avenue of the Americas
New York, New York 10020

Designed by Hyun Joo Kim
Manufactured in the United States of America

10 9 8 7 6 5 4 3 2 1

Library of Congress Cataloging-in-Publication Data
Davis, Douglas
    The five myths of television power, or, Why the medium is
not the message / Douglas Davis.
        p.   cm.
    Includes bibliographical references (p.   ) and index.
        1. Television broadcasting—Social aspects. 2. Television
broadcasting—Political aspects. 3. Technology and
civilization.   I. Title.   II. Title: Why the medium is not the
message.   III. Title: 5 myths of television power.
    PN1992.6.D38   1993
    302.23'45—dc20   92-43243
    ISBN 0-671-73963-8   CIP

ACKNOWLEDGMENTS

When driving from the ocean to the city the other night, I asked myself if I could possibly list here all the people and the teachings that made this book possible. *No,* my inner voice said, *it is impossible.* Well, let me dare my voice by beginning with Jane Bell, who has posed as my wife for some years. But in fact she is my editor and my intellectual guide as well as an example of someone who never gives in to adversity of any kind. Eugene M. Schwartz is another guide, with similar virtues. My recent students at Columbia University, UCLA, and Art-Center College never gave in, either to me or to the fat-bellied God I try here to slim down. Certainly I owe more than I ever thought before to both Rousseau and Pope, unlikely bedfellows. On several occasions I have been able to work and achieve in the shadow of the God's belly, that is, inside television, thanks to men and women like William R. Moll, Mary Perot Nichols, and their rare, exceptional counterparts at PBS, C-Span, ABC, German television, Austrian television, All-Russian TV, and Estonian TV. Several editors at the *New York Times* encouraged me to pursue this thesis in days when it was quite lonely, as did colleagues at *Newsweek* in an earlier era. Jerelle Kraus and Horacio Cardo lent dynamism and grace to the *Times* Op Ed page that announced the myths. Rafael Sagalyn, Jim Silberman, and Dominick Anfuso gave the idea book form. Amy Finkel was one of several research interns from Cooper Union who supplied vital truths. The Rockefeller Foundation supplied vital funds for travel. Merrill Brown, Helen Fisher, and Sandra Ball-Rokeach read the manuscript and inspired me. Charlotte Victoria inspired me. I could go on and on. *No, you can't.* Inner voice, you are right. Again.

New York, October 1992

To C.V. and her sisters

Me-di-um . . . n., pl.-dia . . . -diums for 1–10, adj.-n. 1. middle state or condition, mean. 2. something intermediate in degree. 3. an intervening substance, as air, through which a force acts or an effect is produced. 4. element that is the natural habitat of an organism . . . 6. an agency or instrument of something specified: a communications medium. 7. Biol. substance where specimens are displayed or preserved. 8. also called culture medium . . . 9. Fine Arts, a. painting. a liquid in which pigments are mixed. b. the material or technique with which an artist works. . . .

—CIE Dictionary

CONTENTS

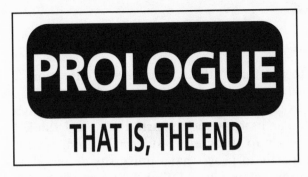

PROLOGUE
THAT IS, THE END

It is important to say right away that I love television, sometimes. No one can change, effectively, a medium he despises. I despise only our perception of this medium, not the thing itself, which we have yet to discover.

I wrote this book to revise that perception. Unless we revise our expectations, none of the extraordinary technological changes now occurring, which make it possible for virtually any of us to send or receive any form of video message, enshrining the dream of the French revolution (to let every man *publish*), will transform "TV."

Yes, I love this thing that I also hate. Both passions date back to my childhood. I grew up in the midst of a family in Washington, D.C., that resisted television longer than anyone else I knew. The TV set came into my sphere of consciousness without endorsement or preconception. As soon as it arrived, I fell in love with Aletha Agee, the late-afternoon hostess of our local news-and-music show. She blew kisses to the viewer. I raced home after school almost every day, for a few months, to receive them. I sent more than a few back to her. At roughly the same time, I also discovered I could watch my local baseball heroes (the Washington Senators, perpetual losers) during the evening.

If Aletha and the Senators lured me inside the set, Luigi Pirandello changed my life. One night, when the Senators were rained out in the second inning, I switched the dial to find a live performance of *Six Characters in Search of an Author* on CBS. Despite myself, I could not turn it off. The next day, I went to the library to find out who Pirandello was.

It occurred to me that without a university education, I might not be able to pursue him, or his six characters.

Here, too, as in the case of the television set, my family's naivete, as well as its resistance, spurred me on. I think I decided very early to study every subject I could. I must have done so partly to prove that a university deserved its hard-earned dollars (my late father had attended one, briefly). But no sage uncle or aunt warned me, then, to take on an academic specialty. Left alone, I gorged on everything, on the arts, on history, on political science, on media theory, as well as on Pirandello. I embraced each with equal respect, if not adoration. The gravity with which I approached "television" is grounded in this innocence, you see. It wasn't until years later that colleagues explained that my early experience of *Six Characters* had been fatally compromised by the vulgar "medium" through which it came. As my Renaissance appetite disqualified me in other ways.

These truths came too late. The American intellectual's certainty that television is not a legitimate subject of analysis either as an art or as a science remains a wonder to me to this day. This prohibition trailed into my life after years of viewing, thinking, and conversing, mostly with myself. The Kennedy-Nixon debates were a singularly fruitful moment. I remember thinking the fate of the nation was resolving itself before my eyes. The debates seemed dense with *content* to me. I noticed that my cantankerous friends and family argued primarily about the policies advocated by each man, not about Kennedy's superior physique, which was a given before the debate. It was too late, again, when McLuhan and others decided the audience had ignored these differences, or when, even later, the essays of Stanley Cavell about television, which I warmly welcomed, were equally compromised, by their subject. What had seemed to me alive, as a child, infinite with possibility, was closed off in the following decades as a serious subject for debate, for discourse, and even for journalism, at a certain level.

While American society dismissed television on one level of discourse, it elevated the medium on another level to imperial heights. We told ourselves that TV's magic powers so engulf our neighbors (if not you and me) that all objective matters of right and wrong, not to say the subtle shadings in between, are virtually irrelevant. This dogmatic conviction, repeated every day in one medium of discourse or another, fatally compromises our political rhetoric, our educational policies, our cultural habits, the often inferior products we design (for consumers who presumably can't tell right from wrong), and even our regard for our fellow citizens.

Let us destruct these myths, as well as the arrogance that supports them. The odds are certainly against me, to be sure, against all of us. There are certain to be cries of disbelief, particularly against my assertion that most of us *hate* what television became for more than four decades. When I am challenged on this score, I often ask my accuser to name a single friend or relative who says the reverse ("I *love* TV," or, "I'm so glad my children spend hours each day in front of my set"). I can't respond to each assailant, of course, in the press or standing near the copy of this book you are holding. And *the numbers* are against all of us, those abstract figures always cited to prove that millions of us embrace our TV sets, like long-lost lovers, every day.

But let me begin by planting a seed of doubt, as you prepare to enter this book. And this seed must be planted in the middle of the conceptual forest that is . . . the Numbers.

In the last days of writing this book, I found myself on the telephone with a blunt and witty executive at A.C. Nielsen, the source of the truly critical Numbers, that is, the "ratings" for each program. I told him I had heard that the new electronic "People Meter" system of audience measurement, introduced in the late 1980s, had altered these very Numbers. True or false? Immediately he laughed, then began to recount the revered months in early 1990, when the new Meters began turning in HUT (Houses Using Television) figures much lower than the old simplified system counted. The networks suddenly found themselves unable

to guarantee the huge Numbers their advertisers demanded, and expected. "The networks announced they
wouldn't accept the ratings," he told me. They began to
"adjust" the ratings, based on the glory days of the past.
The advertisers, naturally, protested. I almost end my Pro-
logue by excerpting from his testimony, which you will read
in full later, in the chapter devoted to the last of our five
myths:

*We'll never know what actually happened or who paid what to
whom in 1990 and 1991. But certainly we know there was never
universal acceptance of this "adjusted" guarantee of audience size.
Now [early 1992] the rates are once again based on the* current
numbers. We are back to reality, such as it is.

Now don't be overly impressed. This is just one seed of
doubt. But . . . if the Numbers are in fact a *subjective*
count . . . closer to Jell-O in truth than solid marble . . . then
perhaps TV is not quite the superpower we have been led
to believe that it is. Perhaps we need to doubt more, and
more, in the pages to follow, moving toward the end of our
blindness, and the beginning of something else. Perhaps
finally all these seeds, planted here years after Aletha first
kissed me, will flower into a fragile, wondrous, totally unexpected thing.

THESIS

THE MEDIUM AS MYTH

> Myth is a true story because it is a sacred story. . . . The recital of myths . . . is part and parcel of cult, because it is a cult itself and helps to gain the ends for which cult is carried on, namely, the preservation . . . of life.
>
> —R. Pettazzoni, *Miti e Leggende*, 1948

> Television . . . is one of the tools modern societies must now use to sustain themselves. In many countries, as in our own, television and the central government are the only national institutions. Television is a baby-sitter, an initiator of conversations, a transmitter of culture, and a custodian of traditions. . . . If it were suddenly to disappear, what would happen to the 20 percent of Americans who watch twelve hours . . . a day? . . . Television is our nightlight.
>
> —Lawrence V. Lichty, "Television in America: Success Story," 1989

We have been told so often that television dominates our minds, lifestyle choices, and political behavior that we believe the telling without conscious choice, without critical attention. This is simply one of the several proofs that this assertion operates on a level analogous to myth itself. Another is that no media event can occur without appearing to support the doctrine of omnipotence, however contradictory it might be. In his classic study of witchcraft, E. E. Evans-Pritchard pointed out that the functional presence of evil spirits is a common daily occurrence for the men and women of the Azande tribe in Africa. When reversals occur—on the equivalent level in our culture of rising street violence, or illiteracy—the witches are blamed in anger, not in surprise or terror. When a young Azande boy stumbled in Evans-Pritchard's company and blamed the spirits, he refused to accept the obvious objection that he fell because he failed to see the stump in his path. The evil spirits "bewitched" his eyes, he said.[1]

Similar justifications are now found to explain the steady decrease in the percentages of viewers watching network television and the decline of voting in the face of huge sums spent by politicians to seduce voters through TV spots. Paradoxically, both failures are used to support rather than demolish our witchcraft—the first because viewers are said to be taping and archiving network material on their VCR (that is, watching "more" television, not less), the second because the "decline of political parties" is to blame, presumably caused by the homogenization of partisan differences inherent in the medium, together with its need to focus on telegenic personalities, not issues. Even when a sophisticated "inside" commentator like Ken Auletta comes to announce, finally, the decline of the Big Daddies, of NBC, CBS, and ABC (in *Three Blind Mice: How the Networks Lost Their Way*, in 1992), he blames it on corporate takeovers— in brief, to managerial incompetence, on high. To date it has occurred to virtually no one with a strong public voice to suggest that the major networks long ago lost psychic touch with the taste of the audience, that the public itself is the aggressor, acting to reject what it no longer needs, or that TV news and political spots are to *blame* for low turnouts, by depriving potential voters of substantial reasons to support any candidate, given the consistent trivialization of political debate. Our cherished myths have led us to ignore the fact that the change is coming from below, that the ground is exploding upward and outward, not imploding downward.

When a subtly contrarian event like the widely broadcast

"home video" recording of Los Angeles police beating up a black man early in 1991 occurs, accompanied by intense coverage in the print media, the means by which the myth is enforced are even easier to find: without the ubiquity of television, we are told, the brutality would have gone unpunished. Like the Azande, we are bewitched, in our denials of a truth for which we are not prepared.

Though this book argues in behalf of this single, focused truth, that TV-as-we-have-known-it is the aging Emperor Unclothed, ready to succumb to leaner, looser, more invigorating competition, it makes the case on a number of levels, like fingers of water spreading through a terraced field, on high, difficult ground, and low, porous marshes. The Los Angeles home videotaping is particularly difficult, but instructive. It occurred at a moment when national attention was focused on the issue of media credibility, in the wake of the Pentagon's finely tuned management of battlefield reports from the Gulf War, confined primarily to videotapes of "smart" bombs hitting their targets and telegenic generals briefing reporters. It was also a time when the Nielsen ratings were constantly reporting a continuing decline in the viewing audience for TV news, network and local. It was also a moment when I was meeting weekly with a swarming body of students in Los Angeles battered each day both by the Gulf War and the incendiary police tape, played over and over on all networks. The skeptical response of the California students to the media overload afforded me an invaluable adversarial view of these events, and their meaning.

The chance hero locked deep inside this swirl of events was George Holliday, manager of a plumbing store in Hollywood, who, early on the morning of Sunday, March 3, 1991, awakened by loud shouts, aimed his brand-new Sony Minicam at the baton-swinging police outside his window. Eager to record almost any "action" that came his way, even a cat licking its paw, as he later said, he simply pushed the start button on the autofocus camera. For several minutes he recorded a ring of policemen kicking and clubbing a prone black man sprawled on the ground not far from Holliday's apartment. When the beatings ended and the victim, Rodney Glen King, an unemployed parolee, was led away, handcuffed, to an emergency room, Holliday put his camera down and returned to sleep.

But of course what he had seen disturbed him. When he saw no news reports of the event the next day, he phoned and offered the Minicam tape to the neighborhood police, who brusquely refused. Balked, he called his favorite local television station—KTLA—and left it off at the reception desk. That night, on the 10 P.M. news, Holliday watched with astonishment as his entire tape was played. Within a few days, the early-morning autofocus images swept the entire nation, triggering a federal investigation, the suspension of all the involved policemen, and a national debate on police methods. Holliday's exuberant lawyer later called it "the most important piece of videotape in the history of this country."

In any event the tape prompts us to ask us why—in the face of amateurism, racial inversion, and defiance both of media and of police authority—it profoundly affected such a widespread audience. In a sense, this entire book will attempt an answer, hopefully as rich as the question. In the winter of 1991, however, we were immediately told that the incident proved again that "television" is the central power in contemporary life. But of course "television" as normally defined refers to the methods employed by the major broadcasting networks here and abroad—all decisively contradicted by George Holliday's tape, which carried not a trace of TV "style," in news, entertainment, or sports. Grainy, badly lit, visually clumsy, without color or voice-over, Holliday's flash recording neither begins nor ends. Like life, the tape that provoked the nation simply existed over a duration in which policemen almost destroy a prone victim who, finally, at the last, rises to his knees. More immediate than *cinema verité*, it is video unadorned, resembling the unpaced banality and horror of real life.

Viewers everywhere instantly believed Holliday's "home

video" on a level that no coiffed news anchor or clipped, elegant film could have matched. Later, Holliday, remembering how sleepy and uninvolved he was at the time, said, "It was almost as if I was watching something on a tiny television—images more than reality." But the nation did not see it as "television." When critics and columnists later credited the medium for the reform of the Los Angeles Police Department—culminating in the retirement of the chief of police and his replacement by a black man—they overlooked an obvious truth inherent in the event: Holliday's document succeeded because of its unquestionable veracity, not because it was delivered through the established television system. One year later, when a feuding jury finally voted to acquit the officers, leading to bloody inner-city riots, their fellow citizens across the nation, including a conservative Republican president, decisively disagreed with the verdict.

Perhaps this home video recording succeeded in spite of the broadcasting system that made use of it. My students, deeply skeptical about prime-time news (which few of them watched), didn't question this videotape any more than they had earlier questioned the sound-only news reports phoned across the world from a darkened hotel room in Baghdad. The room was manned in those early days by three reporters from CNN, the off-center Cable News Network. My thoroughly international class—half were Asian or European in origin—often rhapsodized over the hotel room reporting. "It's real," one of them said, summing up the cross-cultural argot of her colleagues. Later, when Rodney King's beating came into their lives, I heard again this peak of youthful praise: *"Real."* Certain forms of video are *Real* to this generation and its allies abroad surely because they do *not* resemble TV either in its broadcast form or in its deep, internal value structure—and because content in these cases overwhelms the medium in which it is presented. Neither George Holliday nor the harassed management of CNN (who finally decided to "cover" the hotel room voices with text cards explaining their site and origin), tried to gloss the truth, that is, the exact visual reality before them.

If we consider the precise qualities commanded by television—and videotape, its physical extension—we immediately see how the network esthetic has betrayed the premise, and promise, of its medium. Unlike film or print, television can connect viewers to events unfolding directly before them. Captured on videotape, which instantly plays back what it records—unlike film or print, once more—the viewer is in touch with the apparent *Real*, virtually as if he had experienced it himself. Finally, not least, the television set commands a direct, unparalleled access for the producer-writer-cameraman to his audience, which is often one person alone, on a sofa or reclining in a bed. This access is even closer than the golden thread between writer and reader, who are divorced by time: the book, unlike video, must be typeset, printed, distributed, months or years later.

THE FUNERAL BELLS BEGIN TO RING: NO ONE LISTENS

> *The spirit of the truth often dwells in strange places.*
> —Steven Lagerfeld, "History as Soap Opera," 1989

If the American networks have consistently violated the sacred advantage of the *Real*, so have the state-directed networks in Europe, Asia, and South America. The ninety-minute tape recorded in December 1989 of the trial and execution of Romanian dictator Nicolae Ceausescu and his wife, Elena, forms an almost exact parallel to George Holliday's memoir of police brutality in the United States which shook the myth of TV power with its own uniquely powerful mode of delivery. Once again, I found myself on site, in effect, traveling through the U.S.S.R. and the Baltic states when the news reached us that the powerful dictator had been toppled and forced to flee from his palace in Bucharest. My Russian and Estonian friends greeted this news with disbelief. I well recall the astonishment that greeted the broadcast of a short excerpt from the ninety-minute videotape of Ceausescu's trial and execution on Estonian television. "My God," said our host, "he is really dead."

Here again the guarantor of the truth was video that subverted the norms: lacking a narrator, the documentary footage, recorded by still unidentified cameramen working in tense, low-lit conditions, adds only sound to Holliday's barren esthetic. In Estonia, we saw clips of the moments when the "jury" put questions to the dictator, who angrily refused to answer, followed by ghoulish moments when the camera scanned the prone, bullet-ridden bodies of Ceausescu and his wife. In Romania, viewers were allowed a much longer scan of the complete taping, which was finally released, more than a year later, in a ninety-minute version. There, too, astonishment, followed by joy, greeted the undeniable evidence that the revolution had succeeded. It is clear in retrospect that the anti-Ceausescu forces were forced to play back the tape—risking the revulsion of those who might have preferred a "legal" trial—to quell skepticism and fear at once, so that the revolution could consolidate itself.

The authenticity of the "execution" was grounded in the profound spontaneity of the images perceived throughout the homes and streets. Indeed, the Ceausescu trial tape defied the steady diet of controlled, edited, interpreted news that had been fed to the Romanians—and to all of Eastern Europe—for more than forty years. The revolutionaries themselves, engaged in the uprising, produced this document. Telling the "truth" was no longer the province of broadcast TV executives, but of anarchic interlopers, what they offered was closer to home video, even to the family snapshot, than to network "news." For weeks thereafter in Romania, jubilant citizens brought their "amateur" videotapes to broadcast stations across the land, demanding access, which was gladly given, until months later, the new regime began to reorganize "free television" (one of the revolution's main rallying cries) and to control it.

In the United States, it was the ease of consumer access to Minicams that shook the Los Angeles police, pinned random street violence to the wall—and quietly subverted the exclusive network metaphysic. George Holliday's scan of the streets both preceded and succeeded a rash of democratizing surveillance tapes catching the government itself, the primal agent of surveillance, red-handed. In nearby Torrance, California, a "home tape" caught two officers choking and beating a twenty-year-old youth shortly thereafter, but one of a rash of similar sightings across the United States. During the bloody Los Angeles riots of May 1992, home video in the hands of a pedestrian sighted the reverse, four young black men pulling a defenseless white man out of his truck and beating him viciously, leading to their arrest. At first a privileged tool for the elite, home video became in the early 1990s almost as common as the photographic camera, indulged by men, women, children, even the elderly. Networkers and agency mullahs began openly to complain that these grainy recordings of birthday parties, school plays, bedroom lovemaking were eating up network viewing time—according to the Nielsen surveys—competing with high-gloss commercial competition. ABC in effect joined the enemy by soliciting the rankest moments it could find for its prime-time hurrah, *America's Funniest Home Videos*. In a declining market, *Funniest Home Videos* instantly rang up high marks in its first season.

Yet "personal," hand-held video is more profound in its implications than its critics and exploiters allow. At base, in the hands of any free man confronting official power on the street, it is a democratizing agent, however spontaneous or secretive. Personal video makes Everyman an agent of production, as the typewriter renders Everyman a writer and the personal computer turns each of us into a corporate-style accountant. In 1990, the lordly BBC began to provide hand-held video cameras to citizens willing to tape their own personal lives, later edited down for a series entitled *Video Diaries*. No one who has witnessed more than a few of these diaries, which often turn the very men and women who produce them inside out, can deny they operate on the razor-thin line between art and life. Listening to a gay man explain himself to his parents, or to a disabled operator of a wheelchair describe his daily exertions, demands and receives far more attention than "television" has come to mean.

Video Diaries links back to a delicious precedent, *An American Family,* produced for PBS by an innovative young director in 1971. The idea at the heart of this serial twelve-hour drama was to turn the camera on in the midst of the Loud family in San Diego, California—at breakfast, in the car, at poolside—and let it roll for long stretches, without editing. On these occasions, nothing seemed to be said of substance for long periods of time, but when the poignant moments appeared—when husband or wife shouted or lapsed into sullen silence—the emotion hit the viewer as knife-edged reality. Perhaps it was no accident that *An American Family* was revived during the very winter when George Holliday's tape in fact subverted the very networks who used it, by turning their esthetic upside down, on the lip of a decade that may yet belong to the Minicam, not the networks. Raw video is an affront to virtually all the media myths that have impacted us for more than four decades.

LOUDER, LOUDER: THE GULF WAR REVIVES RADIO

> *The government doesn't understand [the role of] the press.*
> —Peter Arnett, CNN, 1991

The seemingly victorious Gulf War of the winter of 1991— often proclaimed a triumph of skillful media management by the U.S. government—is another example of TV's overblown image of power, of a mythic stature that endures even when it stumbles, badly. Though our memory of the Gulf conflict is primarily aural, not visual, I'll never forget my first contact with the conflict, on gleaming TV sets placed high above my head at the airport in Prague, Czechoslovakia. It was early in the morning of January 13. I was instantly attracted to the video images by the enthralled passengers standing beneath them, waiting for flights to depart but momentarily transfixed by CNN's worldwide presence. On the screens were not dramatic images of pillage and destruction but of relaxed American pilots chatting with an ease appropriate for a polished news anchor before another hand-held camera hustled into the desert. We could not see and rarely heard the interviewer. Often, the camera closed in on the affable, sun-lit face, punctuated now and then by a cigarette lifted to the lips. Over and over each pilot—fresh from his first night of bombing raids on Baghdad, Iraq's capital—expressed delight with the mission and wonder over the lack of return fire. "I didn't see any Iraqi planes," one of them said, almost laughing, "except a few escaping off to the north . . . to get out of our way." My fellow passengers, all Eastern Europeans to the man/woman, applauded.

Thus began CNN's radically informal reporting of the heavily censored Gulf War, "manipulated" from start to finish by the Iraqi dictator, Saddam Hussein, and an American military command determined not to permit a recurrence of the negative video images that flowed out from the war in Vietnam during the 1960s and 1970s. But CNN, by discarding the "rules"—most of all the well-lit, fast-talking newscaster propped before static camera mounted on tripod—broke through the censor's veil. The interlopers began by telecasting non-video sound from a hotel room in Baghdad, manned by correspondents Peter Arnett, John Holliman, and Bernard Shaw. Surely the key memory of this war is Arnett holding his microphone out the window of his room, imploring the viewers "Let's listen" to the American bombs falling in Baghdad. This at a time when the Pentagon permitted no on-site reporting and Hussein's government had ejected the entire Western press corps. When the American public was finally permitted to *see* the

American air force in action the next day, they were primarily treated to carefully edited views of "smart bombs" striking their targets on cue through their lenses or through computer-aided simulation.

CNN's view of the war at once countered this image of immaculate control and the big networks' predictable reliance on static cameras and clipped, sound-bite sentences. From first to last, CNN was unbuttoned, so to speak, guided as much by events in the field—and by the ease of access to the satellite through portable telephones, cameras, and transmitting "rovers"—as by the need to polish and perfect. Often CNN caught itself and officials throughout the Mideast in errors of judgment, mainly because its legion of reporters was inside the conflict, not outside, caught constantly in the middle of events still at issue, still unresolved. One day in Israel CNN's hand-held camera focused on Benyamin Netanyahu of the Ministry of Defense. Virtually in mid-sentence bombs began to fall and Netanyahu quickly prodded the cameraman to don his gas mask; next, he grabbed a telephone and called the ministry to find out what was up—repeating what he heard for an audience suddenly empowered, by its presence at a moment where half truths were the truth, in the absence of neat, after-the-fact summations.

CNN's ability to attract influential voices like Netanyahu in mid-war was partly based in its own "local" visibility (by the dawn of the new decade CNN International's twenty-four-hour news feed was being carried on channels throughout the world)—Netanyahu knew his audience was Israeli and Arabic as well as American. But CNN's coverage was also enhanced by the freedom granted its correspondents, who often wielded cameras as well as words, discarding the tripod, pointing the lens through windows and into back alleys. Where the networks insisted—often with labor union prodding—on dividing announcers from cameras, CNN allowed the reverse, turning the camera into an extension of the "reporter," or "author." In comparison, then, network news seemed throughout the war to be stolid, unexciting, a tool of the Pentagon: each night its most forceful voice was the burly American General Norman Schwarzkopf, whose salty apothegms were dutifully compressed into prime-time news bits, leaving his hesitations and indecisiveness on the editing room floor.

It is therefore no wonder that the media and its analysts later proclaimed Schwarzkopf and the Pentagon the victors in a war whose approval rating for several months was sky-high, temporarily escalating President George Bush's approval rating to the same heights. But a minute's reflection reveals the case to be far more intriguing, and complicated. Surely the total collapse of Saddam Hussein's army, permitting a quick, easy exit for American troops, is the main reason why the public fell briefly in love with the Gulf War. And the true media non-victory belongs to CNN, whose ratings on several crucial evenings approached network numbers, for the first time in the history of cable television, which still doesn't reach as many American homes as the over-the-air networks.

CNN's war decisively differed from the "official" war. It presented—despite roars of protest from politicians and rival broadcasters—Hussein's point of view, in a series of interviews with Peter Arnett widely assumed to be the reason CNN's crew was permitted to remain in its embattled hotel, (in fact, CNN offered Hussein both a "window" on the world and a camera to the pan-Arab world). It caught the war and its victims over and over in tragic, bloody situations, far from the briefing rooms. CNN rarely "edited" press conferences and briefings, in the manner of the networks, ceding to the news a temporal luxury that may have barred it from official industry awards (CNN failed to receive one nomination for an Emmy award for its Gulf coverage—on the ground that it rarely condensed events down to "program" form). Long after the American army left Iraq and the victory parades had enlivened network news, CNN continued to report the anguish of the anti-Hussein Kurds and Shiite Muslims fighting alone against a vengeful dictator. By leaving the war unresolved, CNN's coverage insisted—by implication—that the Western media's hero-villain casting was deeply flawed.

Within a few months, public opinion in the United States responded to the plight of the Kurds fleeing from Hussein without U.S. protection. Americans' outraged letters and phone calls in part caused Bush to send American troops back again, briefly, perhaps not for the last time. By July of 1991, well over half of those questioned by *USA Today* believed the United States had quit the field too early— disagreeing with a basic tenet of administration policy—and 71 percent were opposed to further conflict. In 1992, skepticism both about the war and the methods used to "sell" it mounted. Several books fiercely attacking the war's origins, conduct, and motivations were published, among them Stephen Grebaud's *Mr. Bush's War: Adventures in the Politics of Illusion* and John McArthur's *Second Front: Censorship and Propaganda in the Gulf War.* Congress began to probe into the role of Hill and Knowlton, a public relations agency, in parading debatable Kuwaiti "victims" of Iraqi atrocities before the media and the Congress itself. Yet CNN anticipated all of this by leaving its coverage of the Gulf War "unpackaged."

Why did its competitors lust for the reverse? In Peter Arnett's speech to the National Press Club, he argued that the government misunderstood the press's role, believing it to be finally an extension of national policy. But governments have always attempted to control news, in peace as well as in war. The same question is more tellingly addressed to the networks—to "television" itself. Why "package"? Why simplify? Why seek always to personalize news, in comic-book pairing of distinct heroes and distinct villains? Norman Schwarzkopf, for all of his virtues, did not "win" the war; certainly he did not inspire the Iraqis to dispatch their troops to indefensible positions, without adequate food, water, or ammunition—the real cause of the war's speedy end. Surely TV was motivated primarily by what it believed its audience wanted. To the man, and against all the available evidence, the networks concluded that a papier-mâché reality was preferred in America's living rooms. More than any other factor, this tells us why CNN's war turned out to be *Real* while the network's war was false.

SHARPER, SHARPER: THE SOUNDS OF ZAPPING . . . OF RATINGS . . . FALLING

> *The imagery of myth . . . can never be a direct presentation of the total secret of the human species, but only the function of an attitude . . . a way of playing the game. . . . And where the rules or forms of such play are abandoned, mythology dissolves.*
>
> —Joseph Campbell, *The Masks of God: Primitive Mythology*, 1959

If television's failing health was disguised during the trauma of the Los Angeles Police Department crisis and the Gulf War, it was unmasked by the persistent Zapping Debacle, which is clearly related to an even more profound and persistent flaw, the Ratings Scam. Not long after public sentiment began to shift on the Gulf War, new evidence surfaced proving that "zapping"—that is, the use of remote control wands to rapidly change channels—had increased.[2] Insiders in the industry conceded to the press that almost 80 percent of American TV viewers were wielding zappers with élan, mostly to jump away from commercials to other programs, with no end in sight. Some analysts warned that viewers were zapping half of the commercials they saw, or at least muffling the high-pitched sound. Even the venerable A. C. Nielsen Company, which has "documented" the awesome size of the TV market for decades, acknowledges zapping's persistence, while claiming that viewers are hopping from commercial to commercial, rather than refusing to be sold. In any case, the concession to this destructive truth seemed complete. The makers of commercials themselves admitted that zapping called the viability of their product into doubt. The networks admitted the same, indirectly, by publishing a report in July of 1991, *The Gold Standard,* which contended only that viewers zapped ABC, CBS, and NBC *less* than they jumped Cable TV and "independent" stations.[3]

The Zap, in brief, is *Real*—a particularly destructive admission. If television manages and controls our destiny, why do we reject its core commercial function? In our resistance we may be shaking a societal myth placed as precisely in our path as the stump in the road that felled the little Azande boy. Further, its economic consequences are profound. Each year approximately 50 million commercials are designed and aired in the United States at a cost of more than $21 billion—more than the entire national product of oil-rich Kuwait before Hussein's invasion. Given these stakes, it is no wonder that the TV "industry" has reached for extremes at once to defy the zapper and to surveil his wand wielding, hoping to learn more about him/her. Saatchi and Saatchi, the elegant ad agency based in London and New York, began to structure "strong product images" that would prevail even during the fast-forwarding that seems to occur when viewers tape and play back recorded TV programs. As early as 1988, the R. D. Percy Company of Seattle pioneered the TV set that "watches" the viewer, through an infrared scanner lurking just behind the screen, detecting each split-second leap from soap ad to feature film.

Later discarded, the Percy scanner was simply the first of a whole range of fine-tuned "passive" audience measurement systems, which progressively increased electronic surveillance in a vain attempt to record and explain the behavior of a viewer once considered stolid, captive, predictable. Certainly the remote control wand has called dramatic attention to this fallacy. It finally reinforced the mounting critiques of Nielsen's once sacrosanct claim to certify the enormousness of the TV market. A series of investigatory "committees" sprang up to critique Nielsen's methods, concerned both to gird the prestige of audience measurement and determine if late reports of shrinking audience size were correct.

For several decades, academic critics have been challenging the built-in fallacies of numbers based on Nielsen's small, restricted "sample," made up of singular individuals willing to exchange surveillance of their viewing habits for dollars— with its built-in incentive to turn the TV set *on*, whether watched or not. After a particularly incisive study of these techniques at the University of Connecticut, a spokesman made the point flatly, at last. "There's really no telling how closely Nielsen's numbers correspond to reality."[4]

Now, clearly, the viewer is emerging in these incidents as decidedly more independent than we have been led to believe. But what kind of viewer? Are the nay-sayers fleeing to Cable TV, the theater, and jogging simply high-income, high-IQ elitists, as network spokesmen often allege? In truth, the evidence of resistance extends all the way down to the earliest years, to the children who are supposedly transfixed by TV, as legend has insisted for decades. But even the networks have complained that the viewing habits of children are unfathomable and unknowable because they are impossible to count or measure by means of any system—like Nielsen's early diaries and meters—requiring diaries or active button pushing. No matter. The myth insists that TV controls unformed minds with particular insistence, luring unformed minds to worship comic-book superstars and plague their parents for the flashy products beamed at them in endlessly vulgarized commercials.

BONG! BONG! THE CHIMES CALL US TO . . . QUIET BURIAL

> *A proposition is a picture of reality: for if I understand a proposition, I know the situation that it represents. And I understand the proposition without having had its sense explained to me.*
>
> —Ludwig Wittgenstein, "The World Is Constructed on a Logical Scaffolding," 1921

Perhaps no aspect of our obsession with TV power is more traumatizing than the oft-quoted figures that supposedly prove our children spend thousands of hours before the TV set, presumably wiring themselves into lifelong illiteracy. Americans take perverse joy in quoting these figures, along with declining test scores, at each other. Now these shocking numbers—which take no account of the debased curricula now offered our students, nor the impoverishment of many of the public schools they attend, nor the larger social context in which TV is viewed (whether a poor, single-parent kitchen or a comfortable suburban library) or the exact nature of the program (as even the networks agree)—ignore impressive anecdotal evidence available to us all. Whenever we pass by an active video game store we notice instantly that TV is hardly able—on its own—to drug and stupefy our children, of any age or race. The wild whoops of joy and anger from kids pounding, pulling, and pushing images across the screen, trying to "beat the game," is impressive evidence to the contrary. Many more of us have witnessed similar aggression in our homes, or the homes of friends. As of early 1991, the same year that crowned the *Real* forever, one third of American households owned video games. The year before, Americans bought 25 million Nintendo games, each one equipped with active modalities, with buttons, levers, controls.

The spread of these games is occurring at precisely the moment when the personal computer is itself rapidly becoming common fare in many public and nearly all private schools, when the Federal Communications Commission, as well as the Congress, is attempting actively to encourage fiber-optic cabling of our homes, a step that will permanently dissolve TV into the computer, where our keyboards will permit us to refine, store, and control an immense array of choices. My eight-year-old daughter has been typing out letters and tracing abstract flourishes across our Apple Macintosh terminal since she was four. From the age of six she has been spelling, adding, and subtracting for a "junior computer" that chides and praises her by turns.

The notion that the monolithic TV God of yesteryear will find easy prey in a generation reared to process/command the electronic gaming images flashed before them is debatable. If TV is in fact an irresistible *Plug-In Drug,* to borrow from Marie Winn's hair-raising phrase (and book), then all grades of age and intelligence are condemned to insipidity.[5] But if not, if the interaction between what we have come to call "TV" and what we have always called "the viewer" is more complex, even at the earliest ages, then we need a massive dose of revisionist social policy. Meanwhile I propose this test with any handy clutch of children below the age of eight years, analogous to experiments lately conducted by sociologists: offer them a television set tuned to any supposedly irresistible children's program. In the same room, offer them a tussle with Nintendo, a junior computer, or interactive software like *Carmen Sandiego,* where a vagabond mistress of global crime leads her audience on a question-filled chase around the world's geography (you must answer correctly to follow). The odds are definitely on the side of activism.

Those who cede the TV God demonic powers cede him precisely the arrogance and authority he needs. When well-meaning critics like Marie Winn, Neil Postman, and Jerry Mander find TV at the core of virtually every problem, from illiteracy to rape, they indirectly enhance the value of every televised minute, no matter who is programming (or speaking) or who is watching, or listening. They ignore the *Real,* the defining power of history, of personal heritage, of events, of income, of powerful competing media (such as the book, the film, and the computer), of personality—and most of all of the obdurate human mind. Not that long ago, in the year of 1984, many of us were told that George Orwell's vision of a Big Brother world, in which TV acts as the handmaiden of the totally controlled technocratic state, was accurate prophecy.[6] Barely five years later, in November of 1989, the Berlin Wall collapsed. Throughout the U.S.S.R. and Eastern Europe, millions of citizens supposedly subdued by propaganda insistently delivered by the glowing screen took to the streets and overthrew their oppressors. In many cases, in Prague and in Bucharest, they instantly seized the TV stations and ejected their programmers. Rather than striding the world, TV, as God, as Myth, may be near a form of extinction, or, at least, a profound reinterpretation.

LET US COUNT THE MYTHS THAT MUST BE FELLED

> *Language disguises thought.*
> —Ludwig Wittgenstein, "Understanding Depends on Tacit Conventions," 1921

> *Social isolation, poor adjustment to peers, and low self-esteem are associated with high viewing.*
> —Bob Hodge and David Tripp, *Children and Television,* 1986

Deprived of our insistent adulation—our oft-repeated belief in its awesome power—what we have come to call "television" would fall to any halfhearted revolution. In one sense, TV-as-network-monolith, as baby-sitter, as night-light to the nation is already teetering, prodded by the spread of cable television (where a proliferation of channels fragments power and production), by the booming popularity of videocassettes and portable cameras (which have decidedly personalized TV in the home), and by an increase in the appeal of phenomena like travel, sports, theaters, museums, and books that were terminated years ago in the prophecies of countless forecasters, among them Marshall McLuhan, who saw the demise of "print" decades before the personal computer tripled the amount of paper produced by each of us. We ought to welcome this demise. Our overwrought perception of TV's hold on our minds has already diluted the intensity of our educational system, where courses have been adjusted to a supposedly passive clientele, and vulgarized our political campaigns, where politicians have adjusted their rhetoric in a similar manner.

But the extraordinary freedoms now permitted by a medium that bears almost no resemblance to the monolith described by McLuhan and others have yet to reform either our language or our policies, public and private. Our newspapers still breathlessly report on the springtime revisions in prime-time entertainment, in the rescheduling of *Wheel of Fortune, Dolly, Roseanne,* or *Jeopardy!,* as though they still drew 90 percent of the viewing audience, while ignoring the counterprogramming of the three dozen alternative channels, some of which, like CNN or C-SPAN, an unedited twenty-four-hour presentation of the U.S. Congress in action, are steadily increasing their audience. Some if not all of our merchants still regard this variegated, choice-conscious market as the oversimplified "mass" that TV appeared to serve and please several decades ago. Nearly all our politicians—as well as our educators—talk to this audience as though it was still 1955, still sprawled, helpless, before the three or four similar and stultifying options offered by *TV Guide.*

It is not enough simply to detect TV in crisis. We must understand why the myths surrounding this critical medium flourish even today, in the face of the total collapse of the ideas that once girded the belief in an all-conquering "mass" medium decisively pacifying a "mass" society. This book will name these myths, beginning with the notion repeated to us several times each day in varying ways: "TV elects our political leaders." It will debunk as well the prevalent notion that television's omnipotence has weakened the power of the word, or print; that it has driven down the test scores of our students; that it has turned entire societies, like ours, into lumpy couch potatoes, content to witness a distant, mediated reality rather than the real thing. Finally, we will address the most prevalent and devastating myth of all: We, the public, *love* the medium that enslaves us, according to countless columnists and propagandists, with a passion equivalent to the devotion once inspired by the church, the town crier, and the book.

As these myths are dissected, we may also discover why a medium so rich in promise has failed to please the bulk of its audience. When questioned, even constant viewers express dissatisfaction with TV programming.[7] It is a condition that holds throughout most of the world. The profound irony of television to date, as Denis McQuail points out, is that even the "democratic" obsession with courting the public has so far produced content that is universally judged "low in aesthetic and moral quality."[8] In the East, the system of state control—of ignoring, in effect, public demand—has also failed, decisively. Stalinist control of the media did not produce "the new man." Vaclav Havel's speech before the newly liberated Czech nation in January 1990, touched indirectly on this paradox when he asked of the millions who rebelled, "How is it possible . . . that none of them needed any advice or orders?" This paradox links subtly to a furtive secret lately beginning to surface in studies baring the wide differences between the substantial number of hours spent before the TV set by children in barren, uninspiring homes and the lesser numbers indulged by kids on another economic and intellectual level: each viewer consumes and interprets television in his or her own decidedly distinct manner.

As these arguments develop, they will certainly reverse much of what we have been led to believe about the destiny of this medium by authors whom I perversely admire. They include Orwell, of course, whose *1984* unfortunately reinforced the notion that whatever Big Brother sends us will be received in our minds as he intended. As for Marshall McLuhan, his brilliant, wrong-headed metaphors and slogans—among them "the Global Village" and "the medium is the message"—inadvertently confirmed Orwell's prophecy by assuring his dazzled readers that the mere reception of a transmitted image means acceptance. To date, as we all know, the instantaneous TV image has often hindered rather than enhanced reconciliation and unification. In certain parts of the world, indeed, most of all the Middle East, televised access to other cultures has intensified religious fundamentalism and a vigorous retreat from "globalism." McLuhan's uncritical embrace of the electronic age has since been countered by a cadre of equally charming and persuasive Visigoths, eager to cede to television such overwhelmingly destructive powers that they perversely align themselves with the God, and with Orwell's misunderstood novel. Learned critics like Neil Postman and Kathleen Hall Jamieson proclaim at every opportunity the evil impact of TV on all those who behold it, except, of course, themselves. Jerry Mander's deliciously vicious *Four Arguments for the Elimination of Television* as well as George Gilder's *Life After Television* leap into the same black hole, crushing themselves and their doomsday theories—following five centuries after the high-minded church leaders who tried to stifle the secular printing presses.[9] To call for the destruction of a medium that is simply a *means,* not an *end,* is as futile as the wave of Utopian prophecies describing its seductive takeover of the world, without taking into any account the combative and adaptive powers of the human mind, the very powers that drove each of these writers to frame their exuberant, decisively failed hypotheses.

This book will gently but definitively refute each of them. It will attempt to persuade the reader/viewer that the medium is *not* the message, that the ultimate power lies here, in his/her eye and mind, not on the "other" side of the screen. A variety of historical accidents have left the control of television in the hands of those interests, public and private, eager to indulge the thesis inherent in McLuhan, Mander, & Co. Now, at a moment analogous to that very proliferation of printing presses opposed by church and state in the Renaissance, the single voice and the single viewer are both beginning to find each other. They need what this book now attempts to provide: a fresh metaphysic to empower their illicit affair.

MYTH ONE

TV CONTROLS OUR VOTING

Television is more than just another great public resource . . . ruined by private greed. . . . It is the greatest communication mechanism ever designed. . . . It pumps into the human brain an unending stream of information. Every minute of television—commercials, entertainment, news—teaches us something.
> —Nicholas Johnson, "What Do We Do About Television?," *Saturday Review,* 1979

Three people in front of a television set is a political rally.
> —Joel Swerdlow, "A Question of Impact," 1989

TELEVISION'S BLINDING POWER (How it Shapes Our Views)
> —Cover, *U.S. News & World Report,* July 27, 1987

You won't see a lot of our ads. . . . The problems we face are difficult and complex. I believe you deserve more than thirty-second commercials with vague promises. We want you to have a copy of our plan. Call us or visit your local library.
> —Lawton Chiles, TV spot in Florida gubernatorial campaign, 1990

Though widely praised, the campaign of Lawton Chiles for governor of Florida in November 1990—or rather, its radical media strategy—was kept secret, rather like the furtive romance of a priest or philosopher-king. By contemporary standards, Chiles spent a pauper's sum for television commercials, while his opponent, Governor Bob Martinez, poured dollars into TV with the free-spending abandon that has become routine for established American politicians. More to the point, most of Chiles's commercials critiqued the very medium on which they appeared. They urged citizens to look elsewhere for political information. They asked the voters to leave the living room and meet Chiles firsthand, in the streets and in the countryside. Though running in a wealthy state renowned for media bravura, Chiles's soft-shoe campaign toppled an incumbent governor by a healthy margin (56 percent to 44 percent).

The comparative journalistic silence that followed this victory is instructive. On the following day, newspapers outside Florida ran third- or fourth-page headlines that stressed Chiles's low-cost tactics but referred only in passing to his anti-TV strategy: the quick reference to figures alone (Martinez spent $10 million, Chiles only $5 million) was always the core of the story. Few of the national columnists who routinely savage television for its vulgarization of campaign rhetoric noted Chiles's defiance of common wisdom. Perhaps this broadband group of journalists instinctively avoided challenging this most strident and ubiquitous of media myths—that TV dominates every election in the modern era—without overpowering proof.

Chiles's campaign sinned against omnipotence. He not only called TV power into question: he *proved* it wrong. That is why what he did had to be hushed, for a time. To this day, well after the broad-based revulsion against "sound-bite" politics that characterized the 1992 presidential campaign, most Americans have never seen Chiles's anti-commercial commercials. But we are regularly reminded of the flagrant attack spots that allegedly swayed millions of voters, most of all the infamous "revolving door" created in 1988 by Roger Ailes, George Bush's media consultant, to symbolize Massachusetts Governor Michael Dukakis's allegedly permissive attitude toward criminals. Chiles's success certainly discomfited most of all those who profit from the wholesale commitment to TV power, that is, campaign managers and TV exchequers across the land, which share a pie approaching $1 billion every four years. His victory even threatened those who regularly denounce the medium's power, among them academics, columnists, and nearly all politicians who lose hard-fought campaigns. By proving that TV is neither god nor devil, that it is fallible, that a combination of drive, intelligence, and credibility (Chiles had been twice elected Senator in the 1970s and 1980s, retiring only because he was "burnt out" by Washington politics) can overpower supreme power, Chiles forces us to rethink a whole string of easy assumptions.

Even in 1990, when Myth One ruled uncontested, before the signal 1992 campaign, Chiles was hardly the only politician who had resisted TV and still captured major elective office. Throughout his twenty-four-year Senate career, William Proxmire of Wisconsin barely spent a penny on television commercials. Jesse Jackson's low-cost primary campaigns for the presidency in the 1980s were similarly frugal—due at once to necessity and the candidate's own telegenic skills, which won him endless invitations to talk without charge on the nightly news. One year after Chiles's victory, Wellington Webb, an impoverished black candidate for mayor in predominantly white Denver, reversed a twenty-eight-point deficit in the polls to win without buying TV time. Like Chiles he made a fetish out of face-to-face meetings with voters and campaign rallies, in the old, pre-television manner. Indeed, the little-known study by Professor Michael Robinson, a professor of government at George Washington University in Washington, D.C., documents this point with impressive breadth. Professor Robinson isolated sixty bitterly contested primary campaigns in 1988, half Democratic, half Republican: *The candidate who spent the most money on media and advertising lost in well over half the elections (60 percent).* Among the well-heeled losers he discovered were Senator Al Gore of Tennessee, who dropped the primary in Georgia to the impoverished Jackson, and Robert Dole, Minority Leader of the Senate, who outspent but underpolled George Bush in the Maryland primary.[1]

The Chiles Florida campaign is nonetheless singular, mainly because it *directly* challenged our first myth, that TV, virtually unaided, elects and defeats political candidates at the end of the century. It is, as we will see, a mystical conviction, bereft of real proof and countered by facts, by logic, by common sense. Yet Myth One has noticeably transformed both the methodology and the standards of political discourse in the world's oldest democracy, as virtually everyone agrees, even those who doggedly believe in it. The obsession with purchasing time on television for "spot" messages increased the cost of campaigns tenfold between 1970 and 1990. The price for a race for a seat in the House of Representatives leaped *482* percent between 1975 and 1990 alone. The *average* cost of a competitive senatorial campaign climbed to $10 million by 1988, ten times the cost in 1974.[2] In 1988, then Vice President Bush and Governor Michael Dukakis of Massachusetts together spent $50 million on media. By 1992, President Bush alone began the campaign with a budget of $40 million targeted in the same manner. TV now dominates almost every candidate's resources. It soaks up time and staff as well as money. On deeper, subtler levels, it changes the politician's attitude toward the voter, toward himself, and, most of all, the perception visited upon both by those who manage and analyze our campaigns.

This sea change can be easily tracked in the widely read-quoted-and-imitated series of books written by Theodore H. White on *The Making of the President*, which began with the 1960 Kennedy-Nixon campaign. Deeply impressed by the critical importance of the televised debates in that year, which clearly played a decisive role in a tight race joined on the high level of content (largely foreign policy), White began, volume by volume, to focus on style first, content second. What began as a "story" of a clash on issues became the saga of contrasts in self-promotion. By the time he gathered bits and pieces of all these books together in 1982, in *America in Search of Itself: The Making of the President, 1956–1980,* White seemed a wholesale convert to what he called "The Reign of Television." By 1982, according to White, Americans gathered together only before a "thirteen-inch or nineteen-inch stage." The personality of the candidate mattered more than what he said. Party chieftains mattered no more. In their place were "the paymasters of the television specialists at court."

But not even White's enthusiasm could match that of Joe McGinniss, in *The Selling of the President 1968,* which made White, a journalist whose antecedents preceded TV, seem pedantic.[3] McGinniss's book, often cited as the herald of a new, media-conscious journalism, was one long extended TV script. The men who managed the Nixon campaign—and Nixon himself—agonize endlessly over lighting, makeup, timing. Entire chapters are devoted to describing Nixon rehearsing, then taping his spots. In a lengthy appendix, McGinniss reprints one position paper after another, in which media specialists direct Nixon to focus now on this tactic, now on the other. One of them, a compilation of quotes from Marshall McLuhan, heaps scorn on Theodore White because he defers to the *content* of the Kennedy-Nixon debates rather than their visual *appearance.* The book introduces Roger Ailes, Nixon's media manager and later mastermind of the Bush campaign. Ailes's view of the campaign is the view of a sitcom producer, with rarely a word wasted on the meaning of the presidency or the fate of the nation. Near the end, when Nixon performs well on one of Ailes's staged broadcasts, he exults to a friend, "This was the Nixon I met on the Mike Douglas show. This was the Nixon I wanted to work for."

By the onset of the last decade of this century, White and McGinniss had been joined by an awesome parade of critics, professors, and theorists, all similarly convinced that the mere appearance of a candidate or his paid commercials on the TV screen (particularly when primed by eye-catching visuals) exert decisive persuasive powers. Twenty-three

years after McGinniss, in 1992, the very year that shook the
Myth, Kathleen Hall Jamieson, dean of the Annenberg
School of Communications at the University of Pennsylvania, reinforced its premise from the reverse. In *Dirty Politics:
Deception, Distraction, and Democracy,* Professor Jamieson
handed over to the medium, yet once more, killing powers.
Television can erode the mind far beyond the capacity of
"stump speakers, print barrages, and radio," she lamented,
joining the chorus. TV alone, she claimed, can "re-orient
attention" and provoke "strong, unthinking negative responses in low-involvement viewers."[4]

Given this unanimity of expert opinion, it is no wonder
that two-thirds of every competitive campaign's budget—
for President, the Senate, the House of Representatives, and
most gubernatorial races—is being handed over to national
and local TV broadcasters. This commitment leaves most
candidates with almost no incentive to research policy for-
mation or prepare position papers that might define complex political solutions or differentiate one candidate from
the other, on substantive grounds. Nor does it encourage
our politicians to campaign in the streets, to seek the direct
human contact that in the past fanned the flames of voter
passion, not to say participation.

Often campaign managers defend the rush into TV on
"democratic" grounds, on the need to bring more political
news and "information" to more people. But voter apathy
has intensified since Myth One has taken root in our political
life. In study after study, interview after interview, citizens
complain that they are information-starved as to the candidate's positions on matters of public policy that concern
them. Between 1970 and 1990, this passive-aggressive re-
sentment reached record levels: the percentage of eligible
voters going to the polls dropped by one-fifth, or an average
of 20 million people in each presidential election. In 1988,
the year of the highest spending on a presidential campaign
ever, the voting numbers dropped further, to the lowest
level since the tedious Calvin Coolidge–John Davis race in
1924. In midterm, nonpresidential election years, the per-

centages are declining at the same rate, by more than a fifth of all voters between 1974 and 1988. The upswing in voter interest in the 1992 presidential race confirms rather than denies this apprehension: for a variety of unique historical and economic reasons, as we shall see, the campaign deserted monolithic dependence on traditional prime-time/ sound-bite methods. Faced for a change with real issues related to its own survival, the electorate responded by voting rather than sitting out an irrelevant, indecisive media disturbance.

But only a cockeyed optimist would bet against the resilience of mythic power. The future is at best unpredictable, particularly because the younger generations are proving to be more than normally disengaged from politics. Until 1992, the eighteen-to-twenty-four-year-olds voted less frequently than all other age groups. On the cusp of the 1990s, pollster and analyst Curtis Gans testified to Congress that we have entered "the Silent Spring in American politics." Beyond two or three demagogic sentences scripted for his/ her commercial assaults, few politicians care to say anything of consequence to the American voter anymore, primarily because they think of him/her as supine, if not inert. They regard him, wrongly, as "low-involvement." The response of the voter so ignored and degraded is hardly unexpected. He/she trades silence for silence, by refusing to vote.

METAPHOR AS SUBVERTED MEANING

> *If we are right in suggesting that our conceptual system is largely metaphorical, then the way we think, what we experience, and what we do every day is very much a matter of metaphor.*
> —George Lakoff and Mark Johnson, *Metaphors We Live By*, 1980

> *It [TV] holds a mirror to our society.*
> —Edward Fritts, *USA Today*,
> 1988

> *The media system is the new elector of the modern political age.*
> —Austin Ranney, American Enterprise Institute, 1991

> *The personality of the interviewer, the nature and sequence of the questions, the environmental factors of the particular day and setting all produce reactions in the respondent that may not be totally typical.*
> —Doris Graber, *Processing the News*, 1984

If we attempt to reason *why* noble democracy has come to such a pass we must confront hard economic and political realities, yes. But it's also necessary to take account of softer issues, primarily linguistic, psychic, and psychological, the kind rarely considered by traditional analysts. The academic community—and its political allies—prefer the hard factors, easily lined up in numerical rows. When it occasionally searches for the *motivation* behind media or political events, this community predictably ignores the irrational, the metaphorical, the uncountable. The possibility that some politicians might prefer to praise and display their virtues on the tube, for example, rather than think, write, or research is unmentionable as a motive.

As for our language, Lakoff and Johnson's thesis, which reminds us of the formidable power of metaphor, is another key to Myth One's dominance. The phrase "global village," first coined by Marshall McLuhan in the 1960s, crunches every synapse it enters, implying that the advent of television reduces the differentiated complexity of the world's nations to a single commune, hunched before the set, awaiting instruction. When TV is compared to a "mirror" or a "nightlight," when Professor Ranney asserts that TV is our "elector," we scent the same bias. Even Nicholas Johnson, no friend of mindless video, paints TV as an irreversible mechanism, if not a mighty sewage pump. If any of us tries finally to count on his or her hands the number of times we have been confidently told by journalists and anchormen that

"Television" (the self-automated monster) "has changed American politics forever," we will run out of fingers, if not toes.

Each of these metaphors implies that the medium acts on its own impulses, beyond human resistance. Perhaps in the beginning, as in McLuhan's stream of sophomoric apothegms (from "the medium is the message" to, inevitably, "the medium as . . . massage"), this assumption was self-conscious, driven by his desire to shock the monastic community of book-bound intellectuals. By now, however, this conviction is wired into our common language. The "global village" directs meaning exactly as the rosary reinforces devout Catholics. By these lights TV is of course a "blinding power," as *U.S News and World Report* puts it, on the level of superhuman visits from outer space.

Even when the "other" side of the story is acknowledged in public discourse—Chiles's victory or the statistical evidence that most viewers "zap" out commercial spots, political or not—the speaker ultimately bows to Myth One. When NBC News resident Lawrence Grossman came to the Joan Shorenstein Barone Center for Public Affairs at Harvard in 1990 to discourse on the recent elections, he admitted that the deluge of electronic coverage in the 1988 election resulted in failure. Out in the supposedly provincial hinterland, said Grossman, there is unrelenting criticism of TV's role in political reporting:

> *High on the list of complaints were the networks' preoccupation with the "horse race," candidates' private lives, opinion polls . . . love of the flag, death penalty and prison furloughs.*[5]

Grossman concluded his talk with a six-point mandate for "reform" that anticipated the Bush-Clinton-Perot campaign waiting just two years down the road, behind a tree. Though he said little about the *content* of American political campaigns, about *what* might be said or published or broadcast, Grossman called correctly for "more diversified televi-

sion"—for news, debates, and discussions on cable, public
television, and beyond.

He could not have anticipated the change of heart that
appears to have moved even network TV news reporting
in the early stages of the 1992 campaign, as Marvin Kalb,
director of the Barone Center, later noted in *USA Today*. In
the early months, according to the center's studies, one in
five network TV "stories" dealt with issues rather than political guile or strategy, improving on the previous campaign.[6] Yes, the percentage declined, disastrously, later, but
alternative media more than supplemented NBC, CBS, and
ABC in responding to what voters have been telling us—
through passive resistance—for some time: the heart, soul,
and mind of American politics has atrophied in the past
two decades, when Myth One dominated campaigning style
as well as content, leaving our citizens no decisive reason to
support or oppose any candidate, or party.

Though most of us know that political commercials inspire disbelief, for example, the language we use in daily
life, as well as journalistic accounts, implies we are credulous: "TV is a drug," we are told, or say, time and again,
"the viewers are addicts." The oft-told complaint of newscaster Leslie Stahl about the "official" response to her critique in 1984 of the Ronald Reagan campaign media blitz
is yet another example. On *CBS News,* Stahl delivered a five-
minute assault on the disparity between the President's up-
beat, compassionate words, cloaked in flag-waving imagery,
and the specific policies he supported. The next day, a Reagan staffer enthusiastically thanked her for the attack, insisting that her use of their telegenic visuals counted for
more than her words: "The audience doesn't listen to you,"
he said, according to the shocked newscaster, "if you are
contradicting great pictures."

Once more, Mythic power reverses negative evidence in
its favor. In the Stahl case we see the White House itself
boosting the image-as-drug, carrying indefinable messages
that mysteriously overwhelm the same viewers whose

mounting political cynicism is common knowledge. The presumed effectiveness of the infamous 1988 Republican spot linking presidential candidate Dukakis to Willie Horton, a black convict who committed rape while on a weekend governor's furlough in Massachusetts, is yet another heir to Mythic Reversal. Though exit polls tell us only a small percentage of Bush voters could even recall Horton's name, veteran political analysts continue to assume that this spot was a decisive factor in George Bush's victory.

Neither Bush nor Ailes, his media manager, claimed direct responsibility for the Horton assault, which was produced by an "independent" political action group. But Ailes's "official" spots were similarly negative, feeding red meat to all those buying into the Myth and its simplistic view of the voter. The ubiquitous "revolving door" ad, repeated over and over, is typical: while the door spins, the smooth but anonymous voice provides a primordial message: "Dukakis's revolving door prison policy gave weekend passes to first-degree murderers not eligible for parole." At the end lettered words punch the final point home: *"268 escaped."*

On one level brilliant propaganda, this flawed, widely discussed broadside (268 prisoners did *not* escape) suffered the same fate as Willie Horton in exit polling. Most voters couldn't remember it. Few Bush voters cited the "revolving door" as the reason they voted for the vice president. But the press paid little attention to this contrarian fact. Neither did the opposition. One year later, Dayton Duncan, Dukakis's press secretary, maintained that the 1988 election was simply a matter of "how well the two campaigns succeeded in getting their own soundbite on that night's news." When Governor Bill Clinton's alleged infidelity with a woman named Gennifer Flowers, reported first by a tabloid early in the 1992 campaign, next by the mainstream press, and then, finally, in allusion and sound-bite, by political opponents, Hillary Clinton, his wife, called the story "The Daughter of Willie Horton," intended to keep "real issues out."[7]

Victors, losers, accusers, defendants, all seem to see the voter as wired and helpless, awaiting a decisive electronic charge. Even the guardians of print repeat the rosary. One year after Grossman's visit, a panel at the Barone Center joined by the very TV journalists from Texas and California who had patiently deconstructed inaccurate ads on nightly newscasts pronounced themselves failures. *No matter what we say*, they complained, in effect, *the false ads are repeated over and over, brainwashing the voters.* The viler the claim, the more likely, so goes the line, to get "free" TV news coverage, as in the race for the Senate in North Carolina in 1990. Newscasters all over the nation routinely berated—and displayed—a spot by Senator Jesse Helms, the ultimate victor, in which his media managers distorted the sound track of a speech by his opponent, Harvey Gantt, the black mayor of Charlotte, North Carolina, degrading his words into an imbecilic slur.

None of the panelists bothered to explain how multiple plays of a ludicrous thirty-second charge succeed, while careful dissections of its inaccuracy on prime-time news fail. Nor did they concede that Helms's track record in North Carolina was studded with electoral successes. Presumably Gantt's degraded voice laid an undocumented imprint on the subconscious of North Carolinians, as Reagan's flag-waving subsumed Stahl's impassioned words. Needless to say, such assumptions presume the voter is considerably lower in intelligence than the speaker, be he journalist or media manager. They also presume the voter pays devoted attention to political ads, registering every nuance, rather than zapping or ignoring them, which is far more likely, considering his normal behavior.

Myth One ignores as well the fact that voters surprise us over and over. Think for just a moment how often we have experienced contrarian political events in our lifetimes, whether at the polls or in the streets. They include Kennedy's narrow victory in 1960, Carter's upset wins in the 1976 primaries, Reagan's landslide in 1980, the two Chiles

victories in primary and general elections, the completely
unexpected primary victories in 1992 by the low-key ex-
Senator from Massachusetts, Paul Tsongas, once described
by columnist David Broder as "the least charismatic politician I have ever seen," and Governor Clinton's rise from
low approval ratings in the same period to a broad-gauge
victory. In all these cases most pollsters and pundits were
either inconsistent or incorrect. Few experts or opinion
counters predicted the popular revulsion over Vietnam or
Watergate either, or, most of all, the fall of the stolid, all-
powerful Soviet and Eastern European police states, culminating in the destruction of the Berlin Wall and the
reversal of the aborted coup attempt by party leaders in
Moscow two years later. In nearly all these cases the losers—
presidents, cabinet members, and state police bureaucracies—had virtually unlimited access to TV, that "infallible"
agent of mind control.

These and other events argue that the viewer/voter is
hardly the binary "yes-no" creature confidently charted on
TV news. The often errant line graphs and forecasts (errors
rarely recalled in later broadcasts), are normally based primarily on overnight telephone calls that pose simple up-
down questions to a small, harassed sample.

In Doris Graber's *Processing the News*, an impassioned defense of patient, drawn-out, follow-up interviewing of a
smaller sample than networks pursue, the author, a soci-
ologist, and her colleagues present a radically different view
of the simple-minded "public" described for us by the networks. Here we discover that voters continuously adjust
their opinions during a race, occasionally swinging completely around, based on a wide variety of hunches, premises, and life experiences. None of these doubts or
contradictions can be drawn out by a single interviewer in
one telephone call. "Closed" questions that demand quick
yes-no decisions "force respondents into thinking patterns
suggested by the investigator," they contend.[8]

Processing the News studied twenty-one residents of Illinois in 1976 to 1977 over an entire year. The interviewers asked hundreds of questions on repeated visits to homes and to offices. In the Carter-Ford presidential campaign of that year, Graber and her colleagues found voters responding to events and to speeches on a highly tentative and deeply personal level. The book by implication blasts the notion that telephone calls immediately following a political debate or a congressional hearing (particularly "call-in" polls using 900 numbers that require the caller to pay, limiting the response) are valid. *Processing the News* tells us the respondent might well change his or her mind one day later, particularly on complex, emotive events like presidential debates or the confirmation in 1991 to the Supreme Court of Clarence Thomas, following a weekend of testimony focused on his alleged sexual harassment of an employee.

If this full-dimensioned portrait of the American electorate is correct, it further calls into question virtually all the evidence summoned to prove TV power, particularly over political decisions. Combined with the critiques of polling often voiced within the profession itself, and with common sense, Processing the News raises an inevitable yet unprecedented question: why does TV *fail* to change our political opinions? Indeed, why does it inspire us *not* to vote at all?

THE BITE OF THE MIND

> *The culture of critical discourse (CCD) is an historically evolved set of rules, a grammar of discourse, in which there is nothing that readers will on principle permanently refuse to discuss or make problematic; they are even willing to talk about the value of talk itself and its possible inferiority to silence or to practice.*
>
> —Alvin W. Gouldner, *The Future of Intellectuals and the Rise of the New Class,* 1979

Television has generated an exponential increase in self-multiplication. This is true not only in terms of the . . . number of hours in which they [the viewers] are exposed to social facsimilies, but in the extent to which self-multiplication transcends time—that is, in which one's identity is sustained in the culture's history.

—Kenneth Gergen, *The Saturated Self: Dilemmas of Identity in Contemporary Life*, 1991.

The general industry assumption was that no more than three subplots were manageable [by the viewer] within a single episode.

—Todd Gitlin, *Inside Prime Time*, 1983

Polls are like drugs, a kind of political crack: easily available, capable of crowding out thoughts of everything else, and very addictive.

—Dayton Duncan, former press secretary for Michael Dukakis, 1989

Mental images are premises. Granted all the exceptions, network TV sees the viewer's mind as something like a tiny container ventilated with holes—a schoolchild's lunch box, in effect. "The attention span of the average viewer is short," Av Westin, highly respected ABC news producer once said, summing up this instinct and explaining why prime-time news increasingly flashes like a speeding bullet from subject to subject, fearful that delay will bore its audience. But there is another image of the mind, held by a large body of psychologists, teachers, philosophers, brain surgeons, any writer who dares to publish works longer than a page or two in length, or any politician who addresses voters in compound-complex sentences. Among this distinguished company the mind appears considerably larger than a lunch box. Indeed, to them, to many others, it seems a marvel of retentive capacity, able to hold and process dozens, even hundreds of words, images, and memories in a single second. Best of all, the brain has what appears to some investigators an almost infinite capacity to grow, heal itself, and extend its powers.

Clearly, these two images are in profound conflict with each other. At this moment in the history of the republic they approximate the shifting line between appearance and reality that has preoccupied philosophers, scientists, and poets for centuries. On one side, the side occupied by most of those who sell products and politicians to the American public, there is an assumption that we are virtually empty in mind and soul, waiting to be taken. From this perspective, every complex event in public life can be explained in primitive terms: Ronald Reagan's victories were caused by the actor hoodwinking us, for example; the early support for the Persian Gulf invasion was orchestrated by slick press conferences. Here, on this angle, the assumption is that the viewer/voter acts entirely on the basis of immediate provocation. Later, more considered studies and polls provided a different picture, however: the pro-Reagan votes were based on economic well-being (among other considerations), support for the Persian Gulf War changed with events. But these conclusions are primarily noted in academic journals, not in public discourse. Why? Because they don't fit that omnipresent image of the tiny lunch box, hanging in the synapses of too many influential brains.

Not that long ago, both politicians and their managers believed differently. Though pre-TV political campaigns were boisterous and sensational, the candidates believed they had to elaborate positions at length to be taken seriously by the voters, whether the positions were directly read or heard at all. In the 1950s, the 1960s, and even well into the 1970s the genre of the "half hour" film or live speech, when the candidate laid himself on the line in detail, was assumed to be as critical to victory as kissing babies. Even in moments of crisis political leaders once felt compelled to establish their gravity by unveiling positions patiently before the microphone, the camera, or crowd, then passing out bulky treatises to the press. Franklin Roosevelt's one-hour "fireside chats" on radio in the 1930s and 1940s were early examples. Richard Nixon's tortured press conferences and lengthy mea culpas under fire, grist for stand-up comics in their day, seem heroically sober now. The infamous "Checkers" speech in 1952, when Nixon defended his personal financial conduct in detail for thirty minutes, alone before the camera (while praising Checkers, his pet dog), is, by today's standards, a three-act Sophoclean tragedy.

Equally precious in the "sound-bite" era is George McGovern's sober half-hour soliloquy on "morality," produced late in his doomed campaign for President in 1972. Artlessly directed by veteran filmmaker Charles Guggenheim, this valiant testimony, replayed now on tape, is a marvel of straight-ahead talk. It contains barely a nod at what we have come to call "production values." Sitting alone in his Senate office, McGovern patiently lays out in his hopeless monotone a withering list of illegal actions by the Republicans, from the extortion of corporate campaign donations to the break-in by "five men wearing rubber gloves" in the Democratic National Headquarters, the event later known to the entire world as Watergate.

At no point in this vintage event does McGovern pause to sneer or snarl. The facts, the motives, even the precise dollar amounts are unveiled with merciless precision, as if the viewer were eager to punch numbers into his adding machine while the tens of thousands, the hundreds of millions, the billions roll endlessly off the candidate's tongue. When McGovern rises in the end to leave his chair, he is followed off camera not by music or by dancing electronics but by an announcer's voice, whose words are printed out on the screen, insuring that no one misunderstands the gravity of what we have heard: "In this place over the last four years," he begins, "611 billion dollars have been appropriated and decisions have been made that have touched the lives of people in every part of the earth. . . ." At the last, still unmoved by any need to enliven or titillate, the voice reminds the viewer that the election will be decided at least in part by "complex and demanding issues."

Nixon, McGovern, and the generation of politicians they
befriended or opposed—Lyndon Johnson, Barry Goldwa-
ter, Hubert Humphrey, John F. Kennedy, Robert Kennedy,
Edmund Muskie—must appear now to the disaffected, non-
voting eighteen-to-twenty-four-year-old bloc as creatures
from another planet, reared in a time when the program
of a candidate drove the campaign, even when events, emotion, or personality overwhelmed the issues. The incredulity
that greeted Paul Tsongas's constant reference to his detailed eighty-four-page *Call to Economic Arms,* often bran-
dished in primary debates early in 1992, is proof of this
self-enforced state of cultural remission (corrected, quickly,
by his shaken colleagues, who began to issue "position papers" in the old, Victorian manner, too). Some campaign
managers now presiding over huge TV "spot" budgets wist-
fully recall the days when "visuals" in campaign films were
drawn from the events themselves, from rallies, motorcades,
foreign travel. With the signal success in the 1964 campaign
of a Lyndon Johnson spot ad that depicted the hands of a
small child pulling apart a daisy, one by one, while a voice
warned that the opposition Republicans were eager to wield
nuclear power, the new era began to unfold. For some nascent media analysts, the "daisy" spot appeared to properly
service an imperious medium that prefers sensationalism to
detail. Beginning with the 1968 Nixon-Humphrey campaign, the candidate's once lengthy speeches and leisurely
half-hour films dwindled to five minutes, then, in succeed-
ing elections, to one minute, and now thirty seconds in
length. The time for political discourse also decreased because production costs for longer forms increased. TV management further refused to give up lucrative prime time for
long programs that don't produce what is called healthy
"audience share."

The thirty-second frame evolved out of all these considerations, practical and theoretical. Within thirty seconds, the
time slot preferred by most commercial advertisers, the candidates are limited to a dozen sentences at most, the equivalent of one typewritten paragraph. At worst, the candidate

is now reduced to a sentence, or to no words at all, as professional surrogates are hired to enact tiny dramas or speak in theatrical tones, while breathtaking visuals (heirs to LBJ's daisy) or the omnipresent, pseudo-scientific parade of numbers, charts, and "facts" take his/her place. In this brief compass the need to defend or justify charges in the manner of the painstaking McGovern film or even Nixon's agonized mea culpa, dwindles away. The "Spot" becomes the Saturday Night Special pistol of political debate.

Often the Sacred Thirty is taken up with nothing more than distortions of the opponent's record, intelligence, or physical appearance. Jesse Helms's slurring of Harvey Gantt's speech in 1990 is a perfect example. In the campaign for governor of Texas in the same year, Democrat Ann Richards's managers blanketed the state's TV screens in the final week with ads depicting the blurred, grainy face of Republican Clayton Williams on a videotape decayed through several generations—the visual equivalent of Gantt's decayed speech.

When he came to testify before Congress in behalf of campaign reform, Charles Guggenheim, who produced one of the first half-hour television films for a candidate (Adlai Stevenson, in 1956), blamed the popularity of the thirty-second spot on the new breed of "campaign managers." Since few of them are trained in film or television production, he argued, they prefer the simpler forms of huckster-ism and blitzkrieg:

> *Every tool of the advertising craft has been exercised to prove opponents lazy, dishonest, unpatriotic, dumb, cruel, unfeeling, unfaithful, and even criminal. It takes so little skill to condemn someone on radio and television commercials that there has been a proliferation of media consultants—many carrying their wares from one state to another. Only the names in the commercials need to be changed.*[9]

But it is not simply the ease of production that has caused the proliferation of spots. The Myth is at the center of this seismic shift. The conviction that the medium *virtually un-aided* persuades the unwary viewer is what poisons democratic discourse. Paradoxically, when Guggenheim warns in his testimony that viewers will "excuse" a spot for overstatement and inaccuracy, he, too, joins those who assume the TV viewer is mindless, if not helpless. As in many other cases, the evidence denying Myth One, which includes the testimony of the voters themselves, is routinely ignored.

Most reporters and campaign managers point to the daily and weekly "tracking polls" that have become common in recent years as proof of the Spot's deadly power. In the Helms-Gantt and Richards-Williams races, the fortunes of the final winners seemed to zoom during the very days when they mounted negative ads. A similar pattern appeared in the Chiles-Martinez race, with Martinez erroneously reported on the upswing in the wake of his own TV blitz. But such conclusions exclude impressive evidence, logic, and common sense on the other side. Repeated expressions of discontent with political advertising by voters is rarely credited by those committed to the Myth. The obvious presence of a host of competing sources of information, most of them, like newspapers, demanding more attention and respect than television, is also ignored.[10] When TV does impact on a campaign, it is often because the avoidance of substance by the two opponents (cf. Richards vs. Williams in Texas) leaves many voters with nothing except sensational charges to consider, whether seen on the screen, heard in conversation, or read in the newspapers. Predictably, as in Texas, as in the 1988 presidential campaign, the turnout in these cases is low.

When politicians focus on appearance rather than reality, it is no wonder that the medium becomes its own decidedly impotent message. In her study for Harvard's Barone Center of "Soundbite Democracy," Kiku Adatto confirmed the alarming change between the quantitative coverage of the Nixon-Humphrey campaign in 1968 and Bush-Dukakis in 1988. In twenty years, the average sound bite—that is, uninterrupted speech by a presidential candidate—offered on

prime-time network TV news dropped from an average of
42.3 seconds in 1968 to 9.8 seconds in 1988.

What replaced the candidate's own voice, defining his
own position, on the news? A barrage of visuals mixed with
an overpowering emphasis on media style rather than political content: Adatto found that more than half of all TV
news "reporting" in 1988 focused on what she calls "theater
criticism," compared with virtually none twenty years ago.[11]
When we add the marked shift of newspapers toward in-
depth analysis of TV ads *as news,* it's now clear that all aspects
of campaigning, from strategy to reportage, are encom-
passed within the thirty-second infinity. Aware of the shift,
media consultants now regularly attempt to gain "free coverage" on the nightly news, mostly by producing outrageously unfair spots. Roger Ailes himself, who gloried in
the free play granted his Revolving Door, put it succinctly:
"Now guys are trying to produce commercials for the evening news."

This strategy is failing on the one ground used to justify
it: voter acceptance. The sinking rate of participation that
has accompanied the massive investment in television cannot be denied, though it is often blamed on other phenomena (registration difficulties, for example). But the deeper
unease that surfaced in a series of polls, interviews, and
focus-group studies in late 1991, on the eve of yet another
campaign primed to repeat the media patterns of 1988, is
more difficult to dismiss, at least for those outside the armed
political camps. In a week-long series of group discussions
conducted across the United States, two polling firms, Peter
Hart Associates (for the Democrats) and Bailey Deardorff
and Associates (for the Republicans) concluded that respect
for the political process in the United States has plunged to
unprecedented depths. "This is a very dangerous situation
in any democracy," their report concluded. The main cause
of this alienation is the "low level of information" provided
by candidates to the public. And the single remedy most
enthusiastically endorsed by voters questioned in these discussions totally refutes the notion that Political Spots are

beloved. They asked that TV stations *"give candidates free and extended time blocks (e.g., five minutes at a time) for candidates to speak directly to the camera."*[12]

In brief, Nixon and McGovern redux. However amateurish their face-to-camera assaults might have been, politicians used to respond to the electorate's need to hear out issues in depth. In this light, McGovern's long, rolling script at the end of his monotoned speech is as valid a symbol for campaigning on television as George Bush's jail door or Jesse Helms's slurred sound track. Whatever the latter gains in immediate impact, it loses over the long run, spreading disaffection for politics; whatever the former loses on immediate viewing, turning off the uninterested voter, it gains by demonstrating a depth of involvement with "real" issues.

When the electorate asks over and over for "more information," it signifies a persistent desire for a full accounting, that is, for truly democratic dialogue. Both politicians and media ignore this need—this innate sophistication—at great peril. The networks' widely proclaimed return in 1992 to "issues" on their evening news programs (CBS News even announced it would air no "soundbite" less than ten seconds in length) and the candidates' wholesale commitment to long-form interviews and talk shows responded, however inadequately, to this need. Truncated spots by their nature fail the test of psychic complexity and contradiction so admirably illustrated in Graber's *Processing the News*. So do the "yes-no" formats of quick polls on issues like the Gulf War or East-West geopolitical confrontation. In its present form, TV is inadequate to this task. The only exceptions are those moments when highly articulate, impassioned voices are allowed to speak at length on intricate issues. By commercial TV logic, these moments can only be allowed in times of high drama. The prime examples are of course Watergate, Irangate, and the long weekend of charge and countercharge by law professor Anita Hill against Supreme Court nominee Clarence Thomas in the fall of 1991. In these instances, when question, answer, parry, and thrust rip away the shrouds of rhetoric, we sense vividly what we have lost by shortchanging political campaign debate.

Voters confirm this by telling us in many ways they rate print as the most reliable source of political information. It is easy to see why. A major urban newspaper like the *New York Times* can articulate a range of issues rising in the wake of the battlefield victory in the Gulf War. In its Sunday editorial section (on March 24, 1991), for example, the *Times* provided a modest "frame" of only two thousand words, the equivalent of twenty campaign spots laid end to end, for an article, written by a staff writer, that touched on the emerging policy of arms sales to friends and enemies in the re-formed region, on the security of states like Saudi Arabia and Kuwait, on the need to visibly reward allies in the coalition so that the vanquished Iraq cannot dominate public sympathy in the Mideast, on the search for a friendly "policeman" in the region to replace Hussein as an opponent of fundamentalist Iran, on the developing plight of the Kurds (which later forced the United States to recommit troops), on the economic consequences of a slump in military orders from oil-rich nations now out of immediate danger, and, finally, on the prospects for a wider peace settlement in the war's aftermath.

It is virtually inconceivable to imagine network news in the 1990s touching so many bases in one of its nightly newscasts or even in hour-long weekly programs like *60 Minutes*. The occasional "specials" more and more devoted themselves to sensationalism and personalities involved in major news events during the 1980s, nodding again to Myth One. The obsession with polling, sometimes based on nothing more than a few hundred phone calls placed immediately upon the heels of an event, before time for reflection has set in, seems unshakable. Here invented non-news becomes news. Yet it is not only the viewer who senses the implacable gulf between the marathon reality of the world and the short-order esthetic prevailing in television. It is the politicians themselves, whose wide-open embrace of what has come to be called the "think tank" is another symbol of the ironies that have attended the TV takeover. Throughout the very decades when the political parties stooped to commercial TV strategies, they funded and utilized a flourishing new genre of lavishly budgeted institutes dedicated to programmatic research, providing both parties, most of all the Republicans, with a barrage of dense position papers.

The tanks employed a range of substantial intellects. One of them, Jeane Kirkpatrick, authored in 1979 a highly polemic historical essay for *Commentary* magazine, "Dictatorships and Double Standards," proclaiming a distinct difference between "totalitarian" and "autocratic" regimes, arguing that the latter—a nation like Argentina, for example, or the Philippines—was susceptible to democratizing reform, while the Soviet Union was not. This intricately argued and documented paper impacted significantly on U.S. foreign policy in the Reagan years. Though it later proved totally fallacious, as communist regimes converted to democracy a few years later, it is the influence of her pedantic, demanding essay that matters here. It proves yet again that our political leaders, as well as the maligned voter, instinctively reach out for dialogue that is competent rather than short-order, that weighs as many factors and events as *The Federalist Papers* and *The Declaration of Independence*, which launched two centuries ago the democratic system now betrayed by the first of our five myths.

Politics on television is at this moment a mismatch between form and subject. Further, it offends the critical core of its audience, that is, the growing group of adults who are at once college-educated and active voters. Often called "baby boomers," this large and affluent center of the American white-collar class reveals in every study the highest levels of discontent both with network television (which it increasingly deserts for cable TV), for the credibility of commercials, and for politicians. This group, particularly middle-aged males, are the most frequent "zappers" in the TV audience. They are the most sustained viewers of CNN and C-Span, where entire sessions of Congress, of press conferences, of speeches and symposia are presented without interruption, for seven twenty-four-hour-days a week.[13] It's transparently obvious that Spot-mania has totally turned these voters off. Simply because the American voter *views* another ubiquitous "spot," often by chance, does not mean he/she believes or even remembers what he/she sees.

In *No Sense of Place: The Impact of Electronic Media on Social Behavior* (1985), Joshua Meyrowitz points out that the electorate in the 1950s was fiercely partisan—that is, committed to Democratic or Republican voting—but less knowledgeable about a broad range of issues.[14] By the 1960s, the rise in media coverage and of education introduced a new electorate, at once better informed, less committed to a single party, less credulous. At precisely this moment, the American media devised a system brilliantly calculated to alienate the "new class," as Alvin W. Gouldner calls it, this huge chunk of the electorate schooled to higher expectations from discourse. The image of the brain-as-lunch-box is singularly inappropriate for this vital core. If Kenneth Gergen is further correct that the acutely verbal, engaged self in contemporary society is spread thin, alienated by competing claims on its consciousness, then the Spot is worse than the wrong strategy. The Spot is the psychic crisis of democracy.

FROM BITE TO BIT (FROM WORSE, THAT IS, TO WOR—)

It is evident how much men love to deceive and be deceived, since rhetoric, that powerful instrument of error and deceit . . . has always been held in high reputation.
—John Locke, *Essay*, 1680

You can't have it both ways, Jim. . . .
You can't have it both ways, Harvey. . . .
You can't have it both ways, Bob. . . .
—Political spots by National Media, Inc., 1988–1990

*Thirty-second spots are speech. They are po-
litical discourse.*
—Robert Squier, campaign consultant. Interview with Author, 1991

*I'm Bruce Herschensohn. My opponent, Tom
Campbell, was the only Republican Congress-
man opposing the 1980 anti-crime bill. He's
liberal and he's wrong.*
—Bruce Herschensohn, ten-sec-
ond TV "soundbit," Senate primary, California, 1992

Bruce Herschensohn is lying. . . .
—Tom   Campbell,   "soundbit"
reply, 1992

No one questions the massive presence of television. But
what, precisely, is its effect? At base, this question probes
beyond the numbers, into whether TV's quantitative presence in our lives and our politics has triggered a qualitative
change. On the level of numbers, there is no doubt. Though
emotion has always played a profound role in political campaigning, through rumors, slogans, posters, photographs,
films, and mass rallies, no medium ever summoned so large
an audience for single events or images, repeated over and
over. In the fall of 1991, Anita Hill's charge that Supreme
Court nominee Clarence Thomas "harassed" her with sexual innuendos transformed her into a national figure virtually overnight. In the fall of 1992, President Bush's
double-barreled assault on Clinton's avoidance of the Vietnam war draft when he was a student at Oxford in the late
1960s and his week-long visit to Moscow in the same period
also received saturation coverage for several days in all
media, including print and radio.

But do these high-profile moments move viewers or voters to action, or sustained thought? Are the techniques so
readily borrowed from commercial television's prime-time
armory—among them the news executives' unabashed libido for fast-paced, black-and-white subjects (cf. Hill vs.

Thomas, Oliver North vs. the Congress)—proper for what Robert Squier calls "political discourse"? Or do many voters instinctively reject TV news's rush to judge, to identify winners, losers, heroes, villains, overnight? In fact, most Americans remained undecided about the Thomas-Hill standoff in the early days, many asking, as did the Senators on the Judiciary Committee, for time to reflect and weigh all the evidence. It is also likely that many of them waited instinctively to read and analyze the follow-up articles in the press, as the Senators demanded *reading time* themselves, to pore over the transcripts. Finally, in the end, the voters *appeared* to decide in Thomas's favor, once again surprising those who expected Anita Hill's charges to definitively tarnish his case.[15] One year later, to compound the complexity, sentiment seems to have shifted again, particularly among women, in Hill's favor. The Bush charges against Clinton led to a similarly surprising rejection: the President's rating in the polls remained stagnant in the week following his assault. Many anonymous leaders in his own party concluded the attacks had misfired, harming the accuser more than the defendant. Here and there certain polls turned up numbers documenting that a solid majority of voters, nearly two-thirds, believed the attacks to be "unfair."

TV's role in the political process, therefore, is hardly simple. As a political weapon, this medium, like print, is a double-edged sword. TV is the heir and superior to the newspaper headline. It excels in setting agendas, in calling the attention of society to primal questions, like war, peace, the budget, to conflicts between strong personalities. There is no doubt the barrage of early TV "spot" attacks in 1988 against Michael Dukakis's alleged softness on "crime" briefly set an agenda—for the press, for the candidates, for the voters. But it was hardly these spots alone that finally changed the momentum of the campaign, destroying Dukakis's early lead. The primary causes appear to have been the rosy economic climate left behind—briefly—by the Reagan adminstration, which dulled the appetite of those who did vote (primarily the middle class) for change, and Dukakis himself. Dukakis's failure to bring out the Democratic working-class vote, to establish his own agenda, was a failure of content, not of media strategy.

As for Bush, it now seems certain that voters finally decided in his behalf not because he was "tough" and Dukakis was "soft" but because he appeared to be the hand-picked manager of good economic times. Reagan himself had benefited from rising expectations in the mid-1980s, not long after his approval rating had nosedived in the wake of a persistent recession earlier blamed on former President Jimmy Carter. In hindsight, it is clear that neither Reagan nor Bush profited from any noticeable passion in the electorate for their hard-line conservative views on "social" issues like abortion, crime, welfare, or lifestyle, where most voters opposed them. The moment the economy shifted into reverse, in 1992, the oft-proclaimed "Republican lock" on the White House, lacking any deep social or cultural mooring, loosened.[16]

Conclusion one, then: George Bush would have won the 1988 election without the supposedly decisive anti-crime spots. Conclusion two: human error handed the holy medium its apparent victory in 1988, supposedly confirmed in the percentage swings up and down in the tracking polls. Without a single spot, the election would have moved in a similar pattern, as voters finally decided for Bush on substantive grounds.

TV's awesome immediacy can self-destruct its user. Often when we are suddenly inundated by the sweep of instantaneous facts, names, and numbers provided by nonstop hearings or events, we are prompted to deny what we see, to step back, to change our minds, precisely as we do when assaulted by a street vendor. The early and massive "undecided" position on Thomas-Hill is but one example. Throughout the 1992 campaign, public approval and disapproval ratings shifted rapidly up and down for each of the three major contenders. In the beginning, Bush and "independent" Ross Perot scored high in terms of trust and credibility, while Governor Bill Clinton was low. Near the end of the campaign, both Bush and Perot had plunged downward, while Clinton improved his numbers. Away from the heat and high-focus drama of presidential campaigns, similar delays and shifts in opinion are rarely documented by a press days or weeks after the initial emotive event. The slow diminution in the popularity of the Gulf War was less noted than the early "vote" in favor. The rise, then fall of support for Oliver North as he testified before Congress on the Irangate controversy in 1987 is another example, as is the flip-flop of public support for George Bush in his angry rebuttal to Dan Rather's questioning about Irangate on *CBS News* in 1988—at first strongly pro-Bush, then, two weeks later, shifting toward Rather.

The researchers who painstakingly pursued voters for *Processing the News* concluded that their sample consistently "selected and interpreted news in line with the predispositions established throughout life, which were continuously adapted to changing lifestyles and experiences." It stands to reason that these shifting interpretations are moved as much by wary suspicion of the media and the government as by the gullibility assumed within the folds of Myth One. The final swing to Oliver North's side in his trial years later, when the public saw him primarily as a martyr put up for punishment while higher authorities, perhaps President Reagan himself, was prompted by this cynicism.

The demands and the expectations in political discourse differ profoundly from the brutally brief discourse that surrounds products hawked beautifully (on occasion) by TV. The viewer approaches Lawton Chiles or Ann Richards through a web of responses hardly prompted by Obsession commercials or prime-time detective stories (though the complex, shifting plot lines in *Hill Street Blues,* a popular success in the 1980s, demanded an equivalent alertness). The moment a political spot hits the screen is the moment when the viewer either suspends belief, deserts affection, narrows his focus, or zaps away.

These responses describe a division that surely corresponds to "voters" and "nonvoters." Quick cuts, slogans, and imagery prodding into war, peace, and taxes give us pause, or provoke disgust. Note the pressure points touched in this elegant haiku written by Squier, Eskew, Knapp, Ochs Communications and his colleagues for the aging Senator Claiborne Pell of Rhode Island in his victorious, come-from-behind campaign for office in 1990:

> *For more than thirty years this man been one of*
> *America's strongest believers*
> *Claiborne Pell, a war veteran, foreign service*
> *officer, serving under eight presidents, world*
> *leaders*
> *helping shape our nation's foreign policy*
> *when the Berlin Wall went up in 1961. Pell*
> *predicted that the wall and Communism would*
> *crumble*
> *he worked to make it happen*
> *a lean, effective national defense made right here*
> *in Rhode Island*
> *a firm foreign policy*
> *a commitment to arms control and peace*
> *and today America's victory is seen everywhere*
> *Senator Claiborne Pell*
> *he never has to shout to be heard*
> *he conducts himself and his nation's affairs with*
> *something all too rare in politics*
> *dignity*

But rhetorically deft spots like these, which reaffirm rather than attack without validation, are rare in the climate of post-discourse American politics. The Spot now refutes "discourse," bringing it to a halt altogether. To compare the exchanges in the lengthy Lincoln-Douglas debates in 1858, the fevered Kennedy-Nixon debates in 1960, or McGovern on morality in 1972 is like comparing Dostoyevsky with Obsession.

Our fifteen- and thirty-second anti-haikus are filled with half sentences and angry, unmetered prose, sometimes

amounting to fifty words or less. In the 1984 epic fired by
Jesse Helms at his Democratic opponent James Hunt, we
see nothing more than a grainy photograph pairing Senator
Edward Kennedy with Hunt, who is scowling. The words
allege simply that "Hunt is for racial quotas, Jesse Helms is
against." Six years later, in 1990, Helms went after his opponent, the luckless Harvey Gantt, on the same issue, providing a close-up of a pair of distinctly white hands tearing
up a rejection letter, while the anonymous, disembodied
voice says, simply, "You needed that job but you lost it because of racial quotas." In spot after spot, no matter what
the state, the candidate, or the issues, the political opponent
is routinely charged with hypocrisy on the ground of
quotes—rarely identified or dated—that appear to contradict each other.

"You can't have it both ways," has become as familiar in
spot campaigning as the flag, the wife, and a combat medal,
if available. By 1992, the libido of the campaign managers,
if not the voters they allegedly courted, decompressed down
to a mere ten seconds, to what cynics began to call "Sound-
bits." In crowded, expensive primaries like the California
Senate competition, where almost a dozen candidates from
both parties struggled for recognition, these travesties flourished. In the struggle between Bruce Herschensohn and
Tom Campbell for the Republican nomination in June, the
bits simply charged and countercharged, without proof or
grace. Herschensohn finally triumphed, but his bitter "bits,"
widely condemned, dogged him in the fall election, which
he lost to his Democratic opponent.

By no stretch of the imagination are these techniques
"discourse." They do not provide information or provoke
thought. They seek only to stir raw emotion. That nearly
all of them disguise the identity of the attacker, who is represented normally by a mercenary stand-in voice, with his
name revealed only in a tiny tag line at the end ("Paid for
by Bush-Quayle" by "Richards for Governor," by "Herschensohn for the Senate," etc.) is the final proof that neither dialogue nor debate is intended. The debater—the

accuser—is nowhere to be found in the new genre of anti-discourse.

Increasingly, the only defense against a killer spot is to return fire, say the campaign managers, to imitate, in effect, the assassin. In 1982, Republican John Danforth found himself regularly assailed in spots mounted by his opponent, Democrat Harriet Woods, as "millionaire Jack Danforth." The phrase, insistently repeated, seemed to blot out all other issues in the minds of the press and perhaps the voters, who appeared in early polls to be turning against the incumbent. Though Danforth loathed negative spots (and has since sponsored bills to banish them), he agreed to a counterattack. Mounted by Charles Guggenheim, it combined direct on-camera appeals by Danforth with direct assaults on Woods's record. In one of the spots, Woods's face hung out of focus on the screen, a vile visual parody, while the omnipresent, impersonal killer voice recounted her record, bringing the face finally into recognizable focus.

Victorious in the end by a narrow margin, the Danforth campaign is often cited as a model for media counterattack. So is the aggressive policy pursued by Squier, Eskew, Knapp, Ochs Communications for Democrat Richards in her slam-bang battle with colorful Clayton Williams, Republican, in 1990. Williams blanketed the TV air with $6 million worth of ads early in the campaign, portraying himself as a tough, outspoken cowboy crusader, taking a wide lead while Richards staggered through a bruising primary plus runoff election. But the Richards counterattack fed on Williams's electronic campaign like a deadly viper. Her spots refuted his charges and portrayed his blurred, grainy face on a small TV screen in the background. In its last three weeks, the Richards campaign repeated one ad over and over, in which Williams's verbal gaffes were repeated for the viewers—on environmental issues, rape (which he compared to the weather: "relax and enjoy it"), and Richards herself ("I hope she don't go back to drinking again"). Once again, the victim-turned-killer won, by three percentage points (Danforth's margin was 1 percent).

Does the thirty-second spot decide elections? If it does, there is small hope for purifying politics at the end of the century. In its reduction of campaigning to banal charge and banal countercharge, the spots speak to an electorate that appears incapable of distinguishing between false and real issues. Worse, conventional wisdom, or "C.W.," represented by the mainstream press, the TV networks, and the prosperous political managers, accepts this debatable premise. If the 1992 results argue for a reassessment of C.W., there is still no guarantee of change. The aura of Myth One bathes all numbers that confirm the decisive power of the spots—mostly the overnight tracking polls—and drowns "facts" on the other side, most of all the disastrously low turnouts, as well as inconvenient results, such as Clinton's victory, which can be attributed to his undoubtedly canny managers rather than to the public's hunger for a change in government economic policy.

Needless to say, the final answer to this critical question is hardly simple. Deciding on the efficacy of political spots is at least as difficult as the Danforth-Woods, Richards-Williams, and Clinton-Bush-Perot races themselves, which turned on issues that were primarily economic and cultural. But certainly they were not resolved by the superiority of one media style over another. In the Danforth case, nearly all incumbent Republican senators were threatened or defeated across the United States in 1982, due to the continuing economic downturn that had begun four years before, whether savaged by media violence or not. Danforth's victory is logically credited to his record, which closely paralleled the positions held by the voters (particularly on abortion: both Danforth and the state were pro-life at this time). The Richards-Williams race was similarly conflicted by a plethora of competing factors, from the evident distaste of younger Texas voters, many migrants from the North and the East, for the cowboy image invoked by Williams, to the state's economy, which had sputtered under the retiring Republican governor, William Clements. Most of all, Ann Richards as a woman identified with the progressive wing of the Democratic party represented a clear refutation of the past: she was a new voice, a new start; Williams's face was defiantly, openly retrograde, blurred or not. Contrarians can argue that this race, too, as well as many of the costly 1992 campaigns, could have been won without its immense and costly commitment to thirty-second mayhem.

THE POLITICS OF APOLOGY

> *If the media are more acted upon than acting, it has profound implications for the kind of question one asks.*
> —Denis McQuail, 1972

> *In the sixties, Katayama began to sense a change in consumer attitudes, an increasingly powerful undercurrent of resentment. The objections to Detroit, he and some of his American people (and their counterparts at Toyota) decided, were different now. They were no longer just about the size and the price of cars, but more about the quality and, even more important, about Detroit's response to legitimate complaints.*
> —David Halberstam, *The Reckoning*, 1986

> *Mr. Clinton claims he is not like those Democrats in Congress who like to tax and spend, tax and spend. (Waddling mechanical duck quacks.) We say, if it talks like a duck, walks like a duck, it must be a Democrat.*
> —Sean Fitzpatrick, unused proposal for a Republican TV spot, 1992

The case against Myth One is overpowering, based in fact and in experience. This is precisely why the case is feared. The refutation of Myth One threatens the ease associated with beliefs rarely changed, most of all in the media. The assumptions about TV power have been shaken continually in our lifetimes without moving the faithful one inch. Two decades ago, we were told that TV's ability to smother differences and produce homogenized consensus meant the end of political dissent in America. This was followed by the vigorous anti–Vietnam War movement of the 1960s and early 1970s, which soundly challenged institutional authority. One decade ago, we were told that TV's direct approach to the voter meant the end of the imperial presidency. Faced with adversaries challenging him on the tube in fifty states, making their own cases to the voter, so it was said, no chief executive can hope to form a consensus and lead the nation. Yet this cliché was followed by the advent of Ronald Reagan, who single-handedly forced a set of far-reaching economic reforms both on his party and on the nation, in the early 1980s. Then we were persuaded that the Republicans' conservative agenda, combined with their media smarts, would inevitably enlist most of the southern and western United States into the electoral college column into the foreseeable future, another agenda, along with the supposed invincibility of George Bush following the Gulf War victory, reversed in the recent election by swings in the social and economic pendulum that virtually no one prophesied as recently as January of the fateful election year.*

Such reversals must be refuted or ignored because they challenge a well-heeled industry. The presumption of TV power feeds a hungry elite: the consultants, TV networks, independent stations, and cable TV outlets gorging on a billion-dollar war chest in every full-fledged election season. More, the myth "serves the interest . . . of party leaders," contends critic Walter Karp. The leaders want to disguise their own hold on power, he says, by blaming the electronic

---

*Kevin Phillips's *Politics of Rich and Poor* might be considered a contradiction to this statement. But this book, like Phillips's earlier treatise proclaiming a Republican "lock" on the White House, is highly general in its thesis, predicting a slow reversal of the Reagan administration's antipathy toward the use of government power to ameliorate economic distress, aid the poor, the homeless, and so forth. Phillips did not and could not foresee the downswing in the economy in 1992 nor the role played by Ross Perot in whetting voter appetite for change. Surely he would not contend that the 1992 election was largely determined by the complex, deep-seated, long-range change defined in *Rich and Poor*.

monster for their own mistakes. The monster leaps to accept this blame, because it magnifies its apparent power and escalates the prices it can charge the clients:

> *When party apologists blamed the networks for ruining . . . presidents, undermining American foreign policy, and subverting the party system, they knew that television would issue no hot denials.*[17]

Most of the experts who prey upon politics further prefer to ignore the fatal unpredictability associated with any human endeavor. In the political arena, the doctrine of predictable unpredictability recalls a hugely inconvenient fact: the voter has a mind of his own. If he or she can even detect fraud or tedium, if political ads bore him to death, an entire advisory elite is suspect. The growing refusal to vote is a hugely inconvenient case for this elite. The *People Versus Politics* study published in 1991 by Democratic pollster Peter Hart and Republican Charles Bailey does sum up the case for dwindling enthusiasm in neat arithmetical rows.[18] Here and in other studies we find record "dissatisfaction" levels as well.

But evidence of this kind has been quietly mounting for several decades, highlighted by a series of studies conducted with relentless thoroughness by Syracuse University's Thomas Patterson and Robert McClure. From their pivotal book, *The Unseeing Eye*, published in 1976 and based on "in-depth" interviews during the 1972 McGovern-Nixon campaign, funded by the National Science Foundation, we learned that most voters trust written or spoken information more than electronic messages. A subsequent book by Patterson alone, *The Mass Media Election*, which applies the same methods to the 1976 Carter-Ford race, reached the same conclusions. So did a later survey conducted by the Simmons Market Research Bureau in 1986, and Michael Robinson's study, already noted, of sixty 1988 campaigns.[19]

Robinson concluded, bluntly, that "advertising" is the

"single most overrated club in a candidate's pack." Patterson, McClure, and Simmons each found that TV is less
important to the average American than a host of other
sources of information, most of all print, for several reasons:
voters watch TV news sporadically, then can't recall what
they see, whereas readers of newspaper articles typically
retain much more; those who do feast on TV news tend to
be older, less educated and less likely to vote than those who
prefer reading; and the small, influential core of voters who
do change their minds during campaigns change on the basis
of issues and events, not TV ads. In the 1972 campaign,
the Patterson-McClure interviews showed that the Paris
Peace Talks, which identified Nixon with an end to the
Vietnam War, persuaded close to *half* the undecided voters,
dwarfing the influence of TV ads, which ranked down near
"party allegiance" and the "advice of friends" as a deter-
mining factor in decision-making. The Simmons study in
the mid-1980s found that the most consistent viewers of TV
news fell into two distinct categories, neither supportive of
the myth. One group includes habitual viewers who watch
the news along with everything else but are less likely to
vote. The other group, younger and better educated, is
represented by "a heavy reader of news . . . who watches a
lot of news and information programming on TV but little
else."[20] But this critical and activist group uses TV as only
one source among many for decision-making.

The hidden message between the lines in these books,
which touched thousands of citizens, is identical to the explicit findings of *Processing the News*, which focused on a
small body of Illinoisans: that each voter acts actively on the
information he receives, siphoning it through a wide range
of discussion, memory, and changing events. The need expressed over and over by these twenty-one citizens, surely
in league with their colleagues elsewhere, was for media not
confined to simple win-lose polarities: "They often express
great disappointment [with media] because learning seems
to be slim."[21]

Now of course none of these contrarian reports affected

either campaign or media strategy until the halcyon Bush-Clinton-Perot campaign. Even now, when reminded of the incontrovertible decline in voting that accompanied their uninhibited indulgence in buying TV time at escalating rates, consultants and politicians typically respond by blaming other influences—the opposition party, the difficulties faced by a highly mobile population that must reregister every time it moves, the sense of well-being that suffuses an old, self-satisfied democracy ("They [the public] believe whoever wins [we] will do just fine," argued Robert Squier, pre-1992). The debatable response of most major newspapers has been to increase "ad watch" coverage of the spots, focusing yet more attention upon an adversary that now sets the public agenda for nondiscourse. It is an agenda saturated with simplistic bromides appropriate to one paragraph of print—whether Dukakis is "soft" on criminals, Ann Richards drinks too much or, in 1992, whether either Bush or Clinton was guilty of infidelity—slighting the higher destiny of the nation. For several decades Americans appeared to face an apparently unending series of campaigns determined to provide voters what they don't want.

What *do* they want? Every sign indicates that he/she hungers for precisely the sustenance denied by fast-paced network TV news or killer soundbite—or bit—spots. No wonder that in the "People Versus Politics" focus groups, the unanimous call was for "free and extended time blocks" during the campaign. The voter lusts for content, for some deeper handle on his fate, for the kind of content that print handles best, with its unhurried pace, and TV news once tried to approximate. In "Soundbite Democracy," Kiku Adatto recalls instance after instance in 1968 when network nightly news allowed embattled politicians to speak in stretches of time far longer than the 9.8 second average allowed presidential candidates in 1988. She reminds us of the moment when Democratic Senator Edmund Muskie, assailed by student hecklers during a speech, was given a full minute to respond on *NBC News.* Twenty years later, when the networks were following the lead of the killer spots, CBS figuratively gagged Michael Dukakis in the coverage of a similar incident. When Dukakis was confronted by anti-abortion demonstrators, his reply was never heard. The only words came from a screaming woman, sitting on the floor surrounded by small kids. "Do we have to destroy our children?" she shouted as he passed.

Effective television? From one angle, the prime-time entertainment angle, yes. From another angle, this is precisely the kind of noncoverage that has alienated the public from the political process and from network TV news itself, where ratings have been dropping for almost a decade. The wonder is that so few politicians have followed Lawton Chiles's lead in assaulting this system, particularly those facing a well-heeled opponent on the wrong side of the issues. Early in 1988, *TV Guide* asked one thousand Americans which characteristics they most wanted to see in the "next president." At the top of the list they wanted "intelligence," "honesty," and "command of the facts" most of all, while "sense of humor," "youthfulness," and "good looks"—prime-time virtues—sank to the bottom.[22]

Neither the Bush nor the Dukakis campaigns paid attention in 1988 to this ordering of values. The priorities were bequeathed to managers who studiously pursued the ingredients lurking at the bottom of the *TV Guide* chart. The disappointing presidential debates, in which neither man appeared to depart from his prepared text, failing as popular fare as well as serious discourse, is a symptom of this error. Dukakis lost far more by avoiding real discourse than Bush, because his position on vital issues like abortion, trade, and defense aligned with majority sentiments virtually across the board, while Bush's attitudes did not, according to the *Times-Mirror* poll.[23] But Bush also lost, in that his mean, uninspiring campaign failed to attract anything close to a majority of eligible voters: he won with a scant quarter of those eligible to cast ballots.

TV was hardly the cause of George Bush's victory, as we have seen. Without buying a single spot, he would have bested Dukakis in the end, given his legacy of economic success, and his opponent's lackluster case. With the public's widely documented disgust with video campaigning, indeed, it seems likely Bush won *in spite* of television in 1988. Invaluable support for this conclusion can be found in the extensive *Post-Election Survey Among Voters* commissioned by the American Federation of State, County, and Municipal Employees one month after the disastrous campaign ended, and published in 1989. Along with other documents, it proves conclusively that Bush won the election on the few substantial grounds he allowed to surface in his campaign rhetoric, including his greater experience in foreign policy, defense, and military issues.[24] He owned this advantage over Dukakis from the first, even when he trailed in the polls following a tumultuous, carefully managed Democratic National Convention.

Myth One is a myth. When the public senses that any election—for the presidency, the Senate, the House, for mayor, for the school board—is a life-and-death matter, it will strain to see beyond surface or style. Neither President Bush nor his advisors were able to distinguish between the real stakes in the campaign they won and the glitz that accompanied their overbudgeted media strategy. When, four years later, Bush's numbers began to decline as the reelection challenge neared, the administration bought into Myth One again, once more at high cost. In May of that year, Bush's organization hired two successful Madison Avenue media executives, Martin Puris and Clayton Wilhite, to form a private corporation charged with managing a $40 million budget.

Calling themselves "The November Group," this elite task force proceeded to repeat the negative, slashing spots and rhetoric that characterized the 1988 campaign. Each of Bush's tormentors, Clinton and Perot, took turns besting him in the polls. Each was also alternatively savaged with attacks of every variety. In the middle of the summer, the entire Republican convention seemed dedicated to nothing other than the character assassination of Governor Clinton and his family (Perot had temporarily withdrawn from the race). The challenger was accused of everything from tax-and-spend libertinism to draft avoidance to disregard for family values. He narrowly missed being lampooned even for his girth by Sean Fitzpatrick, an ad writer who advised his colleagues to study the recurrent images of Clinton jogging every morning on the network news. "He looks like a duck," said Fitzpatrick, who unaccountably failed to sell his killer duck spot and later left the belligerent November Group.[25]

Yet Bush's numbers remained sluggish, despite occasional spurts. On the eve of the first of three debates in early October, following his unsuccessful thrusts at Clinton's draft record and his one week in Moscow, Bush was offered some startlingly unconventional advice by Edward Rollins, a Republican strategist who had managed several of Ronald Reagan's highly successful campaigns. If Bush wants to restore credibility, Rollins told the press, he should *apologize to Clinton* for the harm done "to you, your wife, to your draft status, to your state, and to your family." Most of all, Rollins contradicted the premise behind the high-priced November Group:

> [They] didn't learn any lesson from 1988. George Bush won because he inherited Ronald Reagan's popularity. But his campaign people thought they won because they destroyed Mike Dukakis. Now they think they can destroy Clinton.[26]

In these words, Rollins shakes, surely unintentionally, the imperial status of our first myth, by implying that the content and demeanor of Bush's campaign mattered more than mere momentary command, of the medium. But the entire campaign, properly seen, performed the same act: demystification. Properly seen, from beginning to end, on levels stylistic, ideological, and cultural, the election of 1992, like a Shakespearean tragedy, brings the final curtain down on our lead myth, and closes out the persistent, highly provincial strain of media strategy and theory that has virtually destructed our political process.

CAMPAIGN 1992 AS SHAKESPEAREAN TRAGEDY (IF NOT COMEDY)

BLASPHEMOUS ART TOO SHOCKING TO SHOW: BUSH USED YOUR TAX $$$ FOR THIS.
—Pat Buchanan political spot, Georgia primary, 1992

Communication and the media—since '84 and certainly since '88—have changed. People . . . get a lot of information.
—Robert M. Teeter, Campaign Chairman, Republican party, 1992

I think it is good to take some questions and to be out there on the front lines. But I think to turn the White House into a clearing house for 800 numbers is a little beneath the dignity of the White House and I am determined to conduct myself . . . with decency and honor and dignity.
—President George Bush, 1992

We hear you do an admirable imitation of Elvis Presley, Governor Clinton. Would you do that for us now?
—Charlie Rose, PBS, conversation with Governor Bill Clinton, 1992

Aren't you sick of being treated like an unprogrammed robot?
—Ross Perot, concluding remarks, Debate 1, October 11, 1992

From beginning to end, the campaign of 1992 turned the apparent lesson of 1988, *negative fast-food media wins,* upside down. As much as the victors—and, occasionally, the losers—wanted to replay the terms of the previous campaign, virtually every significant movement on the part of the new victors and the invigorated voter/viewer reversed them. Whereas in the past, for example, candidates lusted to land one or two minutes on nightly network news, as Roger Ailes recommended, this year many of them aggressively moved to speak at length on radio and cable television talk shows, produced thirty-minute "infomercials" of their own, and managed two-way satellite TV exchanges with voters. The more any given challenger found the means to engage in direct discourse with voters, the better he seemed to do both in the polls and in the endless stretch of primary elections.

In time, this surprising subplot—that neither the players nor the audience wanted to play by the old mythic rules— became clear even to those who wanted to ignore it. "Killer" challengers like Pat Buchanan found their attack ads, focusing on allegedly subversive art funded by tax dollars, turning voters off rather than on, mainly because 1992 was a year when voters, many of them out of jobs or fearing loss, clearly wanted bottom-line solutions, not distractions. In time even Robert Teeter, the Republican party's chairman, openly embraced this "sub-plot" and urged his candidate to enter the talk show fray, right away.

Act I of the 1992 campaign, then, spanning the primaries, might be likened to the first act of *King Lear*, in which the audience is introduced to the main characters and to their main dilemma: whether the kingdom should be handed over by the aging king to Goneril and Regan, his flattering, adoring daughters, or to Cordelia, the daughter who loves him with reservations (she spoke out when she thought him wrong, to his displeasure; her sisters always told him whatever he wanted to hear, rather like a November Group spot). The equivalent dilemma posed in the 1992 campaign—who will inherit the republic, if not the kingdom—was resolved by a range of seductive weaponry as well as by the three human players who remained onstage to the end. Along with satellites, cable TV, radio, and talk shows, these weapons included 800 telephone numbers, electronic databases, fax machines, home videos, and a torrent of printed statements, in the form of books, papers, and notebooks slammed down on the table by candidates during the debates.

The early Democratic primary debates were filled with references to these alternative means of mounting a sustained political dialogue. Taking a cue from Lawton Chiles's call to visit your local library, the unsung Paul Tsongas would often display his eighty-four-page "notebook" calling for economic reform. Jerry Brown, former governor of California, offered his 800 number to voters over and over, insisting that he would finance his campaign entirely through donations from voters of $100 or less, refusing PAC money (from well-heeled political action committees). Brown early announced his antipathy to soundbites, refusing to be interviewed on television for anything less than five minutes. Like Ross Perot, the "independent" Texas billionaire running outside the two major party structures, he frequented long, open-ended talk shows, on radio as well as cable television, mixing it up with call-in voters, offbeat hosts—and winning, here and there, primaries he was supposed to lose. Perot's surprising entry in the campaign actually occurred on CNN's *Larry King Live!* on February 20, when he offered to enter the race "if you, the people, are that serious, you register me in fifty states." Not long after, Perot began to speak with his army of "volunteers" by satellite television links, contacting a spread of distant cities simultaneously. Bill Clinton's early TV spots openly criticized the media, spoke yearningly of "direct access" to the voter, and offered viewers yet another 800 number, where they could hear about his policies and plans at greater length than allowed on television. Later in the campaign, Clinton gave journalists touch-tone access to recordings of entire speeches delivered that day.

In effect, Perot and the Democrats played Cordelia to the press and to the media. Virtually every study or poll during these months indicated that the voters and viewers shared this hypercritical view of the media's inability to cover or analyze the campaign on substantive rather than superficial grounds. The Republicans moved more slowly at first, because they perceived themselves to be in the lead, with President Bush's popularity rating high early in the year, still primed by the Gulf War. But Robert Teeter's advice to Bush finally cracked the November Group's preoccupation with prime-time hits.

Act II—in which the players in *Lear* (and most of Shakespeare) reveal their true spots, narrowing down the issues— was surely the two conventions, which, in their preparation, execution, and aftermath, occupied most of June, July, and August, leading into the final months of the campaign. By the middle of *Lear*, the King has been virtually ejected from his own palace by his ungrateful daughters, while Cordelia, his ugly duckling, tries to care for him, revealing her virtues. Clinton/Cordelia, who trailed the president and Perot throughout much of Act I, ends Act II in a commanding double-digit lead. How did the once-fragile governor of Arkansas, buffeted early with "character" flaws (an earthy tabloid headline accused him of infidelity) and assertions from Republican voices that both he and his wife were "liberal," if not "leftist," in their social and political views, inherit the kingdom?

Certainly the answer to this question is multiple. Certainly psychic and economic factors played a role in forming the public's response to each of the candidates, as is normally the case in any American election. But it is equally clear that Clinton benefited hugely from the active presence in the campaign of a stream of alternative media strategies and tools, which he and his colleagues seized upon, partly because they distrusted Myth One's dependence on the medium-as-arbiter. Like Brown and, later, Perot, Clinton began as early as the Pennsylvania primary in June to purchase and produce his own open-ended video dialogues with the audience, renting the time he needed to explore what he called the "specificity" of his programs, ignored, he and others complained, by the networks. Clinton eagerly agreed to engage in direct Q-and-A with the even larger audience offered him twice by CBS News, which, on one occasion, meant faxes from all over the United States, containing written, carefully considered questioning.

But Clinton, like Perot/Cordelia Two, who became virtually a *Larry King Live!* regular, also embraced unconventional venues and voices, divorced from standard newsfare. Clinton played his saxophone on the late-night *Arsenio Hall* talk show on Fox Television, a beacon for the politically disengaged twenty-year-old class. Later, he answered questions on MTV, which began, between music videos, to cover the campaign, for the first time in its brief, meteoric history. On the night before the New York primary, Clinton had obliged an older audience of PBS-style baby boomers on *Charlie Rose* by imitating Elvis Presley with a hoarse, croaking voice. During the convention in New York in July, the abdication of the networks from gavel-to-gavel coverage resulted in the widely lamented lowest-Nielsen-numbers ever for any Democratic or Republican convention. Later, to be sure, these numbers were reversed during the debates, which routinely outpolled competing entertainment and sports. But in the meantime the Clinton campaign's embrace of alternative media provided multiple points of access for voters, viewers, readers, listeners throughout the Democratic convention, and, indeed, all of Act II. From morning to night the Democrats thronged talk and call-in shows, on CNN, C-SPAN, and radio. They published and distributed an avalanche of position papers to newspapers as well as to high-profile subscribers sitting by their home computers and to electronic data and bulletin boards like Prodigy and Compuserve—which printed out the convention's texts and speeches every day.

Robert Teeter, the Republican manager, may have been the first in his camp to notice that the opposition, having deserted the notion that only *one* medium, network TV, matters (the irreducible core of Myth One), was reaching a decidedly pluralist electorate in an effectively pluralist manner, rather like fingers of water spreading across a dry landscape. Bush's reluctant conversion to Teeter's change of heart, slowed by concern for the "dignity" of his office and his fear that *Larry King Live!*, or worse, mattered less than a formal White House press conference, may have been the

decisive cultural gap that dogged the entire Republican campaign, from start to finish.

By the time George Bush's party convened in Houston
in August, it was far behind in the polls. Instead of taking
a leaf from the Democratic embrace of pluralist media,
the convention focused its money and its energies almost
entirely upon the prime-time network hours, with a carefully staged array of speakers determined to bash and
belabor the opposition, ignoring the wealth of evidence
gathered since 1988 that the public was hungry for substance, not bile. When Pat Buchanan openly proclaimed
"Cultural War" on the convention's second night, he proved
more accurate than he wished to be, as did Vice President Quayle two nights later, when he once again took
on the "cultural elite" in the name of the "family values,"
as he had months before, when he chided the loose
morality reflected in Candice Bergen's popular single-
mother hero, *Murphy Brown*, the CBS serial that will be
analyzed in our discussion of Myth Three ("TV Is [Our]
Reality").

The real, functional divide was not between righteous
Republicans and decadent Democrats or Perotistas. In their
media strategies and goals, the candidates for the moment
reflected most of all two vastly differing assumptions about
that critical one-eyed god in the living room. The Democrats
chose to circumvent Him, running around God's back and
between His legs whenever possible. Though Republicans
also dutifully appeared on cable, radio, and print media in
Houston in August, it was clear from their intensively
planned final "show," featuring tens of thousands of bal-
loons floated down from the top of the cavernous Astro-
dome, that they saw themselves as prime-time
entertainment. More than persuading voters, the Republicans were reaching for a big Nielsen number.

The big number never came. The Republicans attracted
slightly fewer total viewers than the Democrats in July, and
plunged to the lowest Nielsen for a single political conven-

tion ever. Traditional Media Values didn't work. Worse, the set speeches and flag waving represented "nothing new." They provided nothing innovative to speak or write about. They didn't spill over into hours or pages of follow-up commentary, as did the stream of Clinton-Gore position papers or the low-cost, low-key bus tour taken by the governor with his new running mate, Senator Al Gore of Tennessee, rolling through a string of small, little-known towns immediately following the Democratic convention, eclipsing the balloon barrage.

Perot in his own rowdy, irreverent manner was similarly effective. His continued call for two-way satellite-delivered "town hall meetings" between political leaders and the citizenry, a borrowed concept he called, blithely, "electronic democracy," always provoked applause. At once exhilarating and simplistic, Perot's proposal envisioned a parade of political options—for confronting the deficit, say—being offered over the networks, cable, and radio to the voters. By pressing on touch-tone phones, the public responds, selecting its own course of action in advance of Congressional decision making. Whenever Perot presented this scheme during campaigning, he was vigorously applauded, even by those who obviously might not find the time to watch or vote. His frequent exhortations to "face the medicine" and accept higher taxes almost always met with approval as well, contradicting those who believed the electorate would only respond to wine, roses, and flattery, in the manner of Goneril and Regan.

In *Lear*'s final act, the kingdom is brought to near ruin by the sweet-talking sisters, who ultimately take their own lives in despair. In the 1992 campaign, the mood of the electorate, which clearly responded eagerly to every step taken by Clinton and Perot to involve it in direct dialogue over decisions that seemed certain to affect their lives, seemed a form of antidote to Shakespeare's tragic denouement.

Teeter, Bush, & Co. caught on too late to effectively re-orient a media policy hopelessly ensnarled in the flawed assumption that the medium inherently overpowers the viewing mind, if not the message. But surely the November Group was or is not singular in this commitment to our myth, particularly as it infects political strategy. On the red-letter night of Thursday, October 14, 1992, when for the first time in history the public voice was given presence in presidential debating, it was not the Republicans alone who were found wanting, if not astonished. In any case, it is a signal lesson.

Let us recall the setting, as well as the players. After months of wrangling, a bipartisan committee had agreed on a series of four debates. Responding to widespread criticism of the lackluster 1988 debates, the commission finally persuaded the two parties, as well as Ross Perot, the independent third candidate, to accept reforms, some mild (as when a single moderator replaced the standard panel of star journalists), at least one radical, at least in premise: the voters were invited to question the candidates directly, with only one intermediary, Carole Simpson, an ABC News reporter, to "manage" the flow of questions and the length of the responses.

Neither the mythmakers nor their retinue was prepared for what happened during this session, the third of the four debates, sited in Richmond, Virginia, where 209 "undecided" voters were selected by the Gallup organization to attend and propose questions. Where the earlier debates, primarily controlled by mainstream journalists and candidates, returned again and again to "hot" issues like character and abortion, this session was cool, serious, civilized. The questions were unfailingly devoted to *survival*, to what each man intended to do for the voters about crime, gun control, health care, jobs, and the deficit. Indeed, the only moments that neared the emotional fault lines dear to our myth were those in the beginning, when two speakers exhorted the players to avoid attacks on character. The first, a woman, said:

"Why can't your discussions and proposals reflect the genuine complexity and the difficulty of the issues to try to build a consensus around the best aspects of all proposals?"

The response of the three principals varied sharply. Perot and Clinton both enthusiastically agreed with the lady. President Bush, lagging in the polls, was less enthusiastic, surely because his media advisors had urged him to go for the jugular. At first he attempted to argue that Clinton's demonstrations against the war in Vietnam while abroad were an insult to his country. "Probably a lot of kids here disagree with me," said the President, "but that's how I feel." The audience, clearly restive, broke into scattered applause when the next speaker, a middle-aged man, obviously impassioned, asked, "Can we focus on the issues and not on the personalities and the mud?"

At this point, neither the November Group nor the President had a leg to stand on. The Voice of the People had demanded a serious, even-tempered debate, which is what, for the remaining sixty minutes of this ninety-minute event, they got. Now, I do not recount this affair to belabor Bush, who was honestly deluded by the belief that fierce, negative campaigning had won for him in 1988 and would again in 1992. It is most of all to call attention to the behavior of the media that closed in around the October 14 debate in the following weeks. Over and over again we were told that the third debate—though it attracted one of the largest audiences in the history of such contests—was a failure. One journalist called it "as boring as C-SPAN at midnight." About the warmest praise it received was a *New York Times* headline: "A No-Nonsense Sort of Talk Show Sticks to Issues." Immediately afterward, on ABC's *Nightline*, following a cursory review of the issues analyzed at length by the three candidates, the host focused almost entirely on "who won?" calling in press spokespersons for each man to answer.

On the political level, however, it seems certain the Oc-

tober 14 debate established a precedent that will be difficult
to ignore in the future. From now on, the public voice,
entirely discredited by Myth One, will slowly, steadily le-
verage the political dialogue. To a certain extent, the determination in the 1992 campaign to extend the temporal
scale of political discussion, through the thirty-minute in-
fomercials that highlighted the last weeks of Perot's campaign in particular, also attracted sizable audiences, often
to focus on bitter truths ("the $4 trillion debt," for example),
is similarly irreversible.

None of these events exhaust or even describe the full
meaning of the 1992 election. Nor do the significant reversals in the expectations of voter passivity and avoidance
indicate continued public vigor in the attack on the overpowering difficulties facing the new administration. What
occurred in the 1992 election was complicated. The results
responded to an interlocking swirl of economic, cultural,
technological, and demographic changes probably unprecedented and certainly unexpected. But the least we can conclude is that the viewer/voter never played the withdrawn,
unresponsive role predicted in the beginning. Over and
over his resistance to "killer" spots, his appetite for reading,
debating, talking, going out to rallies, as well as viewing
unconventional coverage on television, and *listening* to it on
radio, surprised media and political elites. Even Ms. Jamieson, a staunch supporter of Myth One, was impressed.
"What you're seeing is a very self-protective electorate," she
told a reporter during those last heated days. "We may have
the first set of conditions to lead to a backlash."[27]

Again I concede that the events in 1992 were exceedingly
intricate. Their implications for our thesis and this book can
only be defined by speculation, below. But Ms. Jamieson's
last-minute recognition of the power of the message, rather
than the medium, recalls Lear, who also sees the truth at
the end and burns to say it: *Howl, howl, howl! O! You are
men of stones:/Had I your tongues and eyes, I'd use them so/That
heaven's vault should crack.*

THE MYTH IN FINAL FLUX

> *Yet that does not mean that one would have
> to lie. What is needed . . . are tact, instinct,
> and good taste . . . of knowing how long I
> should speak, when to begin, and when to
> finish . . . how to maintain a balance between
> the serious political subjects and the lighter,
> relaxing ones, of knowing when and where
> to appear and when and where to remain
> silent.*
>
> —Vaclav Havel, speech at New
> York University, 1991.

How, permanently, to change? How to return the democratic discourse to the politicians and the people rather than
the commercial TV monopoly that guarded the gate for so
long? Even in the wake of the unique lessons of 1992 we
can already sense an obdurate refusal on the part of the
mythmakers to give in. Already we are being told that it
was Clinton's media managers, sensing early the critical importance of venues like Arsenio Hall and C-SPAN, or Perot's
addiction for CNN, that decided the campaign, not our
hunger to search and plunder each one of the candidates
for hard, decisive content.

Of course there are proposals for reform, for setting into
stone the enlightening events that stirred the campaign.
Many years ago, Charles Guggenheim proposed that politicians face the camera and identify themselves at the end
of all spots, accepting responsibility for negative claims. The
ambitious plan devised by Marvin Kalb and Harvard's Barone Center to provide for "Nine Sundays" in the concluding
weeks of each presidential campaign, during which the candidates will alternatively discuss and debate one subject at
a time on ninety minutes of free television, donated by the
three major networks in collaboration with CNN, C-SPAN,
and PBS, is similarly enlightened. Further, the "debates" in
the Kalb plan would be one-on-one dialogues, with a single
moderator in a bare studio, sans the galaxy of star reporters

and primed spectators that have diluted nearly every presidential debate up till now. Late in August of 1992, this
writer proposed that the debates give up intrusive moder-
ators entirely, handing the question making over to the voters, not gathered into a studio but permitted to speak and
fax from their homes, free from the need to "perform"
before a camera. The third Richmond debate may have
begun an evolution toward this full dialogue.[28]

But finally the critical lesson of the campaign is that a
profound cultural change has occurred in the electorate,
not the media. What we want, what we expect now from
the means of communication and of the political leaders
who serve us is totally different from what was expected,
or delivered, in the past. Needless to say, these needs are
highly individuated. They are looser, freer, less iconic, verg-
ing on the anarchic. The resistance to the imperious au-
thoritarian personality once defined by Hannah Arendt
seems irreversible, save in rare instances. The distaste for
prying into the private affairs of politicians, often attributed
in the 1992 campaign to economic duress, is surely
grounded in the widespread belief that each man, each
woman deserves the heaven or hell he or she prefers. It is
the tendency to attribute these changes to impersonal technology, not to say impersonal market forces, that must be
resisted. Why are we served now by multiple channels, as
well as multiple products? Because we *demand* them, with
our dollars, and with our impassioned zapping, and channel
switching. Our message to the Medium is: *Break into a thousand parts. Serve me, not yourself.* Now it is responding, slowly,
imperfectly, to us.

This is very far from saying that TV has no power at all.
As long as we *perceive* TV to be powerful, as long as our
press follows every killer spot, every nuance in campaigning
style, the medium will act, in the calm, managed center of
the political discourse. But the 1992 campaign taught us
that the discourse is better compared to an angry river than
solid ground, on which one beacon beams to everyone.
Around the edges of the roaring river's center there are

streams of infinite rage and range—print, radio, computer networks, long-winded "talk," as well as the unpredictable psyche of voters now primed to speak, and think, for themselves.[29]

Again, we can only speculate at this moment. But it seems inconceivable that both politicians and their managers won't begin to realize that a cache of critical votes awaits them in the discursive forms implied by these "marginal" streams. And "discursive" means time—time to talk, listen, reply, the essence of political dialogue. On the highest level, what used to be called "rhetoric," what is now called "style" or "pitch," is essential to the humanity of such a dialogue, as Vaclav Havel, the playwright-president of Czechoslovakia testified, after a harrowing, accomplished year in office.

Now humane rhetoric, tact, and manners, the final style of styles, cannot operate within inhuman thirty-second bursts. To continue to reopen dialogue and rhetoric, to keep prodding into temporal structures approaching the open quality of the printed page, may be the last and certainly the least expected destiny of electronic discourse: to become "the library" that Lawton Chiles recommended, not the spot he defied. Now very little of what I am saying here has yet been anticipated by any of our sacred media prophecies. But the cultures of commercial network or state-managed television as we have known it and of democratic politics are contradictory. One must die, so the other can live.

MYTH TWO

TV HAS DESTROYED OUR STUDENTS

In the decade of the 1950's, television came to dominate the nonsleep, nonschool time of the North American child.

—Wilbur Schramm, Jack Lyle, Edwin B. Parker, *Television in the Lives of Our Children*, 1961

Whether the program being watched is "Sesame Street" or . . . "Fantasy Island," there is a similarity of experience about all television watching. . . . It is a one-way transaction that requires the taking in of particular sensory material in a particular way, no matter what the material might be. There is, indeed, no other experience in a child's life that permits quite so much intake while demanding so little outflow.

—Marie Winn, *The Plug-In Drug,* 1977

A complex picture tends to elicit parallel processing, while words elicit serial processing. It seems to me likely that watching television . . . cultivates parallel processing as a strategy for taking in information.

—Patricia Marks Greenfield, *Mind and Media: The Effects of Television, Video Games, and Computers,* 1984

Welcome. I'm sure you'll find your assignment here exciting, interesting, and VERY dangerous.

—Broderbund, Inc. *Where in Time Is Carmen Sandiego?,* 1991

Not long after *Where in the World Is Carmen Sandiego?* appeared on the PBS network in the fall of 1991, I happened to sit down at my Macintosh computer while my daughter, aged nine, and one of her friends, a boy, aged eight, were "glued," as the mythmakers say, to the television set. But I hadn't even opened my directory when they rose from the TV and clamored for what they called "the *real Carmen Sandiego.*" They meant, of course, the interactive software program that preceded the television series by several years and more than 2 million customers. Both of the children played with *Carmen* regularly and claimed to great proficiency in the game. "Just watch," they told me, "we'll catch her." As soon as I agreed, they turned the TV set off, soundly.

Carmen Sandiego herself is a clever, animated thief. In the series of programs first devised by Broderbund, Inc., of San Rafael, California, solely for the home computer network, she is the center of the plot and the motivating force for interaction. Every child wants to "catch" her by responding to questions asked on the PC screen as any one of the hundreds of plots buried in the software unfolds through the keyboard. By sitting, focusing intensely on the screen, reading the questions asked, interpreting the verbal and visual "clues" provided, and tapping out replies on the keys, the viewer-player tries to apprehend the thief, who is sometimes Carmen, sometimes one of her colorful colleagues, among them Aunty Bellum, Lynn Gweeney, Len Bulk, and Nick Brunch, each simply one of a parade of V.I.L.E. Henchmen.

On this late afternoon, I watched daughter and pal chase the bandits. It was a demanding chase, beginning with a series of questions that required typewritten replies, first of all the "name" of the agent invited to "solve" the crime (after a fierce dispute, the children decided on "Victoria," my daughter's name). While they were engaged in the chase, I switched the discarded TV set back on, and plugged one of the headphones into my bad left ear, permitting myself the luxury of watching both the computer program and the television program play out, side by side.

It was an instructive experience. I recommend it for all those committed to Myth Two, those who believe TV is by its very nature the cause of educational ennui in the United States, in particular the almost unbroken decline in literacy and arithmetic skills reflected in slumping scores reported across the nation in elementary and secondary schools since 1963, most of all in the SAT (Scholastic Aptitude Test) given each year to the next crop of potential college freshmen. In my left ear, I was treated to the cheers and shouts of a studio audience that duplicated almost to the decibel the sound level of similar audiences heard on prime-time adult "game shows," surely most of them SAT dropouts, or so I thought. They were being entertained by an equally familiar pair of hosts, a young man and woman exuding charm and cheer. They were convulsed with laughter over what they saw and heard from the "contestants," in this case three students playing detective, as were Victoria and Co., answering questions in pursuit of a villain fleeing through films and cartoons, while live music roared in the background.

In the other, better ear, I heard only two voices, equally vibrant, rising from this, the "other" side of the screen. For Victoria and her friend Arthur the line between "computer" and "television" screen is nonexistent. By the advent of the first grade their entire generation has already worked out on dozens of interactive "video games" in drugstores, toy stores, restaurants, train stations, and airports. The word "video" may safely be said to subsume virtually all images seen on a small electronic screen. While I watched, Victoria and Arthur quickly typed their way from San Francisco, where the home office of Acme Detective Agency, Time Crimes Division, dwells, back through time and space to the Peru of the Incas, to sixteenth-century Spain, and twentieth-century Holland. At every step, Victoria and Arthur are required to read, plot, and make decisions based on verbal clues—to choose between times and places where the criminal might be hiding, his or her hair and eye color, hobbies and passions, even between an array of those ominous names.

None of these decisions can be made at leisure, for the program continually reminds the player that time is passing, that the deadline approaches. Finally, on that particular day, when PBS's program was completely forgotten, Victoria and Arthur nabbed their suspect, a blonde, snaggle-toothed vixen named Lynn Gweeney, just in time. Before our very eyes, the heavens opened and a helicopter, hovering just above Ms. Gweeney, opened and sucked her inside, like an airborne vacuum cleaner. "Congratulations, Victoria," announced the program. "You are being promoted!"

The cheers, needless to say, almost reached the levels attained by the two-hundred-plus studio audience in my other ear. Further, they erupted in response to events on the screen, directed from the receivers to the senders, not in the reverse ratio maintained by PBS. It is difficult if not impossible to reconcile this increasingly common interactive rambunctiousness with the chilling solipsism described by Marie Winn and others; further, it is a solipsism that is seemingly predestined and impervious, that characterizes "all television watching." Winn might argue that *Carmen* on my Macintosh is not *Carmen* on "television," but TV, or "video," as the Victorias and Arthurs prefer, as we've already noted, means both less and more than she means. Of course it means a *screen* of many sizes and shapes, on which imagery, symbols, and even sounds cavort. Increasingly, it also means, as millions upon millions of PCs enter our homes, a screen equipped with means of interaction far more demanding than the generic Nintendo games that flooded the market in the 1980s. On this higher level of intense interaction, eyes truly glued to both images and words, hands on the alert to strike the keyboard, our Victorias and Arthurs are as alert, as focused, as open to learning as they are before a printed page.

To say this, to go further and argue that video, that even broadcast television itself, sans keyboard, is inherently *two-*

way in its nature, not one-way, that even the retiring PBS version of *Carmen* could have roused its youthful audience to touch, tap, or dance on the screen simply by asking, is sacrilegious, of course. It is particularly satanic at the end of the century, when virtually all informed opinion repeats the incantations enjoined by Myth Two, that most of all the kids spend, count them, more hours before a TV set, presumably enthralled, than hours in the classroom—presumably hours that differ not at all in substance from watching comic elephants bash tragicomic dogs during late-afternoon or early-evening cartoons.

But there is greater sacrilege to be said, in the service of historical accuracy, if not logic. The particular kind of intelligence demonstrated by Victoria and Arthur in nailing Lynn Gweeney is in fact several notches above and beyond mere "literacy," as it is conventionally understood. In one sense, this conclusion is perfectly obvious, though rarely noted in our official pedagogics: *Carmen*-on-the-Macintosh requires the use of simultaneous spatial, temporal, and linguistic skills. The viewer-reader in this situation, responding to verbal and visual demands at once, is also an actor. He/she must respond on several levels, not simply one, not simply what may be called the sequential, reflective mode of reading.

TV IN FULL DIMENSION: VICTORIA AND ARTHUR REDUX

> *The . . . tendency . . . which is decidedly my own . . . is of a constructivist nature (attributing the beginnings of language to structures formed by the pre-existing sensory motor intelligence). It recognizes neither external preformations (empiricism) nor immanent preformations (innateness), but rather affirms a continuous surpassing of successive stages.*
> —Jean Piaget, *To Understand Is to Invent: The Future of Education,* 1973

> *From this fundamental error—the idea that*
> *our understanding of reality is primarily ver-*
> *bal or symbolic . . . flow many other errors,*
> *and not just in the classroom.*
> —John Holt, *The Underachieving*
> *School,* 1969

In a provocative dispute with Jean Piaget, the Swiss theorist who impacted decisively on American educators in the postwar years, John Holt argues in *The Underachieving School* that Piaget's classic test of a small child's intelligence is exclusively verbal[1]: the master would hold out two rods and ask nursery school children, "Which is longer?" Their repeated failure led Piaget to conclude that the preliterate mind is incapable of dealing with the "real" world and its driving, decidedly abstract notions until he gains an inner conceptual hold on that world. Holt believes that the question, because it is framed in an entirely verbal way, overlooks an intelligence fully capable of deciding between up, down, long, short, smooth, rough *on its own,* without words. And it is precisely this dimension of the child's—that is, the student's—mind that is ignored in our official approaches to teaching and grading.

Until recently, "television" ignored this intelligence as well, or, to put the point more properly, *hid* from it. It is neither the medium nor the audience that is one-way. The proponents and guardians of passivity are the programmers—until recently—and the educators, for whom television has beome a welcome rationale for the uninspired, underfunded school turning out underachieving children. Holt went on to insist that any pedagogy that ignores the child's intellectual survival instincts, that is, his drive to make sense of the world *in his own way,* based upon his instincts, his intelligence, and the world of his home and parents, is doomed to failure. The moment when words like "longer" become weapons for the child to employ in an adult manner, or what Piaget might call one of those predictable "stages," is hardly the moment when intelligence dawns. Raw, primal, reaching intelligence is there from the beginning, in front of a gleaming screen or seated at a table filled with food, knives, forks, and spoons. Piaget's error, the error of those who see TV's impact as inexorably and always the same, ignores the manner in which Victoria and Arthur finally nabbed Lynn Gweeney, one "hour" before the time period allotted to them by Broderbund, Inc. elapsed.

THE MYTH BARES ITS FANGS

By about age 15, the average American child has spent more time (about 20,000 hours) in front of a television set than in the class-room—or doing homework.
—Joel Swerdlow, "A Question of Impact," *The Wilson Quarterly,* 1989

In England and other industrialized coun-tries, it is not unusual for academic high school students to spend 8 hours a day at school, 220 days per year. In the United States, by contrast, the typical school day lasts 6 hours and the school year is 180 days.
—National Commission on Ex-cellence in Education, *A Nation at Risk,* 1983

Primary schooling and literacy are necessary, it is so often repeated, for economic and moral development . . . democratic institutions . . . and so on. All this, regardless of its veracity, has come to constitute a "literacy myth."
—Harvey J. Graff, *The Literacy Myth: Literacy and Social Structure in the Nine-teenth-Century City,* 1979

How does the hidden curriculum relate to cul-tural acquisition from television?
—Bob Hodge and David Tripp, *Children and Television,* 1986

Though Myth Two appears to reinforce the critics of tele-vision, it acts in fact as a subversive double agent. Myth Two further strengthens the flawed perception that TV is omnipotent. Here, TV programs take on the power of social life (and death), wielding a sword that supposedly slays every nascent mind able to turn the on switch. Further, like Myth One, this sacred text presumes a universally credulous response to whatever appears on the small screen, and ignores the vast social and economic disparities that fragment the audience, in this case children between the ages of three and the onset of adolescence. It makes no allowance for critical response, which is certainly strong among teenagers, who watch far less TV than small kids, adults, and senior citizens.

Myth Two bares its fangs most blatantly when its disciples repeat over and over that American students spend more hours before television than before their teachers, not to say the pages of the books assigned them in class and at home. We are deluged with frightening figures—here "20,000 hours," there "hundreds of hours per year"—with none but the barest reference to the source or confirmation of accuracy. As in the continued assumptions that "killer spots" reach more voters than any other source or the sweeping claims made for the size of prime-time audiences (the standard bearer for Myth Five), of course, "proof" in the normal sense is unnecessary. Myth thrives on declaration, not evidence.

But a moment's reflection instantly reveals that the mere counting and numbering of hours tells us almost nothing about TV's relevance to growth or to education. What happens during those twenty thousand hours? Of course we don't know, even assuming that our method of counting is accurate. Surely most children alternately focus upon, then ignore the TV set. Anecdotal evidence—Victoria and Arthur rejecting PBS for the Macintosh—ought to inspire doubt in each of us. Neither TV nor hapless parents, relatives, and friends command the undivided attention of the child. More to the point: daytime classroom hours, managed by teachers, set in the context of the school, are clearly more demanding than relaxation or play before TV at home. Counting classroom and homework hours as the equivalent of TV viewing, no matter what the subject on the screen, is clearly wrongheaded, bordering at once either on stupidity or on rhetorical strategy.

If the latter, who gains from the assumption that television simultaneously rules and decimates the minds of our students? In addition to those who sell commercial time to toy manufacturers, the obvious answer is: educators and politicians. Battered and buffeted in recent decades by mounting evidence that American students appear to be losing ground to their counterparts abroad, particularly in Europe and in Asia, our teachers, administrators, college deans, and not a few critics have increasingly blamed television. Marie Winn, Joel Swerdlow, Neil Postman, and others have even discerned physical changes in the student physique. The eyes of American students can no longer concentrate on a stationary page of print, we are told, conditioned as they are to shifting electronic motion; they lapse into an unfocused "alpha state" barely thirty seconds after tuning in to the medium; they have become "couch potatoes," weighted down with fat, not muscle. Marie Winn's popular *Plug-In Drug*, with its apocalyptic cries of rage, sums up this veiled paean to TV power; *Television in the Lives of Our Children*, by Wilbur Schramm and colleagues, which emphasizes the "disengagement" phase in adolescence, goes unread beyond the academy.[2]

Yet even Marie Winn, read closely, concedes that Myth Two ignores the overwhelming universe of motivations and influences playing upon the child beyond the TV set. No "fair sample" can be taken, she says, to prove or disprove TV's guilt in a range of social crises, from violence to slumping SATs to sexism.[3] To prove or disprove Myth Two, the only proper "sample" would require matching our behavior with a similar society deprived of television. At the end of a momentous century, when more people have been born, educated, empowered—and massacred—than in all the previous history of mankind, it seems specious to single out one medium as the single molder of boys and girls of sharply contrasting backgrounds.

Not even polling or interviewing kids will provide us with significant evidence, as noted by Bob Hodge and David Tripp, who interviewed six hundred of them over three years in the preparation of their sophisticated study, *Children and Television* (1986)[4]. "One cannot ask them academically precise questions," write Hodge and Tripp, "or hand them a questionnaire form to fill in." Further, every act of communication is both social and interactive, conditioned by time, place, and circumstance. If children are deprived of certain defenses assumed in adults, they are also guarded, by the overpowering influence of home and parents. To compare the influence of TV on a highly literate Japanese middle-class student, required to spend hours alone in his room at night studying, with its impact on a poor teenager in the Bronx, one of a swarming family of six or seven barely attended by a poor, working mother, is farcical. All attempts to compare the test scores turned in by a heterogeneous, multicultural society like that in the United States with older, more homogeneous class-conscious nations like England, Germany, or Japan partake of this blindness. In each of these cases, TV is as much receiver as sender, acted upon as vigorously as it acts, by the viewers, youthful or not.

By adumbrating this rich complexity, Myth Two drives us to errors in judgment, yes. Worse, it tends to discourage positive action, particularly among the humanists and traditionalists who guard education here and abroad. Since TV is assumed to be dangerous to intellectual health, our school systems and universities have tended to ignore its powerful potential as a teaching medium. Though we are obsessed with the so-called decline in print "literacy" in the United States—surely conditioned by the massive influx of non-English-speaking labor since 1965—we spend almost no time talking to children in the suburbs or the inner city about the esthetics of content of TV, during the day, during the night, on cable, on PBS, and throughout the world. Nor has it occurred to many of us to *listen* to children talk about the programs they watch, and why. If John Holt is right, if the child is capable of thinking beyond words alone, then the flight from a medium able to marry print and image, particularly in its late video/PC linkage, is profoundly misguided. When the Department of Education produced with intense fanfare early in the last decade its call to arms, the report portentously entitled *A Nation at Risk*, its authors, the cream of the nation's educational establishment, did not once so much as mention the word "television."

THE CHILD AND MEDIUM: STATES OF BEING

> *We need a purposeful populist uprising, in the sense that people buy into behavior changes that range from what schools do to what employers do to how people spend their evenings at home.*
> —Chester E. Finn, Jr., *We Must Take Charge: Our Schools and Our Future,* 1991

> *In the last thirty years . . . there has been a remarkable change in the image and roles of children. Childhood as a protected and sheltered period of life has all but disappeared. Children today seem less "child-like."*
> —Joshua Meyrowitz, *No Sense of Place: The Impact of Electronic Media Upon Social Behavior,* 1985

> *Literacy was both act and symbol; it was neither neutral, unambiguous, or liberating. Its value, in fact, depended heavily on other factors. . . . The role of literacy in the life of an individual . . . is contradictory and complex.*
> —Harvey J. Graff, *The Literacy Myth: Literacy and Social Structure in the Nineteenth-Century City,* 1979

It is quite possible to see the state of education and of the child in two radically dissimilar ways, one in which TV overwhelms both, as we are often told, the other in which the larger context—as well as the sacred inner preserve of the

104   The Five Myths of Television Power

mind—prevails. The latter view, rarely voiced, at least matches the complexity of the society we now inhabit, where prodigious feats of learning and research occur in the face of the insistent doomsday reports of rampant illiteracy. Certain forms of knowledge are readily available in the information-rich postindustrial society that cannot be measured or counted in conventional testing. Between the lines of prime-time programming and open appeals to sensuality in commercials, the child rapidly acquires a precocious perspective on marital, sexual, and professional relationships. The enormous appeal of the MTV network all around the world, particularly for teenagers, young adults, and virtually every prepubescent child (as well as post-pubescent elders) who nears the screen when a compelling "music video" by Madonna or Michael Jackson swinging or clutching her or his own anatomy, is self-evident. Few adults can recall a time when the most sophisticated parameters of sexual attraction, homosexual as well as heterosexual, were so easily accessible, to every age and economic class.

In this sense the enormous psychic distance between childhood and adulthood has begun to narrow again, returning to the closeness common in preindustrial societies, when young men and women in their early teens mated, married, and spawned (Romeo and Juliet were fifteen and fourteen, respectively). Through radio, film, print, and jet flights, as well as video, the child's visual command of the world has heightened immeasurably since the end of World War II. We know more about European and Asian music, dance, clothing, and personal customs than ever before, often firsthand, thanks to the quantum leap in travel. Our command of athletics has similarly expanded—soccer, for example, is now a popular pastime in the United States, while baseball is spreading to Eastern Europe. Finally, the child's *sense* of political drama, compounded by immediate access to demonstrations, speeches, assassinations here and abroad, has also been intensified by the rapidity of informational exchange.

In such a world, "literacy" is hardly the simplistic functional tool it became in the nineteenth century, when public schools first attempted to teach entire nations to read and write, by hand. Even then, as Harvey Graff shows, in *The Literacy Myth*, his rare study of literacy as a symbolic code for progress, reason, and civility in the context of urban, industrialized Britain in the Victorian age, the standards of "literacy" varied widely, from class to class.[5] The workers of Manchester were driven simply to read, spell, and write basic documents. The sons of aristocrats were force-fed Homer and Aristotle. Even now, when democratic norms prevail, "literacy" is a shifting, weaving skill, often badly taught in schools below the poverty line, as Jonathan Kozol reminded the nation in his blistering book, *Savage Inequalities*.[6] Kozol points out that in Chicago alone the funds spent on poor, inner-city students amount to barely half the level maintained in the wealthy outer suburbs. Is television or crowded classrooms, poorly trained teachers, and inadequate books the cause of the fact that a mere 3 percent of these students read on or above the national norm attained in wealthier schools?

When we blame television for rampant illiteracy, for college students who score below norms attained abroad, in compact societies like Sweden's, or Japan's, we not only pay it undue homage. We ignore the discordant economic realities inherent in a sprawling society. We ignore as well its multicultural nature, the divergent languages and learned habits of thought that often contradict one another within a single classroom. The same causal patterns persist even in the infamous log of hours spent "watching" the TV tube. The poorer the household, the more time its children spend before the tube.

No poll or study that does not take proper account of wide variations in income ignores the most crucial distinction that can be made about any human pattern of behavior.[7] Economic constraints narrow the field of choice and impose behavior. Often, as is the case in violence, poverty is the clear cause of action while watching television is simply an effect, or symptom. Yet even *TV Guide*, in its admirable series of studies aimed at persuading the networks to cut down on violent programs during youthful viewing hours, crowns TV as the muscular *provocateur* of rape and murder, virtually ignoring the virulent social ills affecting poor kids and neighborhoods.[8]

Our prognoses on education are similarly crippled: TV addiction is not the origin but the *result* of broken families, crippled schools, and pedagogical malaise. Both TV and FI (or "functional illiteracy") have become pawns in the public debate over the destiny of the nation. For those who see that debate in stark black-and-white terms, TV and FI are veils that can be drawn over a host of unmanageable crises few of us dare either to analyze or to confront.

By defining these phenomena in conventional terms, furthermore—TV as the one-eyed, one-way monolith, literacy as traditional reading and writing—many of our social prophets have induced us to ignore the unparalleled activism of our nascent viewers and readers. That words are no longer words alone but ingredients in the moving landscapes wrought by video, computers, and optical discs, provoking alternative skills, is ignored. When a child learns to type, draw, and store words on his personal computer at the age of seven or eight, he taps powers of invention and recall beyond anything available to the average student, chalk and tablet in hand one hundred years ago. The wide-ranging, cultural sophistication of the younger audience—the assemblage of songs, images, psychic nuances stored inside their minds—is also missed, under the welter of invective seeking to find mechanistic explanations for deep structural flaws.

In their intensive study of students watching television in Australia, Bob Hodge and David Tripp concluded that "there is a two-way interaction between the culture of the school and the culture of television"—that is, between inside and outside, between mind and medium.[9] Now of course the medium can prod and inspire from inside to outside. The lively, involving drawings, cartoons, and skits generated by *Sesame Street*, America's premier early-morning offering for preschoolers, have demonstrably improved test scores among disadvantaged minority kids. In a different sense, MTV has altered social attitudes, manners, clothing, and behavior, primarily by responding vigorously to changing values.

But we have almost totally ignored the powerful contemporary outside culture brought *to* the screen by those who watch and respond to TV at the earliest age. If *Television in the Lives of Our Children* warned long ago that life itself replaces the TV screen in the center of most adolescent lives, the authors understated the dynamic state of growing, learning, and living as the century closes. More and more, as alternative means of seeing and living present themselves in the postindustrial era, children are beginning to find these replacements earlier and earlier in life, as we shall see. Far from acting as a surrogate pacifier, what might be called "traditional" or "orthodox" over-the-air TV programming is becoming an increasingly intolerable agent of ennui, boring our children, provoking them into new realms of life, media, and action. Any "reform" of American education that fails to respond to this change in the preschool mind and style is doomed to yet more underachievement.

VIDEO GAMING

Totalitarianism involves a systematic effort to control every aspect of social and intellectual life.

—Michael Walzer, "On Failed Totalitarianism," *1984 Revisited*, ed., Irving Howe, 1983

Ted Arthur, a successful professor and author . . . finds himself irresistibly drawn to embark on a true-life journey. . . . What follows is an outlandish spoof where you're in the writer's seat . . . through the new experience of interactive literature.

—*Adventure 101*, electronic book for Sony Data Discman, 1991

I am both man and woman.
—Madonna, *MTV 10th Anniversary, ABC-TV,* 1991

Makes no difference if you're black or white.
—Michael Jackson, "Danger,"
MTV 10th Anniversary, ABC-TV, 1991

*10 years . . . 120 months . . . 3,265 days . . .
87,646 hours . . . 5,258,880 minutes . . .
312,532,280 seconds . . . millions and millions of images . . . memories . . . the image factory.*
—Music Television, *MTV 10th Anniversary,* ABC-TV, 1991

Implicit in the multibillion-dollar video game industry from the first was the clear option of moving toward a confrontation with print, that is the Word. The activism required in the games implied a mind, a child's or an adult's, that might be activated by content, if the game could become as flexible, as easy to handle and carry as the book, most of all the paperback. The spunky Sony Data Discman, which appeared on the market in 1991, took that step. Equipped with a three-inch optical disc, the tiny Discman, roughly the size of a fat paperback, could play back up to one hundred thousand pages of text on a single disc, with thirty thousand graphic images. But the complexity of the narrative or report unfolding on the tiny screen surpasses the simple flipping of pages in a book. At point after point, the "reader" is presented with options that allow him to pursue any lead he or she wishes. In the paunchy *Adventure 101* novel issued by Sony to its early, surely bemused market, the reader found himself empowered to send the hero, Ted, on a safari to Africa or a tour of the historical icons of Great Britain. Within those adventures, the reader is given the option of examining Ted's wallet, searching through his suitcase, or reading his love letters.

What drove Sony to issue what is in effect a small TV set for reading only? The same question might be asked of the schools and teachers who combined with New York's PBS station, WNET, to form a telecommunications *Learning Link* in 1990. Beginning with simple data transmission from computer to computer, the *Link* quickly established ties to almost nine hundred elementary and secondary schools throughout the United States. Teachers, schools, and libraries began to exchange text, images, entire courses. Students as well as teachers "talked" to each other via keyboards. As the software evolved, the schools began to exchange live as well as videotaped images, sometimes as many as four or five "windows" filled with video appearing on the screen at the same time. The ease and relative economy of the *Link* made this process a formidable competitor to the "long-distance" learning that began to evolve at the same time in cities like Lexington, Kentucky, where specialized teachers used TV—and push-button keypads—to contact students across the city,[10] and in Whittle Communications' controversial "Channel One," an early attempt to transmit current events programming by satellite to secondary schools across the U.S. through video systems donated to the schools, all subsidized by commercials.

In each of these cases it is not only a form of literacy that is emerging out of what used to be "television"—and is now, increasingly, a hybrid, half video, half computer. It is the activation of personal choice. The easier, the simpler the means by which we address the screen, the less critical it becomes. Where once he merely received what the networks chose to send us on two, three, or four channels, the child now sits at a keyboard and directs his own plot. Rising in the place of the medium, then, as the source of power, is the mind. The advent of hand-held video books and computers, the inevitable appearance in classrooms of TV screens as flat—and as portable—as sheets of paper means the exaltation of choice. Precisely as kids now select grades and colors of chalk to use on a blackboard, they are selecting "video" images to see, correct, and modulate.

And the purveyors of these means are supplying them in order to survive. The Sony Data Discman has arisen with the

Learning Link in the face of Myth Two's totalitarian implications, and insistence. So has the more sophisticated series
of "Expanded books" produced by Voyager, Inc., of California for laptop computers in 1991–92, which reached toward
the "New Class" audience for serious fiction and nonfiction.

Michael Walzer's prophetic essay on the failure of totalitarian systems in the postmodern world, written a year before 1984, when convention insisted that the police states
fashioned by Stalin would never fall, argued that no crack
could be allowed in the ethic of total control, or the entire
system would fall. But the cracking began in the culture, in
the music, in the clothes, in the lifestyle increasingly pursued
by young people throughout Eastern Europe, rarely noticed
in the depth of the Cold War by the Western press. It is
conventional now to say that television brought high-spir-
ited Western music to the East, but this overlooks the far
more widespread presence of audiocassettes, live music,
magazines, and the underground *samizdat* press at a time
when state TV was totally closed.

Further, the key response was always to the content of
the music and the films still in evidence in what can only be
called a form of "global" culture. In this sense the historic
tenth anniversary of the Music Television Network in 1991,
in which this global culture was celebrated, was a confirmation of its historic power. Though MTV congratulated
itself as the cause of the values rhapsodized in its ballads—
freedom, reverence for nature, for the human body, for
racial equality, for the right to protest, the right even to
license or hedonism (Madonna's gospel)—these values were
generated centuries ago, in the Enlightenment, at the onset
of rapid information exchange, through the printing press.
In broadcast television, many of these values have been at
the heart of *Sesame Street*, which has been broadcasting to
generations of children for more than twenty years.

But MTV's insistence on *quantity*, on the sheer number
of songs and images it has sent around the world, to Kuwait
and to China as well as Western Europe, is what finally
shakes Myth Two, if not MTV itself. The impatient activism

evident in Victoria's and Arthur's refusal to simply watch rather than type out words is a literacy grounded in unbounded choice (they sneered at Madonna herself not a few weeks after rejecting PBS). It is a literacy of sharpened tastes, of particular needs. The teachers and students who receive data via telecommunications are already able to store, then edit and change whatever information comes their way. It is quite simple now to distort voices and rearrange imagery with the flick of a keyboard. Lectures provided from afar can be enhanced and advanced in a matter of minutes.

It would be an error of fatal proportions to assume that all of this is occurring because the technology makes it possible. This is precisely the mistake made by the Communist bureaucrats who assumed that the one-way press and media had transformed the citizen into a "new man." Or that television erodes the desire to think and to read. The demand for something else, here as always, comes from the user, from the other side of the TV screen. Whetted by education, travel, information, these demands are increasingly personal and increasingly qualitative. In the end the Stalinist states fell in part because they had bored the public to death. The repetition of phrases, of images, and of content built an impenetrable wall of skepticism. The extension of literacy into a form of visual-verbal Möbius strip means that no form of television or education that simply declares—rather than interacts—can hope to survive.

LITERACY UNBOUND

> What would happen if the whole world became literate? Not much. . . . But if the whole world consisted of literate, autonomous, critical, constructive people, capable of translating ideas into action . . . the world would change.
>
> —Johan Galtung, quoted in Harvey Graff, *The Literacy Myth*

*What the reformers . . . do not see is that each
of us has to forge his own master key out of
his own materials, has to make his own sense
of the world in his own way, and that no two
people will ever do it in the same way.*
—John Holt, *The Underachieving
School*, 1969

*Whatever we see could be other than it
is.
Whatever we can describe at all could be
other than it is.
There is no* a priori *order of things.*
—Ludwig Wittgenstein, *The Lim-
its of My Language Mean the Limits of My
World*, 1921

In *Mind and Media,* Patricia Greenfield argues the extraordinary case for teaching "TV literacy." It is extraordinary
simply because the case still must be argued, decades after
the extension of the electronic medium into every home,
accompanied by doomsday warnings that have empowered
the enemy they seek to oppose. But she is careful, unlike
many others, to point out that the literacy we sorely need
ought not to be focused on the attributes of the "medium,"
but upon our own needs and minds. As the means of education interaction spread, to include "virtual reality" systems that envelop the student in a totally artificial
environment, generated by computer software and transmitted directly through electrodes into the brain, the pur-
poseful self becomes its own critical agent.

In its fullest dimension, TV literacy has primarily to do
with us, with our society, and with our world, not with TV.
Seen in this way, the first question we ought to put to interactive television, to the Data Discman, for example, or to
the Expanded Book is to ask what service it provides *us*—
and, later, how we can reach beyond its borders. Further,
this is a question that increasingly must be asked on the
most specific level. We need to choose our media as we
choose pencils, pens, homes, and even lovers. This is the

reverse of the notion that students need to learn a received vocabulary of virtues summed up in the phrase "good television" or that the evolution of youthful taste will follow in the predictable paths charted by Piaget and generations of educators. John Holt's metaphor of each master key turning in its own lock is precisely the metaphor that is needed, as Wittgenstein's emphasis on the need to take the uncharted and unexpected into account (denying his own premise) is the proper emphasis. TV—rather, the uses we have made of it—has impacted on our minds and our students. Now we must leave these limitations far behind.

MYTH
THREE

TV Is (Our) Reality

Television is the great certifying agent of our time. Most Americans do not believe in the reality of any event or emotion that they have not seen, at one point or another, on television. This is the first commandment in the Age of Television.
—Frank Mankiewicz and Joel Swerdlow, *Remote Control,* 1978

Overexposure to manufactured illusions soon destroys their representational power. The illusion of reality dissolves, not in a heightened sense of reality as we might expect, but in a remarkable indifference to reality.
—Christopher Lasch, *The Culture of Narcissism,* 1979

TELEVISION IS THE CAMPAIGN
—*New York Times* editorial, 1991

Though the power of print has been praised and feared since Gutenberg, the notion that any medium can effectively replace reality, enveloping us within itself, dates properly from the advent of television. Only then did the artificial, created world seem to overpower the real world. I vividly remember the appearance of TV in the neighborhood I grew up in, during the 1950s, in Washington, D.C. While each of the families on my block spent hours reading newspapers and listening to radio, no one warned me, on the street or in Sunday School, against the pernicious powers of word or of sound. But I recall uncles and aunts grumbling about the pervasive spread of Lucille Ball coiffures in offices, schools, and even church pews, as soon as the TV set became ubiquitous. Once I heard a sermon in which Satan and the new medium were clearly linked. Never had the Lone Ranger, who thundered through my living room radio every Sunday night, been so maligned, or feared.

For weeks thereafter, I kept my eye out for upswept batches of Lucy's red hair but couldn't detect a single strand. Her nonpresence on my block matched the invisibility of the loud Ranger, who couldn't be found around the corner, either, despite his ubiquity. As I grew up, I was constantly lectured to the contrary by journalists and authors like Marshall McLuhan (anticipating Frank Mankiewicz and Joel Swerdlow's *Remote Control*), who found Lucy, Desi, and Milton Berle in their morning cereal, dictating social trends, the news, and even the weather. As the paradoxical gap between the omnipotence of TV and the real world sharpened in the years following, I began to think it was the *visual* reach of TV that had traumatized the pundits. We *read* a newspaper, I told myself, turning away from the world. When we *listen*, we have again left the world behind for an imaginary landscape. But TV, we *spectate* TV, as we spectate the world outside, every day, or so it must appear, to my distinctly one-eyed prophets.

These ruminations helped me to understand the elitist hysteria implicit in Myth Three, whose premise has by now totally entwined our brain cells, and our language. Once in the aftermath of the revolutions that swept Eastern Europe in 1989 I attended a panel at a large university assessing events like the totally unexpected overthrow of Romanian dictator Ceausescu. "Nothing that happened in the streets or countryside in Romania mattered," I heard one of the experts say, blithely dismissing the blood spilled all over that nation. "The revolution took place on the TV screen." Nearly everyone around me seemed to agree. Many of us do now assume that for the vast majority of the TV audience, the screen, in effect, is a window. What we see on the other side of the window we believe, if not imitate, according to Myth Three.

The historic roots of this credo reach back into my adolescence and early adulthood, that is, the late 1950s and early 1960s. These were the years when what is now known as the baby-boom generation emerged in nurseries everywhere, when neither the Vietnam War nor civil rights nor feminism were yet in full flower or full roar. The demographics of the nation, and of the mass-produced goods that served it, were stable: two parents, two children, a home, a garden, the suburbs. In his touching, slightly bewildered lament, *Whatever Happened to Madison Avenue?* Martin Mayer recalls the days when a giant corporation like Campbell's could market a soup with a logo and a visual concept (the plump and sprightly "Campbell's Kids") that lasted at least half a century, feeding a social structure that stayed in firm place.[1]

It was the same family structure served by manicured network news, broadband comedians like Milton Berle, and primal sitcoms like *I Love Lucy, Father Knows Best, Leave It to Beaver, The Adventures of Ozzie & Harriet,* and, later, *Family Ties,* which somehow managed to adopt the counterculture, followed, finally, by *The Cosby Show* in the 1980s. I remember thinking in the early halcyon days that the audience was not outside looking in but the reverse, that Network TV had its nose pressed to the glass of the window, seeking to reproduce what it found on the other side, the *inside,* that is, the real world. In these early programs, the heart and soul of Myth Three, the nuclear family prevailed against all odds, centered, as Hal Himmelstein points out,[2] in one of two classic personality types, either the "loser," the genial mom or pop who is half buffoon (Lucy, for example, Ozzie, for another), or the victor who is superior in mind and spirit, though trapped in the same mundane circumstances as the presumed viewer (cf. Robert Young, the father who knew best, and Harriet, the mother who occasionally knew).

But this imperturbable society, enforced at once by the

dictates of fiction and of demographics, proved temporary. Sociologists tell us that the GI Bill generation, those who fled to the green suburbs in retreat from the vicissitudes of a world war, began to splinter as early as the late 1950s. The single-parent family multiplied as the divorce rate rose, empowered by rising incomes and mobility. If the networks moved slowly to recognize the perils of raising kids alone, this may account for the complaint by many viewers—when they were asked, occasionally, in polls—that the sitcoms, though beloved, ignored them. Meanwhile, the resident mother, TV's staple "market," began to leave the home in the late 1960s and throughout the next decade, for occupation, travel, friendship, and extra- as well as postmarital adventuring. Men and women in their mid-twenties and thirties returned to the campus in these years in droves, driving the average age of the college student way up.

In *The Culture of Narcissism,* an august jeremiad against the dissolution of sober work-ethic values, Christopher Lasch, in company with those who accuse TV of dictating reality, rails against a culture bent on hedonistic dissolution.[3] But surely these massive social shifts, finally acknowledged twenty years after the fact in single-parent, working woman, fragmented family sitcoms like *Mary Hartman, Mary Hartman, Kate & Allie, Who's the Boss?, Blossom, Davis Rules, Baby Talk, Full House,* and, in the 1990s, both *Roseanne* and *Married . . . with Children* reflect real choices made in the real world beyond the fictional frame. In *Blossom, Davis Rules, Full House,* and *Drexell's Class,* divorced or widowed fathers raise children, often daughters, on their own, precisely as I somehow managed two daughters as a bachelor father in these very same years. Which side of the TV screen is here impacting upon the other? When Marlo Thomas contrasted the worldliness of the heroine she played in a comedy special in 1986 with her demure Ann-Marie in *That Girl,* fifteen years before, she saw it as a maturation in the medium, not in the public, a sign that TV is imitating life ("It seems astonishing to me how TV has grown up").[4]

Yet even earlier, in the heart of the laugh-track era, there were signs that human reality would ultimately deconstruct the nuclear family universe. I recall casually tuning in *An American Family* on PBS in the early 1970s. By chance I landed in the fifth episode, when the father, Bill Loud, was dialing a restaurant in Santa Barbara, California, to make a reservation for dinner, with his wife, Pat. The simple tedium of dialing, waiting, and passing mundane pleasantries with the restaurateur seemed immediately out of place on episodic television, if not life. But what followed was equally shocking: a long, ambling, meaningless conversation between husband and wife in the midst of a deafening restaurant. When we could hear what Bill was saying to Pat or Pat to Bill, it was hardly worth the effort. Husband and wife were talking to themselves, glassy-eyed, about subjects the other didn't care to entertain, whether it involved the deteriorating state of the family pool or a daughter's decision to sign up for ballet lessons. But of course I was attracted to what I saw even here, in the presence at last of a "family" on the TV screen that appeared to be a part of my imperfect world, not the gilded universe of Desi and Lucy.

Later, I learned more about *An American Family*. This slow-paced "documentary" was indeed attracting a large audience, by the PBS standards of those days, and a vigorous press, which split right down the middle on its virtues. The young producer, Craig Gilbert, had somehow persuaded this large family (with three teenaged sons and two daughters) to allow him intimate access with his hand-held camera for up to seventeen hours every day. Gilbert's mammothian filmed memoir of affluent, southern California life covered the last six months of 1971. In the broadcast I later saw, Gilbert let the hours of tedium speak for themselves, though the stresses inherent in the Loud family dynamic (as well as the project itself) finally exploded with a dramatic force rivaling the network fantasies. Pat Loud's evident unhappiness, her husband's boredom, the void in the center of the children's lives (none seems committed to a goal or profession, save to pass time or meet "artists," in the case of elder son, Lance, or "dancers," in his sister, Barbara), all these burst into moments of high anguish that can't be matched in fiction.

It was not only that Mrs. Loud's decision to tell a gathering of friends she is leaving a husband who sits, shocked, beside her—because she just found evidence of his wanton infidelity—is arresting. It comes after almost ten filmed hours of pretense to the contrary, enhancing the poignancy of her decision. The same is true when Lance announces (to the camera, not his parents) that he is a homosexual, and wants to live with his male friends in New York. *An American Family* touched the "real" rhythms of life in its relaxed, seemingly unedited pacing. Of course those who assumed that the "mainstream" audience would never endure the slow pace, the cacophonic sound track, and the jumpy camera derided it as marginal television, suited only for an elite PBS clientele. In time, however, broadcast television in the 1990s adopted an esthetic dangerously close to *An American Family*.

At its core, Craig Gilbert's unpaced strategy of recording and, later, editing, seemed to present everything, baring the existential quality of life itself. When I asked myself two decades ago *why* this revolutionary series reached the air, or *who* allowed it to be seen by an immense audience, reaching much of the world in the end through replays, revisions, and videocassettes, I erred in looking for a specific villain, or hero. I made precisely the same error made by the proponets of Myth Three, coming from another pole, or premise. We all wanted to find the hand of the medium itself or its proprietors in the evolution of video. We demanded a Caesar or at least a Cecil B. DeMille. In the highest sense, however, the life of the Louds—the very same life most of us endure—made the crucial, telling cut. The Louds forced their boredom, pain, and passion onto a resistant industry. *An American Family* reminded us that the unplotted world on this side, our side of the screen, is the proper business of the medium it happens to occupy.

REALITY AS PLEASURE FAR TOO ABUNDANT

> *Nothing in our research or interviews sug-*
> *gests that commercial television programming*
> *in the U.S. is going to change significantly*
> *in the foreseeable future.*
>   —Frank Mankiewicz and Joel
> Swerdlow, Remote Control, 1978

> *Exhortations by political and religious leaders*
> *to adhere to traditional virtues have had*
> *little impact. President Reagan and . . . the*
> *"Moral Majority" were successful at the ballot*
> *box, but not in the bedroom.*
>   —Sara Levitan, Richard Belous,
> and Frank Gallo, What's Happening to the
> American Family? rev. ed., 1988

> *That is how a picture is attached to reality;*
> *it reaches right out to it.*
>   *It is laid against reality like a measure.*
>   —Ludwig Wittgenstein, Tractatus
> Logico-Philosophicus, 1921

Though it is rarely noted in the many articles and books written about the decisive shift that occurred in the content of prime-time network programming between the 1950s and the 1980s, the nature of the audience changed decisively first. By the time TV began gingerly to recognize single-parent households in shows like *My Three Sons* and *The Andy Griffith Show*, they were spreading rapidly in the land beyond, a consequence at once of education, the rising divorce rate, and the "liberation" of women from confinement in the suburban villa. The unprecedented increase in college graduates, caused first by the GI Bill, acted as a jump start in sophistication. In each of the decades beginning with the 1960s, Americans increasingly read more books, traveled more extensively, and attended more theater, live and film, than their grandparents and parents. The nouveau elite saw to it that their sons and daughters did the same. As for the "liberated" woman, she was now able to make a series of decisions all on her own, rather than waiting for Father/ Husband to act first. According to anthropologist Helen Fisher of the American Museum of Natural History, this more than any other social change insured that the American divorce rate would reach the same level (approximately 50 percent) as that of virtually every other postindustrial nation. In her book *The Sex Contract: The Evolution of Human Behavior*, Fisher notes that historically women who have won economic independence have always preferred a series of husbands or lovers, that is, "serial'" rather than pure monogamy.[5]

Given this fact, it is no wonder that television began to loosen its marital and sexual codes in the mid-1970s, in product commercials as well as sitcoms and even news documentaries. "Reality," or what appeared to be the real world, demanded this change, which lagged considerably behind events on the other side of the screen. Though *An American Family* seemed prurient to some reviewers and an affront to the nuclear family code to Christian fundamentalists, the mere incidence of divorce was hardly uncommon, anywhere in the United States. "Gay rights" was not yet a political movement, but homosexuality was widely discussed, in private and in public, particularly by the generation emerging from the free-speech 1960s. By the mid-1970s, barely a few years after Lance Loud bared his soul, virtually every prime-time "family" show had devoted itself to the subject of gay sex, nearly always in positive, understanding terms. *Soap,* a nighttime serial that appropriately satirized its own name, boasted a gay son in the heart of its "family." The few exceptions, like *My Three Sons,* were clearly holdovers from the stolid ethics of the 1950s.

It is difficult to overestimate the functional importance of this libidinous change in the character of the medium's audience. To date, it has only been sensed—and critiqued— by writers like Lasch or Paul Hollander, in *Anti-Americanism: Critiques at Home and Abroad, 1965–1990,* who are engaged on differing levels in moral outrage.[6] But in retrospect, the reversal seems inevitable. While Bob Hodge and David

122 The Five Myths of Television Power

Tripp argue persuasively in *Children and Television* that economic class often determines viewing response, they and others overlook the power of what might be called "cultural class." Though the aging baby boomers gradually assumed economic power and respectability, they never entirely deserted the belief, rooted in the songs, literature, and politics of the decade in which they matured, that lovemaking was primarily to be indulged for pleasure.

Often dismissed as mindless Aquarianism, this belief boasts a lineage that stretches back as far into the Judeo-Christian past as the reverse. Elaine Pagels's widely read *Adam, Eve, and the Serpent*, published in 1988, revived the heated fourth-century debate between Saint Augustine's harsh interpretation of the Book of Genesis and his several eloquent opponents. The early Aquarian opposition denied the doctrine of Original Sin based in Eve's temptation of Adam. The Gnostic Christians considered Eve a hero, since she awakened her mate to the glories of God's universe. Bishop Julian of Eclanum, who debated openly with Augustine in a losing cause, spoke for the postindustrial class that followed him more than a thousand years later:

> God made bodies, distinguished the sexes, made genitals, bestowed affection through which bodies would be joined, gave power to the semen, and operates in the secret nature of the semen—and God made nothing evil.[7]

The network programmers followed this early Christian lead with timidity, lagging far behind the makers of commercials and films. By the time a popular dramatic series like *Cagney & Lacey* allowed its two heroines to wave nonchalantly (in 1989) at a flasher, implicitly certifying his behavior, or granted the cuckolded husband in *Civil Wars* the right to graphically describe what he saw when he found his wife being entered from the rear by a Korean karate instructor (he recognized her only by her "moans," he said, as her blouse had been pulled over her head), almost two decades had to pass. The Planned Parenthood Federation cited statistics in 1987 that were surely intended to frighten us (sixty-five thousand "sexual references" a year in prime time; one in six "TV families" indulging "extramarital sex").[8] But the audience did not seem disposed to reject what it saw and heard about sex on the networks. "America's not running from that," said one executive. "America is embracing it."[9]

Women became the prime agents of change and its prime symbol. If Pat Loud denounced the philandering of her husband, she—and her sisters—retaliated with activism, not retreat. Mrs. Loud herself became a career woman, moving to New York, where a flotilla of new men presumably awaited her. Fictional prototypes like Chris Cagney, Mary Beth Lacey, Allie (of *Kate & Allie,* played by Jane Curtin), *Murphy Brown* (Candice Bergen), Mariel Hemingway's dour feminist lawyer in *Civil Wars,* together with a squadron of major and minor women in *St. Elsewhere, L.A. Law,* and *Spenser: For Hire* were similarly aggressive throughout the 1980s. Lacey may have been the first woman to pronounce the word "condom" on the nets and Allie was surely the first to behold one in front of the camera. Murphy Brown found herself single, forty, a member of AA, and pregnant in the opening fall episode in 1991. By the time she gave birth to her child, nine months later, she had risen to the status of single-mother-as-political-icon, as we shall see. When Rosie of *The Trials of Rosie O'Neill* first appeared on CBS in the same season she immediately announced that she intended to "reformulate" her breasts, presumably with dread silicon.

In brief, the liberated woman who struck American society with such political and economic force in the 1970s found her symbolic form in these and similar characters exactly one decade later. In place of the sweet, good girls prominent in early decades, the new TV woman was often defiantly "bad," glib, and fast-talking, in the manner of Roseanne Barr Arnold, whose hard feminist edge reportedly led to the sacking of her "sexist" male director. But Roseanne, Cagney, and Lacey paled beside the vigor of the women's movement out beyond the screen. This era saw outbursts of radical feminist rhetoric in the larger political and social world. Writers like Andrea Dworkin and Catharine MacKinnon preached nothing less than a form of pitched war against "paternalism." That most of their sisters preferred the tactics of moderation and reform, moving into the centers of paternalist power, was rarely noted, but significant: the 1970s was a decade when the "first woman"—elected governor, appointed general, named astronaut, rabbi, priest, minister, and corporation president— was everywhere. Advanced paternalism seemed destined to be replaced either by an androgynous elite or a nascent matriarchy.

The new woman's sexual activism both preceded and engulfed television: she bought hundreds of thousands of pornographic videocassettes, as well as copies of Dr. Alex Comfort's *The Joy of Sex,* which specifically encouraged women to innovate in foreplay and positioning, rather than simply accept male prerogatives, like the rear entry described on *Civil Wars.* Every survey of family life indicated that the traditional working-pop, stay-at-home-mom structure was fading. Long before the single mom with her shrinking family hit the sitcoms, she was flourishing in Altoona, if not Skowhegan.[10] Though routinely lamented, these patterns show no sign of reversing, even if the decades of drastic change are behind us. In *Embattled Paradise* (1991), Arlene Skolnick concludes that our present tiny family size, 3.17 people (way below the 4 to 6 TV sitcom families of yore), is stable; further, she predicts a continuing if gradual decline in the annual *increase* in the divorce rate.[11] But this does not mean that the American people are eager to "return" to the sedate lifestyle recommended by Lasch, Hollander, and certain discredited fundamentalist TV preachers, several of whom, like Jimmy Swaggert, were dismissed or jailed for sexual or fiscal indiscretions in the late 1980s and early 1990s.

It is long past time for us to discard moral fervor and reassess the meaning of "the transformation of life on television," as Linda Lichter, Robert Lichter, and Stanley Roth-man put it in *Watching America.* Their simple answer, that "sex sells,"[12] hardly justifies or explains changes in living habits that reach far beyond the bedroom. The fact is that an alternative pattern of life and thought has been exchanged for an older one. It is this pattern in all of its many dimensions that needs our analysis, as well as the halting attempts made by network TV to emulate it.

MEN/WOMEN/WOMEN/MEN

> *In the past . . . the onstage roles of masculinity and of femininity were seen as the reality. But dozens of popular television programs . . . give both sexes a "sidestage" view of each sex role. . . . They show males moving from a backstage area of doubts and fears into an onstage area of fearless masculinity. They reveal women plotting among themselves to attract and control men.*
> —Joshua Meyrowitz, *No Sense of Place: The Impact of Electronic Media on Social Behavior,* 1985

> *A New Class of the culturally disadvantaged is now created that is not integrated with, and not as dependent on, the old class of the moneyed rich.*
> —Alvin W. Gouldner, *The Future of Intellectuals and the Rise of the New Class,* 1979

TV is a tempting target for moralists and journalists. It is easier to use vivid examples of licentious behavior in prime time—teenagers losing their virginity, for example, on *Beverly Hills 90210* or *Doogie Howser, M.D.*—than to patiently pick apart mountains of often conflicting data, or quote the cross-cutting conclusions of psychologists, and therapists, to say nothing of progressive changes in religious practice: while the Moral Majority made headlines in the 1980s, many

mainstream Christian and Jewish faiths revised their teachings on sexual behavior, within and without the bonds of
marriage. Even so patient and skilled a writer as Joshua
Meyrowitz in *No Sense of Place* invoked Myth Three to explain the dramatic shift in male-female role models in the
past two decades. Facing the complex truth about the economic and political transformation of what used to be called
"the middle class," Meyrowitz concluded that TV, by lifting
the veil that once covered the male and the female psyche,
as well as their confidential discourse, had caused the merging of masculinity and femininity, that is, the long-predicted
androgynous lifestyle.

But surely the epic shift in the means by which the "middle" of American society earned its living, cared for its children, and came into direct contact with a world it never
visited before (through a quantum leap in international
travel) dwarfed the influence of prime time. Not that TV
ever fully commanded the allegiance of this "new class,"
which did not duplicate the settled habits of its parents. If
it means anything, "middle class" denotes a certain sense of
stability, of families living in state, in place, with roles clearly
defined. Now, in an era when jobs, homes, and parenting
responsibilities are evolving with the speed of light, the appeal of a "stability" that is rooted in a single place (or function) has disappeared, perhaps forever. Surely it is the
fragmentation of the Middle, brought on by these deep-
seated cultural, economic, and occupational changes, that
provoked seismic change in the body politic, not the medium
that reported and recycled them.

Prime among these changes, charted in part by critical
tracts like Daniel Bell's *The Coming of Post-Industrial Society*
(1973), Peter Drucker's *The Age of Discontinuity* (1969, 1978),
and Alvin Gouldner's *Intellectuals and the Rise of the New Class*
(1979), is the proliferation of education and of literacy. During the very period when analysts like Meyrowitz and others
saw *Dallas* and Calvin Klein *Obsession* commercials revising
each sex's view of the other, the economy virtually demanded that change. As American dependence on indus-

trial production changed to a need for software and services, for literacy, patience, and detail, trained, educated women became prime commodities in the work force, which is crucial to marketplace performance. It is no accident that the 1960s and the 1970s also saw a quantum leap in the number of women admitted to universities. By the mid-1980s, the sexes were virtually equal in their representation on campus, whereas before World War II, women made up less than 10 percent of the college and university student body. Men were similarly affected by these massive shifts in employment supply and demand. More and more they saw their livelihood dependent on knowledge, not brawn.

For the first time, perhaps, American men and women began to share equally in a culture based in print, in travel, and a multiplicity of professional contacts, as well as TV viewing. Chronologically, this change swept through the very generation weaned in the 1950s that suffered the slings and arrows of the civil rights struggle, the Vietnam War, and the assassinations of the Kennedys and Martin Luther King. This combination did not bode well for the simple monochromatic morality that attended early network TV. Producers and directors in the generation following hard upon *An American Family* had to deal with an audience packing a relatively sophisticated sense of how the world works. To say that this worldview was subtler, less given to the acceptance of stereotypical myths is an understatement. Many young adults felt themselves betrayed by a government that prosecuted what seemed an unwinnable, immoral war; they did not believe in sheriffs with white cowboy hats and generals with braided visors. They demanded and instead received the very supply of ambiguous demi-heroes/villains that to this day continue to portend moral decline for TV preachers—lawyers and doctors who cheat, sadistic police officers, priests who are sex offenders. Once revered, authority figures became in these years suspect. *Watching America* documents, for example, a sharp rise in instances of workers ridiculing none other than the boss throughout the 1970s, without suffering any adverse consequences.[13]

It is easy to see why the logic of this shift, as well as the emergence of a more relaxed sexuality, has been routinely condemned by the media analysis industry. The conservative commentators who dominated many of the nation's editorial pages and talk shows in the 1980s, thanks to Reagan's sweeping electoral victories, blamed these iniquities on TV and Hollywood, or, at best, on subversive opinion-makers, as we have already noted.[14] Vice President Dan Quayle's fulminations over the "cultural elite" in the 1992 campaign was a predictable consequence. Equally predictable, *Murphy Brown* became the pointed object of his rage when Murphy, pregnant in fall 1991, decided to have her child, fatherless. She gave birth in May 1992, before an audience swelled to motherhood size (38 million viewers) by her tormentor's fulminations. Myth Three also flourished, paradoxically. Though Quayle's political opposition rushed to defend Ms. Brown, few vigorously applauded her decision on social, moral, or intellectual grounds in the mainstream press, on the opinion pages, or on the central talk shows (Ted Koppel's *Nightline*, ABC, or the *MacNeil/Lehrer Newshour*, PBS) during this time. No one seemed to care or dare enough to argue that a behavioral change in the moral code for relations between and within the sexes was historically inevitable, hardly an invention of the electronic elite, and, from one point of view (the Gnostic/early Christian view), even justified by Holy Scripture. In the years when the press and the media were echoing the Reagan thesis about a "return" to simpler, more righteous days, this view seemed irrelevant. The stridently righteous voices became newsworthy, even the hard-line feminists (MacKinnon, Dworkin & Co.) who alleged that sexual congress perpetuated paternalism. In some cases, these feminists demanded that the publishers and disseminators of pornographic books and films be prosecuted.

That there are feminist voices on the other side is hardly known to this day by the larger public. Organizations like Feminists for Free Expression, a coalition of scholars, artists, writers, filmmakers, actresses, lawyers, and businesswomen opposed to censoring pornography in any form are rarely heard from. Many of these women contributed to a vital collection of articles and essays, *Pleasure and Danger: Exploring Female Sexuality*, edited by Carol Vance in 1984. Unlike those demanding a "return" to the days of Ozzie and Harriet, these women maintain that the approach of social and economic equality argues for a renewal and rediscovery of sexuality, not its abandonment. This mild feminist hedonism, however, is hardly confined only to feminist intellectuals. Though rarely noted, there was no evidence in any reputable behavioral studies during the 1980s and 1990s that the liberated woman shied away from either the company or the embrace of men, even among the "twenty-somethings," whom *Time* also found—predictably, and without any hard, discernible proof—to be engaged in a "return" to the old moral code.

It was also difficult during this period to find anyone defining or defending the pluralist cultural and consumption tastes in evidence in the generation that incubated in the 1960s. With unprecedented access to disposable income, these New Class Americans, ranging from age thirty to fifty, have increasingly pursued multiple, often contradictory, directions in living, traveling, loving, eating, reading, voting, or viewing. Increasingly, these patterns daunted pollsters, marketing analysts, and evangelists. They still do. But in fact, this evolution ought to be celebrated, not excoriated. The informed freedom to think and to choose has been the central premise of mass education, not to say literacy, dating back to the eighteenth century and to the Enlightenment. Indeed, it is precisely this freedom of thought, acquisition and movement that attracted the citizens of repressive regimes in Eastern Europe and in Asia. Their pent-up desire exploded in the late 1980s, leading to the fall of the Berlin Wall and the tragic drama of Tiananmen Square, in Peking. "Choice" on levels both mundane and high has become something approaching a sacred value at the end of this century, approaching the citizen's right to "elect" his own leaders in the eighteenth century. This conviction, which easily predates television, informs virtually everything taught, written, filmed, or set to popular music in Western culture, though it rarely informs those who prefer to see our life choices guided by the nightly network serials.

Coincident with the rise in the economic and political power of women, "free choice"-as-ideal stoked the already heated controversy in the United States—and other countries—over the right to decide for or against abortion. When CBS decided in the fall of 1991 to allow its *Murphy Brown*/Candice Bergen to give birth out of holy wedlock (though the father turned out to be Murphy's ex-husband), we were once again warned by fundamentalist pressure groups like Turn Off Television (who sponsored "black-out" days in the state of North Carolina that year) and journalists committed to our myth that prime-time TV was subverting the morals of its audience. Diane English, the award-winning director and writer of *Murphy Brown*, defied critics in advance of the broadcast. Unmarried pregnancy is widespread, she pointed out to the press, quoting a female viewer who had written in asking "What's the big deal?" But Ms. English also confessed that Murphy had no choice but to give birth; if she aborted, *Murphy Brown* would be finished, bereft of sponsors surely frightened by right-to-life protesters.

My own conviction is that *Murphy Brown* would have stayed the storm, just as then Governor Bill Clinton later survived those who predicted that his alleged extramarital affair would ruin his political career during the Democratic primary season of 1992. Ms. English underestimated both her fictional heroine and her "real-life" audience. A decision to abort would have seemed entirely logical for the aggressive, independent Murphy. Furthermore, she would follow, not trail-blaze, in the path worn by her audience. By the early 1990s, the advocates of choice outpolled their anti-abortion opponents by margins ranging from 10 percent to 30 percent, depending on the state. When a male colleague attempted on the fall premiere to persuade Murphy Brown to abort with a crude joke, offering to accompany her "to some back alley," she replied, coolly:

"There is no back alley. Women in this country legally have a choice . . . at least I think they do. I haven't checked the papers today."

This is hardly radical doctrine. Though the press often portrayed Brown as a marginal, challenging figure, because of her wit and spectacular self-reliance (a TV news anchorwoman, she draws a hefty salary; further, she easily fields a cadre of attentive males), it is by now almost impossible to argue that she is unrepresentative, at least in attitude, if she ever was. In hindsight, it's clear that the pregnancy episode distressed the nation not at all. Rather, it pulled the highest rating the program had ever enjoyed to that point, and the follow-up mail was overwhelmingly favorable. By the time its heroine decided to speak out directly against the vice-president's dark lament (that she threatened old-style "family values," Murphy had moved even more securely into the mainstream. On September 22, 1992, when Candice-as-Murphy-Brown-fictional-TV-anchorwoman rebuffed Quayle, she attracted 44 million people, a larger audience than watched the Republican convention one month before. One of the viewers was Quayle himself, who began to speak reassuringly about his "respect" for single parents, perhaps because his aides had reminded him that more than one-third of American families, potential voters to the last, were commanded by single mothers and fathers. Who, in this exchange, represented fiction, who fact?

Certainly "Murphy" in the end spoke at least for the "fact" represented by her huge market. American life, in a sense, had molded *Murphy Brown* and what she came to represent. Granted, these forces made her into a complex figure, compared with the popular heroines who preceded her. Often, she seemed in these episodes neither male nor female, left nor right, yin nor yang. The decision she made earlier—to have the child in the face of all her misgivings ("What do I want with a baby?" she asks herself. "I'm living a highly complete life here.")—is precisely the kind of impossible choice often presented by postindustrial life to a new class

that swims in a sea of options. In conditions of poverty, or
of wealth, the options are simpler, if not softer. But the life
now endured by most of us is neither. It offers an endless
terrain of criss-crossed, cutting angles.

THE REAL REAL

> Camille Paglia: *There's no sense to reality.*
> *It simply happens. Television is actually closer*
> *to reality than anything in books. The mad-*
> *ness of TV is the madness of human life.*
> —Camille Paglia (in dialogue with
> Neil Postman). "She Wants Her TV! He
> Wants His Book!, *Harper's*, March 1991

> *Believe me, when the viewers tell the networks*
> *that they would rather watch their own home*
> *videos than the product of the six-fig-*
> *ure . . . talent of Hollywood, the networks pay*
> *attention.*
> —David Poltrack, CBS, lecture,
> 1991

Though *Murphy Brown* was labeled "entertainment" and
functioned dramatically as "fiction," the show had more
than one link to what came to be labeled "Reality TV," the
catchphrase of the early 1990s. Murphy, a TV journalist,
referred freely to the pressing political events of the day
(cf. the Supreme Court vs. Roe v. Wade). And the themes
she dealt with—from late pregnancy to alcoholism to single
parenthood—were the themes that swept through the doc-
udramas, expanded news hours, and intimate on-camera
revelations defining Reality TV on its mainstream end. She
also intruded on certain provocative forms near the cutting
edge, primarily the unbounded, unedited attempts by cable
television to host news, trials, and conversations in their
entirety. Certainly the last decade of the century found television in all its forms attempting to embrace a new, discor-

dant sense of the *Real*. In its willingness to risk the patience
of the viewer as well as occasionally challenge his eye with
rough, hand-held Minicam images, this genre flatly contradicted the spherical view of the world associated with network television, as well as Myth Three.

The immediate external causes of this shift were numer-
ous. The presence of cable television itself, which offered
unlimited channels and time, allowed burgeoning phenomena like CNN, C-SPAN, and Court TV to offer unlimited
access to events that over-the-air networks insisted on con-
densing in brief live segments or editing for prime-time
news. Born in 1979, C-SPAN began as a "public service" of
the cable TV industry, modestly bankrolled to provide nonstop coverage of the House of Representatives. Within a few
years, it was turning its anchorless eyewitness camera on the
Senate, State Department briefings, congressional committee hearings, political meetings, and debates. C-SPAN also
began to offer direct two-way call-ins linking politicians and
reporters with viewers who questioned and disagreed with
them by telephone. In time, C-SPAN became an alternative
emblem for TV that defied TV. Instead of offering single-
focused "hosts," C-SPAN allowed the unedited camera to
dialogue with the viewer, free from mediation. In its election
coverage, C-SPAN often pinned wireless microphones on
candidates as they made their way through mobs of voters
in shopping centers and crowded city streets, providing
spontaneous insights into character and mood.

The miniaturization of video technology makes the wireless microphone and the tiny, low-light camera possible. As
TV equipment becomes less and less obtrusive, the world,
as well as the new, open-ended, long-form cablecast relaxes.
The 8mm Sony TR81 camera, which does not require crews
and heavy lighting rigs, allowed CNN to merge the roles of
reporter and camera, of eye and brain, in the Gulf War. By
wiring the politicians, C-SPAN empowered the viewer, who
became his/her own analyst, as the candidates unveiled
themselves in action. The invisibility of camera and microphone allowed Court TV, which premiered in 1991, to po-

sition itself inside unfolding trials without disturbing judges, juries, lawyers, and witnesses. The informality of home video is replacing the imperial presence of the bulky TV camera, the director, and the crew.

In virtually all of these instances, from war to politics to the push-and-tug of the courtroom, life has revealed itself to be, as Camille Paglia argued in her debate with Neil Postman, long-winded, indecisive, and unpredictable. We saw rampant confusion in the heat of action in the Gulf, candidates flubbing or flustered in the Iowa primary of 1988, lawyers rebuked by judges or even their own clients in courtroom trials after days of testimony. We saw the headlines contradicted in the midst of the womanizing charges against Senator Gary Hart in the early days of the 1988 campaign. When the traditional press and television focused almost entirely on his alleged affair with model Donna Rice, C-SPAN stolidly cablecast the entire text of his foreign policy address to the National Press Club in Washington, D.C., without comment, of course.

Before this surreal landscape, the audience once deemed impatient and inattentive showed itself to be obsessive when challenged or aroused by content. Of all the empirical causes for the rise of the *Real*, surely this is the weightiest. While the network viewing share declined, CNN, C-SPAN, and Court TV, all of which began with tiny market shares, boomed, doubling and tripling their modest audience shares, year after year, finally reaching millions of households and holding their viewers in front of the set for long stretches of time. Demographically, the spread of this audience responded almost exactly to the aging of the white-collar New Class, whose appetite for information in the place of fiction is clearly expanding with age. Marshall Cohen of MTV made the point vividly to a reporter, as 1991 ended. "When you walked up the hall this year, the things people were talking about were the war, the hearings on the confirmation of Supreme Court nominee Clarence Thomas, and the trial of alleged rapist William Kennedy Smith. Nothing was made in entertainment that made people talk like that."[15]

But it is precisely this inclination to think of "Reality TV" as an analogue to entertainment that blinds us to its deeper significance. The predictable reaction of the networks has been to seize upon the codes of the new genre rather than its actual substance. The 1990s rushed to enshrine the rough-grained home video/docudrama esthetic in a bewildering variety of forms. High-profile discussion shows like *Phil Donahue* and *Oprah Winfrey* reached for any event or topic that declared itself "controversial" or titillating: Donahue wore a dress to decorate a show devoted to cross-dressing; Winfrey jogged around the block each day on camera to lose weight; incest and the sexual abuse of children, once taboo in polite conversation, became commonplace jargon among viewers of these shows, as well as in the establishment press.

On *America's Funniest Home Videos,* the ABC network enshrined family video by tightly packaging the most absurd of the thousands of tapes it received each week, playing them like hits on the hit parade before a studio audience clearly coached to laugh and applaud on cue. "Tabloid" news programs normally featuring a loud, aggressive host— *A Current Affair,* with Australian reporter Steve Dunleavy, and *Now It Can Be Told,* starring the combative Geraldo Rivera—aggressively sought and paid for "stories" tending toward the sensational, with a particular fondness for sexual violence. NBC's *Unsolved Mysteries,* Fox's *America's Most Wanted,* and CBS's *Rescue 911* blatantly courted viewer participation, offering prizes for solutions, arrests, and rescues, in prime time.

But in each of these cases the *Real* was unreal, that is, invented, or forced upon us, as a simulation of various truths, political and personal. C-SPAN, CNN (during moments of crisis, when the coverage was continuous), and Court TV followed the gait of life itself, turning the camera on from beginning to end, no matter how long or, occasionally, how tedious. Court TV, the last of these pioneers in the new Long Form, depended for its life on the slow, patient acceptance of the camera in courtrooms in states across the United States. By the time Court TV began to transmit its twenty-four-hour, seven-day coverage in July 1991, forty-five states allowed TV into the midst of both civil and criminal cases, with a variety of restrictions. The new network's backers claimed on the one hand to be engaged in serious, uplifting education, rendering the law, if not justice, public exposure; on the other hand, they boasted that the vivid, compelling drama of real trials bringing real victims and criminals to the screen would soon eclipse popular dramas like *L.A. Law* and even the daytime appeal of the sophisticated soap operas.

What in fact the unedited trials seem certain to achieve is a change far more basic, rich with prophetic implications about the shifting relationship between medium and eye, between sender and receiver. Within the first half year of its appearance, Court TV handled two epic confrontations that succinctly defined the meaning of Long Form—the Clarence Thomas–Anita Hill confrontation over his nomination to the Supreme Court and the tense, emotional rape trial of William Kennedy Smith, scion to the great political family. Drawn to the Long Form by the dramatic stature of the participants, as well as the unveiled sexual implications basic to both disputes, the audience in the end learned as much about itself, perhaps, as it did about the forces arrayed against each other in these two events.

LONG COMEDY/LONG TRAGEDY

> *Tragedy is poetry in its deepest earnest: comedy is poetry in unlimited jest. . . . Most perfectly, the greater the display is of intellectual wealth squandered in the wantonness of sport without an object, and the more abundant the life and vivacity in the creations of the arbitrary will.*
> —Samuel Taylor Coleridge,
> *Greek Drama* 1818

> [Today] *actual scenes of newsworthy events*
> *are presented and interviews of participants*
> *are given when these persons can be assumed*
> *to be still in the quick of their involvement*
> *and still able to exude the reality of their con-*
> *cern.* . . . *But* . . . *what is involved is the*
> *transformation of political and tragic events*
> *into raw materials for scriptings.* . . .
> *Events* . . . *can easily be used as a resource*
> *for plot materials. Apparently, a way to*
> *smother live events is to give them live*
> *coverage.*
>
> —Erving Goffman, *Frame Analy-*
> *sis: An Essay on the Organization of Experience,*
> 1979

The marathon conflicts between Supreme Court nominee Clarence Thomas and medical student William Kennedy Smith and their female accusers in the fall of 1991 tested at once the medium, the television audience, and the press that preyed upon all of them. Each of these "scenes," to borrow Erving Goffman's term, covered day after day of live television attended by millions upon millions of viewers, on several networks, commercial, public, over-the-air, and cable. The dispute between Judge Thomas and Anita Hill, a former employee, engulfed a mere weekend but it served as epilogue to the confirmation drama that began months before, parts of it previously televised live on C-SPAN, CNN, and PBS. The rape charges brought by Patricia Bowman in Palm Beach, Florida, against Smith invoked a trial that lasted several weeks and summoned many hours of testimony by dozens of witnesses.

Neither the "hearing" or the "trial" reached a definitive conclusion. The Senate finally voted to confirm, while the Florida jury dismissed Bowman's charges, but few observers, including the Senators and the jurors, would later claim they knew the final truth. In this sense, the new marathons did not completely link to the classical dramatic tradition with which they were often compared. Perhaps the only

proper analogy was the total involvement of the audience,
which, if we are to believe the scribes of ancient Athens,
not to say Elizabethan England, was total: as the grand tragedies and comedies unfolded in the lips of actors not recorded for later replay, the viewer sat rapt by the
importance of each spoken line, as did the Court TV audience, as well as its relevance to his/her own life.

Recent analogies are the marathon segmented dramas
composed by German filmmakers Rainer Werner Fassbinder and Edgar Reitz in the early 1980s for German
television. Fassbinder's powerful and mordant *Berlin Alex-
anderplatz,* a chronicle of life in Berlin in the 1930s, before
Hitler, ran for fifteen and a half hours over fourteen con-
secutive evenings. Later, like the sixteen-hour *Heimat,*
Reitz's generational saga about an entire town, *Berlin Alex-
anderplatz* was often seen in one epic, uncut screening in
theaters. But each drama, like its countless episodic "mini-
drama" imitators that followed in the United States, was
structured to carry a home viewing audience from day to
day, anticipating reversals in plot or continuities in theme
in advance, unlike the unpredictable Thomas-Hill/Smith-
Bowman epics.

Yes, the hearings and trials that dominated the fall of
1991 were "documentaries," not fictions. But in time the
actors assumed an almost mythic stature, like Fassbinder's
Berliners or Reitz's villagers. Their stature was enhanced
by the press's penchant for assigning praise and blame, for
casting roles that seemed to heighten the "drama" on the
simplest tabloid level. The European press almost without
exception scorned these events, most of all Thomas-Hill,
which it interpreted as a primitive witchhunt, primed by the
prurient American obsession with the private affairs of public men and women. These intimate details are ignored in
societies more tolerant of human nature—or so went the
line. "Puritan America," announced *La Republica* in Italy,
"watches television as if it were looking into a mirror."
French and German commentators routinely called the

Thomas hearing in particular "humiliating," beneath a great democracy.

But all of these complaints overlooked the specific context within which the events played out, late in 1991. Certainly the decisive shift is in the temporal structure of television programming, which now allowed events of terrible complexity to totally unfold. This shift gave both the players and the audience time fully to measure each other's multiplicity of roles. So did the mounting debate generated by the women's movement over male sexual violence, fired by angry feminist voices before these two cases began to unfold.[16] At a public conference shortly after the Thomas hearing, Susan Brownmiller, author of a widely respected study of rape, declared to a large lecture audience, almost shouting, that "All men are potential rapists!" Scandalized by such remarks, Barbara Amiel in the London *Sunday Times* announced that "Extreme Feminism is now a state religion in America."

For all these reasons, Erving Goffman's seminal investigation into the theater of daily life, *Frame Analysis,* is perhaps the best guide to the events that seemingly reinforced the all-powerful presence of TV in American lives, but in fact subverted that presence. Goffman sees our social "reality" not as independent of us but always dependent upon how we view or play our own roles and understand others in the same process. Each of us "frames" whatever we see or hear in terms of our own needs or understanding. Nor do we always play our role in a straight, one-to-one manner, directly stating our convictions, even when we know them. The moments when we joke, report on the convictions of another, or change professional roles in the office (from employee to ally to manager, for example), are constantly shifting.

"It seems that we spend most of our time not engaged in giving information," writes Goffman, "but in giving shows."[17] Goffman's book, based on a wealth of analyses of differing perceptions of real and reported events, sees the media as a crucial framer, particularly in its lust for "human interest" stories that quickly convert unusual occurrences—a little boy tripping a large, marauding male on the street, for example, or a famous movie star asking a bellboy for his autograph—into tiny morality plays, with the little boy as hero, the famous star as humble pie.

By detecting these frames, even in the most painful circumstances, such as the fall 1991 video marathons, we can begin to see how we perceive, rearrange, and identify "reality." *"Their telling,"* says Goffman, *"demonstrates the power of our conventional understandings to cope with the bizarre potentials of social life, the furthest reachings of experience."*[18] Goffman would surely say that the extraordinary weekend confirmation hearing in October 1991 began with each side furiously attempting to "frame" the events that ensued in his or her own way. Clarence Thomas immediately portrayed himself as *l'homme naturel*, as a decent, hardworking black man who had overcome racial prejudice, and paint his opponents, among them Ms. Hill, also black, who had charged him with sexual harassment, as immoral extremists:

> *This is un-American, this is Kafkaesque. . . . I am not here to be further humiliated by this committee or to put my private life on display for prurient interests or other reasons.*

Anita Hill, of course, framed herself as the calm, professional, and righteous—though aggrieved—citizen in her very first press conference, when she went public with her charges, disclaiming any interest in the sensational implications of what she revealed to the world about a Supreme Court nominee:

> *Believe me, I'm not trying to set any kind of precedent. That's not my motive. I want to provide information. In my affidavit I never used the term "sexual harassment"—that's not my agenda. I don't have an agenda, except to provide information . . . about his behavior.*

There were equivalent "frames" in the Smith trial, with the accuser often bursting into tears, confirming her helplessness before the tall, strong, and privileged male that allegedly overpowered her, while the sober and serious Smith constantly deferred, smiling, eyes cast down, to the female judge and prosecutor and to his male attorney, demonstrating that he was a "good boy," in effect, not a monster, that he knew his youthful place, before women and his elders.

But what happened on television was not entirely a manner of role playing. Goffman is careful to distinguish what he calls "natural" and "social" frames. The latter is manmade, moved forward by "actors" like Thomas, Hill, Smith, Bowman. The former includes "occurrences" that appear to be "undirected, unoriented, unanimated, unguided, 'purely physical.'" At its most extreme, a "natural" frame encloses disasters like forest fires, storms, shipwrecks at sea. Moving closer to the "social" frame, certain actors are driven by events or by their own instincts in ways that blur the line between cause and effect. These last frames are the most difficult to identify when the media insists on compressing and explaining what has already occurred. The media is not comfortable, moreover, when it must confess to irresolution—i.e., when it cannot explain the events it portrays.

Court TV and its occasional allies (CNN, PBS) allowed just such an enigmatic demi-frame to unfold during the fall of 1991, leaving its vast audience with an experience of seriocomic public tragedies that verged on the unmediated. Though it zealously bracketed and analyzed everything said in the trials, Court TV to its credit kept mum for long stretches of time during both the congressional hearings and Palm Beach trial. During these moments, the mystery that is sexual appeal (and expression) was unveiled in all of its irrationality. At these times, the "social" frame, brilliantly constructed by the principal actors—with their lawyers and interpreters—was replaced by the "natural" frame, unwinding like the reverse of a Möbius strip.

The "conventional understanding," to borrow another

phrase from Goffman, insistently repeated by reporters, anchormen, editorial writers, and politicians, including President George Bush, was that the actors' revelations horrified the audience. Bush asked, pointedly, "Why send all this filth into family living rooms?" The attempt to name villains and heroes, to point the finger of blame, first at the accusers, later at the accused, was a symptom of this notion. When later it became obvious that the audience was far from disgusted, that all across the United States men, women, and children were listening to virtually every word, then phoning and wiring their congressmen, the ready explanation had to be this: that mainstream America was titillated, no more, by sexual revelations.

In fact, Court TV's scrupulous log of viewer calls during both nonstop spectacles, as well as the polls that followed both events, indicated quite a different level of understanding, attuned to the ambiguities inherent in the testimony. On this level, they were well served by the open-ended means of presentation. From beginning to end, the medium surrendered itself by default to the rules and the pacing of larger frames. No ratings-minded TV director would have allowed the Thomas-Hill saga to ask the same repetitious questions over and over, propounded by Senators often devoid of charisma or camera presence. In one notable case, Senator Orrin Hatch, Republican of Utah, even read pages from a novel to reinforce his testimony. Others openly assailed and insulted the initially sympathetic accuser, Anita Hill, alienating her large body of supporters. In the Palm Beach case, to take just one example, days were spent listening to tedious testimony by fingerprint and forensic experts called primarily by the defense—to prove, among other things, that there were no grass stains on the dress of the accuser, thus lessening the probability that she fought or struggled with the defendant.

How did the supposedly inattentive viewer handle these vast stretches of boredom and detail? The anecdotal evidence, backed by polls and Court TV's call-in logs, is clear: for the most part, he and she remained glued to the screen.[19]

In my own case, I had friend after friend say, in effect, *I never watch TV but I couldn't turn the hearing* (or trial) *off*. Once again, the law of contradiction asserts itself: as the length and tedium of the baseball season maintains as loyal an audience, year after year, as fast-paced professional basketball, the defiantly anti-"TV" hearings and trials in the fall of 1991 conquered the screen, and its audience. The boredom, the slow pace, the weight of detail obviously accomplished two ends rarely attained by sound-bite coverage: they confirmed the *reality* of the events occurring on the other side of the screen: the Long Form presentation was so bad, so clumsy in comparison with the slick prime-time trials in *Perry Mason*, let's say, or *L.A. Law*, that it had to be "real," thus ensuring the viewer's belief, and attention. Second, the marathon story gradually enfolded the audience *inside*, not outside the event. Instead of merely spectating, the viewer, now apprised of all the nuances, all the conflicting testimony, all the minutia available to the Congress and the jury, became a full participant, left virtually alone to reach his/her own verdict.

In both the Thomas-Hill and Smith-Bowman cases, this inclusive complexity led to an interesting evolution in the attitude of both the lay audience and the professionals directly involved, that is, politicians, lawyers, and press. Hill's first public complaints about Thomas's behavior were devastating, causing many observers to believe that his confirmation, always a close call, was now unlikely. But she clearly lost ground over the long weekend, particularly with women. By the following Monday, when the final Senate vote shaded in his favor (fifty-two to forty-eight), the consensus, based on intuition, mail and phone calls flowing into the Senate, as well as several polls, was that Thomas's fiery denials, spiced with insinuations that Senate liberals were out to "lynch" a poor black man, had completely overwhelmed the cool, detached professor from Oklahoma. Hill could never adequately explain why she had continued to work for Thomas after the ugly incidents she described so graphically had occurred. Some Democratic Senators complained that in the end she was neither heroine nor martyr. Once again we were told, in brief, that appearance subsumed reality.

But is is also possible to see the response of the viewers here (and in the later Smith trial) as both skeptical and responsive to the content of the case. While the percentage of those polled by the *New York Times*/CBS the next day in favor of Thomas's nomination had slightly increased (from 38 percent the previous week to 45 percent now), more than half were *still* opposed or undecided. Thomas did clearly triumph on "believability" against Hill, 58 percent to 24 percent, with only 26 percent of women siding with her, while 24 percent believed Thomas and a whopping 50 percent remained undecided. But the key result, rarely mentioned in the press, was the majorities of both sexes who were certain that neither actor was telling the "entire truth." Few respondents were sure they knew everything. "I believe there is something that has not come out," said a woman in Biloxi, Mississippi, quoted by the *Times,* summarizing this pervasive doubt.

Neither men nor women, Democrats nor Republicans, left nor right, responded as the advocates of Myth Three or the ideological partisans arrayed around Hill and Thomas, or, later, Smith and Bowman, predicted, or expected. Though Betty Friedan and other feminists threatened electoral defeat to Senators who dared to speak, lobby, or vote for Thomas ("We're going to recruit a Wild West woman to come up and run against Alan Simpson in Wyoming" was a typical threat), there was no evidence that women across the United States shared her outrage in anything like the numbers needed to swing a multiple-issue election. Court TV's logs, which record comments made while the live custody unfolded, showed persistent doubt of Professor Hill's credibility among women callers:

I don't think Professor Hill is lying but I think she is, like some women in the work force, she has an idea that every man is

attracted to her. . . . I believe she thinks in her mind that all
this really took place. I believe Judge Thomas.[20]

The same was true for women reacting to the agonized
testimony of Patricia Bowman, often punctuated by sobbing.
Over and again they questioned Bowman's right to remain
anonymous, with an electronic "mask" covering her face,
while Smith, the accused, was publicly identified; other
women pointed to the lack of grass stains on her skirt, meaning she did not struggle during intercourse. Male callers
were equally unpredictable, often complaining about
Smith's ability to command Kennedy wealth in his defense.[21]

Most revealing of all, male and female viewers alike were
apparently undisturbed, at least on any profound level, by
the explicit sexual details revealed on the television screen.
Court TV's logs are silent on this supposedly traumatic issue
while the callers devote many minutes to a battery of details,
including the political opinions of the networks' commentators during the Thomas-Hill hearings and the persistently
loud pouring of water into a drinking glass by the judge in
the Smith trial. As for Smith, his innocent verdict, though
reviled by some feminists—Catharine MacKinnon argued
in the *New York Times* that the Smith decision called for
reform in our rape laws—was widely approved, though
doubt as to the "real" truth about what happened in the
two sexual interludes that occurred near the ocean in Palm
Beach remains high.[22]

As for Long Form sex, its lengthy presence on the TV
and cable TV screens was marked by an unpackaged informality that is the antithesis of the slick and skillful innuendos inserted into TV commercials and Hollywood
films. Here is Ms. Hill describing her encounter with the
judge, which is reminiscent of the inexplicable natural disasters associated by Goffman with the "natural" frame:

Thomas was drinking a Coke in his office. He . . . looked at the
can and asked, "Who has put pubic hair on my Coke?" On

other occasions he referred to the size of his own penis as being
larger than normal and he also spoke on some occasions of the
pleasures he had given to women with oral sex.

Certainly Thomas's motivation here, the cause behind the effect, will never be known, perhaps even to Thomas himself. Certainly here in these alleged remarks Thomas violated what might be called the "gender frame," where Hill was concerned. It was a classic mismatch between speaker and listener. Whatever "social" frame Thomas may have imagined himself in, Anita Hill was somewhere else, listening in long-suppressed horror. But the response of America was hardly unsympathetic to either actor. Even in its ultimate decision to favor Thomas, the audience withheld final judgment: the viewers were sure the "something missing that has not come out" would have told us more about Thomas's intention, about Hill's visual or bodily response to these words (as opposed to her verbal silence), about the unspoken dynamic that moved each of them over the previous months, weeks, and days, bringing about this moment. By denying these words, by refusing even to comment on Anita Hill's testimony, Clarence Thomas unwittingly encouraged his audience to place a wider, less-focused "frame," at once natural and unnatural, on this event.

Two months later, in the Florida State Court, Patricia Bowman and William Smith, by means of conflicting testimony, constructed a similar "double" frame. Ms. Bowman's tearful testimony rarely rested on a single verbal point. Smith's words, clear, linear, repetitive, verged on the comic, not the tragic, thanks to the relentless passion of the prosecutor for meaningless detail:

LASCH: At that point you took her panties off?
SMITH: We took her panties off. She lifted herself up and I helped her get her panties off.
LASCH: When you say she lifted herself up you're saying

she lifted up her dress and that you pulled down
her underwear?

SMITH: Her dress was up and to get her panties down she
had to move the weight off of her hips and I had
my hand inside of her panties and I moved them
down her leg and she pulled her leg up and took
her panties off. . . .

LASCH: She took off your pants?

SMITH: She helped me take off my pants.

LASCH: And she massaged you?

SMITH: We massaged each other at different points, I'm
just telling you different points. I put my hand in
her panties and massaged her and she was very
wet. . . . I don't know what you want me to say?

LASCH: Did you insert your penis in her vagina at that time?

SMITH: No, I didn't.

LASCH: So you're stating that you did not have your penis
in her vagina on the beach?

SMITH: Yes, I am.

LASCH: Now when you say that you ejaculated, where did
you ejaculate?

SMITH: I ejaculated onto myself.

LASCH: At any time on March 30, 1991, was your penis in
the vagina of NAME ERASED?

SMITH: No.

LASCH: So you ejaculate on the beach. What happened at
that point?

SMITH: After a few minutes I sat up. . . . I got up, took off
my shirt . . . and I went swimming.

LASCH: So any semen you had on yourself would be washed
off in the water?

SMITH: I don't know. . . .

LASCH: So we have this conversation, we have this act.
NAME ERASED is hugging you, then you ejaculate, and then you say, well, I'm going into the water
and take a swim now?

SMITH: Yes.

LASCH: That sounds not too romantic, Mr. Smith.
SMITH: I don't know how I'm supposed to respond to that.

How did the ingenuous American public respond to Smith's fumbling defense of himself? With humor, doubt and compassion, if we are to judge from follow-up polling conducted by CNN and others, together with the jury's unanimous decision to pronounce him "not guilty." Ms. Bowman's fate, enhanced by a sympathetic follow-up interview, together with lucrative book offers, seems similarly benign. Left to the mercy of two-minute summaries on the nightly network news, neither adversary might have escaped the moralizing fate predicted by the European press. But the newfound concession made by television to the pace of life, not itself, allowed all the dimensions that attend any tragedy (or comedy) in the outside world to unfold, for eyewitnesses everywhere.

The apparently superfluous appearance of Senator Ted Kennedy in Palm Beach, called by the prosecution for reasons not apparent to legal strategists, is the final link in this chain. In his gravity and grief, in his choked, monosyllabic replies to questions about the old friends and family on hand in the beach house on the evening when Smith allegedly raped Bowman beneath his window, Kennedy lent the aura of tragedy to a frame that might otherwise have remained the province of comedy. When the audience was left to judge or to discuss what they had seen, it became virtually impossible to leave out any of its contradictory dimensions, from what Edmund Burke might have called the sublime to the ridiculous.

The standoffs between these four actors were equivalent to lifetime decisions made by all of us, decisions that are nearly always tentative. The roles they played were similarly close to us, to the masks we wear each day, as Goffman suggests, in conversations and meetings. In its deepest sense, then, "Reality TV" is not the manipulated tabloid style, engineered to appear spontaneous, but in fact weighted by heavy in-out, good-bad, right-wrong labeling, by the need to identify and cast heroes and villains. Reality TV is rather a situation in which the medium literally disappears, as in the reading of a long, detailed novel, or the printout of a congressional hearing, in behalf of the content. In these instances, the audience senses that it is beholding, not judging, a truth situated on the near side of the screen.

LIFETIME TV

> *Our primitive impulse is to affirm immediately the reality of all that is conceived, as long as it remains uncontradicted. But there are several, probably an infinite number of various orders of realities, each with its own special and separate style of existence. . . . The popular mind conceives of all these subworlds more or less disconnectedly, and when dealing with one of them forgets for the time being its relations to the rest. But every object we think of is at last referred to all these other subworlds.*
> —A. Schutz, "Multiple Realities," 1945

> *Marriage is a relationship which depends on sex and not on gender.*
> —Mr. Justice Ormrod, "Sex," *The Law Reporter* (Great Britain), May 1971

> *Media theory "speaks for the audience," but in ways which seriously malign it.*
> —Conrad Lodziak, *The Power of Television*, 1986

Television as we know it does not make our world. Rather, it is our world, as we perceive it, that increasingly remakes, remolds, and finally destroys "TV." The notion that it works the other way, nourished by those nourished by the Myth, is increasingly difficult to maintain in the presence of Long Form television, a plethora of channels prompting the airing of the special, single voice, and, most of all, the transformed audience. The assumption that Thomas-Hill or Smith-Bow-man would scandalize the nation is left over from the era when the American TV family translated into the nuclear sitcom. Now we live in an age when both serious, sustained attitudinal polling and the evidence of our own eyes document a consistent widening of the concept of the forms of marriage.[23]

It is furthermore no accident that a number of cities, counties, and states have gradually accepted the legal and custody rights of unmarried couples. No one can say for sure what the ultimate results of the feminist revolution will be, but it seems certain to continue the loosening of the traditional codes governing love, sex, long-term living patterns, parenthood, masculinity, femininity. In both the popular and the elite cultures, Camille Paglia's books, the aggressive love songs of Madonna, and the androgynous appeal of Michael Jackson are rough equivalents of these social-political events. In his unintentionally comic decision against a male transsexual who wished to mate as a woman with another man, British justice Ormrod declared that marriage can only exist between two opposite sexes, effectively severing his court off from the new world that began to grow barely one decade later.

Life, not TV, now drives the world. It is quaint in such a time to continue to hear that the all-powerful electronic God will not change its forms or its content for the market and mind it must serve. This market is not merely driven by men and women who are open and tentative about sex, but about virtually everything. Faced with revolutionary changes in politics, medicine, science, and culture, they prefer to make and remake their own minds. At the core, this market prefers non-heroes like the pregnant, single, ex-alcoholic Murphy Brown. It prefers non-anchors when it watches the live news. It demands access to the special, singular voice, to its own home video camera, to the open cable television channel mandated in many cities and towns, allowing its citizens free options to broadcast. This postmodern, post–mass audience adores the *Real*, yes, but it means by that term fiction or nonfiction witnessed and reviewed over long stretches of live C-SPAN, CNN, and Court TV time, or, at worst, with a remote control–driven VCR beside the bed.

Now the catch is . . . even this *Real* is eternally elusive. William James knew this long ago, when he propounded his theory of multiple realities, later refined by A. Schutz, his brilliant disciple. In one sense, the all-knowing fathers of the 1950s responded to an authentic perception of reality shared by its audience. The raw, unmediated vision now on the rise is potentially as easily manufactured as the laugh tracks of another era. It is easy to imagine judges, lawyers, and witnesses orchestrating even the open-ended rhythms of Court TV. The eminent appearance in computer and home video stores of what is now called "virtual reality," in which viewers are wired through electronic headsets into a totally artificial computerized world, where they "feel" as well as walk through raw, created worlds, may become the final corruption of the new ideal. But if this happens it may simply mean that "the audience," forgotten by media theory, according to Conrad Lodziak, may well flee all media, in order to reinvent its present world on this side of every known screen, camera, or fantasy.[24]

MYTH FOUR

TV Pacifies Us (We Are Couch Potatoes)

TV has become the ritual. . . . Now, each Thanksgiving morning, Kellie Zemlicka gives her husband, Brian, a card that celebrates this meaningful new tradition. The card depicts a Thanksgiving table. At one end, a woman sits eating turkey. At the other, a man wearing a football helmet stares at a small television.
—Bob Sipchen, "Tuning in the Spirit: Like a Garrulous Patriarch, TV Now Presides at Most Holiday Gatherings," *Los Angeles Times*, November 12, 1990

The set created its own light, its own color, its own time. . . . Everything on TV was tangled and mixed and yet smoothed out: night and day, big and small, tough and brittle, soft and rough, hot and cold, far and near.
—Jerzy Kosinski, *Being There*, 1978

The emotional isolation from others that starts in front of television may continue in school. Eventually it leads, if not to permanent instability, then to a reluctance to become active in learning or in relation to other people.
—Bruno Bettelheim, *The Informed Heart*, 1960

The presumption that TV inevitably transforms its attendants into passive endomorphs is another cardinal contemporary faith. In this state, the faithful viewers of television already resemble the soft and happy tribe described near the end of *Brave New World* (1932), Aldous Huxley's powerful anti-Utopian novel. Journalists, filmmakers, and academicians cleave fiercely to the implications of this myth, surely because it demarcates the line of status, reserving the near and aloof side for themselves. When Bob Sipchen, an accomplished reporter for the *Los Angeles Times*, set out to enshrine Myth Four in 1990 during the Thanksgiving season, he didn't hesitate to proclaim the "couch potato" families he found in his city as representative of the entire culture: the Zemlicka family, that is, of Manhattan Beach; Kevin Aucello, a Los Angeles businessman who allegedly called his friends on the phone only to discover which TV show they're watching; and Bill and Dana Schreiner, perched on the top of Mount Washington in the same city, whose once-verbose family Christmases had been overwhelmed by network football, according to Sipchen, and the Myth.[1]

Had the *Los Angeles Times* looked around the corner in any of these neighborhoods, it might well have found darkened apartments and homes, deserted by residents who had "gone out," to bowling alleys, health spas, movie theaters, libraries, adult education classes, and restaurants in greater numbers than ever before. "Fitness" is fully as celebrated an American addiction now as TV viewing. The Gallup Poll that has been auditing American "leisure" habits since 1959 records a steadily increasing activism: the percentages of swimmers, bowlers, softball players, golfers, and tennis players have all risen since the spread of TV sets into virtually every home. Both Gallup and the Amerian Book Publishers Association record a similar rise in reading, through the per capita sales of books,[2] though mythologists can attribute the rise to classroom assignments in a society apparently fleeing to schools, colleges, and universities in record numbers. Not even the TV dinner is able to keep the family in the kitchen, according to the Bureau of Labor Statistics, which maintains that the percentage of expenditures for food eaten "away from home" has multipled since the 1950s.[3]

Sipchen's article ignored these inconvenient facts. Rather, it feasted on a new and brilliantly surreal film, *Avalon*, produced and directed by Barry Levinson. *Avalon* tells the story of an American couch potato family—very much like Levinson's—growing up through the 1950s in Baltimore, Maryland, monitored by a giant new TV set. The big, tough TV plunked down in the middle of the family's living room inexorably turns off all talk at the dinner table. Slowly, surely every member ceases talking and simply begins to watch, without any interaction at all, presumably the destiny of the medium. At the end of the film, the youngest son sits alone in a darkened room late at night. Though the station has signed "off," he keeps the blank, humming set on, hypnotized by its drone, its flickering glare. Jerzy Kosinski's novel, speaking for Chance, the semiliterate hero, reinforces this omnivorous image. TV eats *other people* alive, or so we are told. Even the fiercely polemic psychiatrist Bruno Bettelheim, who defined vividly the primal drives inside the child, saw TV as a surprisingly efficient pacifier, without qualification, of those drives—without regard as well for home, parent, school, friends, neighborhood, each a potent influence.

Let us for a moment reverse the widely accepted deconstructive rhythm enshrined in *Brave New World* and thousands of media stories very much like the one that appeared in engaging form in the *Los Angeles Times* on November 12, 1990. Before investigating the reasons and the proof, why not posit, simply as an article of common sense, that the TV audience has surely learned, over decades of viewing time, how to *resist* as well as *worship* a medium no longer viewed as an irresistible miracle, as it was in the 1950s—in brief, that Huxley reversed the reality cycle in the service of fiction. Of course there are small percentages of the population totally addicted to television, in the sense that they actually sit, rooted before the set, watching *and* listening, whenever they are at home. But recent studies indicate that not even these addicts, perched on an endless couch, are without critical detachment: doctors report them "dissatis-fied," like habitual drug users, with the fix they switch on, often in search for companionship alone, for a sound to ward off loneliness.[4]

Elsewhere, of small interest to Huxley or Kosinski or Bet-telheim enthusiasts, or to journalists and academicians im-bued with the Myth, adult Americans are jogging, traveling, and flocking both to football games and art museums, to repeat, in record numbers. One might logically argue that TV has driven us *out* of the house rather than kept us walled within. And when we do tune in TV now, as I have already noted, we are far more selective, in terms of what in fact we watch or zap, with attention, than before. This evolution into a state of free, impatient choice is in part a function of the technological abundance of channels not available in the 1950s. It is equally the result of a mounting sophistication based in cultural and educational upgrading throughout the immense "middle" of American society.

Myth Four is even fragile on its own ground, among the families so unfairly cited to prove the case, that is, the Zem-lickas, the Aucellos, the Schreiners. Are they in fact drawn to television like the moth to the flame? Is it indeed possible that they cannot invent or indulge in conversation while the set drones? Most of those reading this book will recall that the reverse is more often true: save in moments of high drama or moment (the last minutes of a close football game; the first minutes of a key political crisis, such as the wound-ing of a President), most of us habitually indulge *something else* while the TV set is on, from reading to preparing a meal to talking on the telephone. Rather than a god, TV has become something like a little brother or sister: he/she fol-lows us from room to room, lurking now near beds and bathtubs as well as sofas. Occasionally, he or she is annoying, occasionally delightful, most often simply *there*. As we move through this chapter, we will hear testimony to this fact from viewers precisely like the Zemlickas and Aucellos, as well as the Schreiners themselves. What they have to say will surprise the mythologists. More important, we will also hear testimony from the kind of critical, active, intelligent citizen or viewer who is routinely ignored by those who mismanage this medium or seek to profit from this most demeaning of all the myths.

TV AS RITUAL: THE PRESUMPTION

> *"Everyone knows" that television is addictive—Marshall McLuhan (1978) said so himself. From 65% to 70% of adults surveyed believe that TV is addictive ... although far fewer appear to believe that they personally are addicted.*
> —R. McIlwraith, R. Jacobvitz, R. Kubey, A. Alexander, "Television Addiction," American Behavioral Scientist, November–December 1991

> *And now ... no words from the sponsors. SAY GOODBYE TO MINDLESS ADS FOREVER.*
> —Advertisement, Vidicraft CCU-120 Commercial Cutter and Event Timer 1989

It is always salutary to test one's conclusions by immediate recourse to the world beyond. Long ago this method was enshrined by the sage lexicographer Samuel Johnson in a rambling discourse before James Boswell, his faithful biographer: "Sir, look first always to experience." Though I was thoroughly convinced after years of reading, observation, and not a little direct contact (through letters and telephone calls responding to my own appearances on television) that the TV viewer is simply not the gelatinous blob we imagine him or her to be, I decided to test myself at the moment of writing this chapter. On a week's trip that would take me from Los Angeles to Chicago to the suburbs of New York City, I would visit as many completely fresh TV households as I could, in order to view viewers viewing.

Admittedly my sample would be small—I could barely hope to visit and observe at length more than half a dozen households in a single week. It would be biased, too, in the sense that my presence alone (an "author" writing a book about TV) might alter conventional routines. But surely the bias would lean toward Myth Four, or so it seemed to me, as I wouldn't be welcomed into households that ignored television. If anything, my presence might lead people I did not know both to *watch* TV and to claim varying forms of expertise in the subject. As for my exquisitely microcosmic numbers, they would surely outnumber at the very least those homes "visited" by most TV critics and analysts, who rarely refer to front-line experience in any of their writings.

And so I set off, beginning in Los Angeles in February 1992, where the *Los Angeles Times* began. I had decided to attempt to visit the very couch potato families earmarked by Bob Sipchen, if I could find them. Alas, neither the Zemlicka or Aucello families were listed in the Los Angeles phone book less than two years after the article was published. But I struck gold when I phoned the only "William Schreiner" listed. "Yes, I'm the man," he said, "and I remember the article very well. Bob Sipchen lives not far from me. By all means come over tonight. We'll be here, probably watching TV on two sets, my wife upstairs and me downstairs."

As if this were not fruitful enough, I found when I arrived at the door of the Schreiners' casual, wood frame house high on a rare hill in the midst of the city that I was in the hands of a "media family," their own term. Schreiner, thirty-nine, directed a highly sophisticated children's program, *Mathnet,* for PBS, the public television network. Dana Schreiner, twenty-eight, his wife, was an actress who often appeared in films produced for television. "I guess that is why Sipchen called us," said Bill Schreiner, an affable man in jeans and soft blue shirt, beckoning me to sit beside his lighted TV. "He knew we were involved with media and entertainment. We had talked about *Avalon,* I remember."

It was immediately clear to me that the Schreiners violated

any "scientific" pollster's creed, on several levels. They were "insiders," far too coiled inside the media to represent the naive audience that is the staple target both of journalism and of academic research. Worse, they were implicated, slightly, in the definition of the Myth I proposed to assail: they had posed as "couch potatoes" for the *Los Angeles Times.* But I couldn't refuse to interview them. I was committed after all to Johnson's dictum—to see precisely what was in front of me, not some poll-taker's model. And of course I didn't believe in the potato model at all. In my heart of hearts, I was fairly sure the educated, baby-boom Schreiners echoed their class down to jeans, house, and taste, if not profession.

It even seemed that their direct involvement in the definition of my myth was particularly apt. "I said, Bob, you know TV has added a new event to the set of rituals you're discussing," Schreiner recalled. "In the end I contradicted the theme of his article, though it doesn't appear that way in reading. Television hasn't replaced the Christmas ritual in our family. It has added one: watching football. I have six brothers and sisters. We all gather at my father's house over the holiday. If we weren't watching football, we'd never find so much time to sit, and talk."

Talk? Was football necessary to promote conversation? "Yes," he replied. "Before the National Football League began to land on TV, we never talked at Christmas. Now my father follows the game intensely while the rest of us discuss everything, from personal life to politics to philosophy."

I knew I was on to something here. What the Schreiners said, as you will see, ranged across more than football, into the core of the ambiguous, double-coded link between the medium and its audience. So did the comments of nearly everyone I finally saw, coast to coast. I believe their words are at least the equal of the bloodless Nielsen statistics used to sum up viewing habits, not to say the often ingenious means used by dedicated researchers to measure this mys-

terious phenomenon, *watching television*. Their means range
from telephone interviewing, highly suspect for the same
reason that few courts of law recognize it as valid evidence,
to written questionnaires, similarly flawed, to the radio-
transmitted beepers employed by a team of researchers to
"catch" viewers unaware, and pelt them with questions.[5]
Upon reflection, it is clear that each of these methods, including mine, reveals the viewing experience to be deeply
layered, if not twisted, in precisely the same manner.

It was in Los Angeles indeed that I found in a library the
enterprising study on TV addiction. It was based on research methods more scientific than mine.[6] Directed by four
sociologists and professors of media, it took its lead from
the revised third edition of the American Psychiatric Association's *Diagnostic and Statistical Manual* (1987), in which
the clinical definition of the term "addiction" had been
broadened, to the point where habitual TV viewing seems
quite eligible.[7] *DSM-III-R* listed nine criteria that demand
a diagnosis of "substance dependence." The authors of "TV
Addiction" applied five of these criteria to their subject, and
medium, among them *"Substance often taken in larger
amounts . . . than the person intended"* and *"Important social oc-
cupations . . . are given up."* Though the fresh new report
tended to substantiate Myth Four in its use of addictive
"criteria" and in some of its conclusions, the actual facts laid
out inside contradicted the Myth.

Most of all, the findings in "TV Addiction," if not their
interpretation, confirmed what I saw and heard. Each of
my reports gleaned from my tiny survey will therefore be
unveiled in response to the official *DSM-III-R* addictive criteria, one by one. In the end, we will see not only that Myth
Four is desperately flawed but that the TV audience is capable at once of dependence and independence. This *divided*
state is the antithesis of addiction. The same viewer who
swallows football whole in the Christmas season—the
Schreiners, say—would eagerly buy a Vidicraft home VCR,
which promises to automatically "erase" TV commercials

from a recording, if he or she could get one. This device was first placed on the market in Japan in 1989, but angry Japanese corporations quickly chased it away. The moguls understood what the mythmakers do not: even the "heavy viewer," even the weakest link in the market chain, is fatally critical of the medium as presently constituted: he knows precisely what is wrong, as well as what is right, with the drug that only appears to enslave him.

1. "SUBSTANCE OFTEN TAKEN IN LARGER AMOUNTS OR OVER A PERIOD LONGER THAN THE PERSON INTENDED."[8]

> *42% of the 1,241 adult Americans surveyed reported that they "spent too much time watching television."*
> —Gallup and Newport poll, 1990

> *I guess I watch one and a half hours of TV a day. It surprises me I watch that much.*
> —Bill Schreiner, interview with author, February 1992

Gloria Gonick and Harvey Gonick, M.D., Los Angeles, are, like the Schreiners, role models for the viewer rarely discussed in press or pulpit. Each is highly intelligent, professionally active, and personally "overcommitted," in their own worlds. Dr. Gonick, sixty-one, is a nephrologist, or kidney specialist, active both in practice and in writing and lecturing. Mrs. Gonick, fifty-five, is a consultant to museums and collectors in Japanese textiles, which she continues to study, photograph, and videotape when she travels abroad. They use television in totally different ways, he as "background" while he reads or writes in his comfortable study, perched in the rear of a large, comfortable house on the tree-lined west side of the city, she as "foreground," watching by herself only when specific programs—the news or

PBS documentaries—lure her attention. They watch television together only for brief periods of time, usually movies, broadcast or taped, save in rare instances when a public crisis, like the Gulf War, enthralls them both, on CNN.

GLORIA GONICK:

> His patients are often acutely ill and he identifies strongly with them. He will want to watch TV late at night simply as a distraction, then fall asleep. I can't turn it off because I only watch to listen. I never turn TV on for background, except in hotel rooms, when I am alone. I mostly watch PBS. About once a week I will watch the 7 or 11 P.M. news. We both love movies. We rent a film once a week, sometimes two or three times. I think movies have more impact on society than television. Sometimes I watch them to keep up.

HARVEY GONICK:

> I have been playing television in my study for thirty years. It is on all the time. When I go to the bedroom at night I also watch TV for twenty mintues to unwind. No, I can't tell you the next day the names of the programs I watched.

Mildred DeFelice and Carmen DeFelice, Massapequa, Long Island, New York, more closely approximate the presumed national viewing model. Carmen, forty-five, drives a sanitation truck for the town of Oyster Bay, rising each morning at 3 A.M., a job he has held for almost twenty-five years. His wife, forty-six, manages the house, drives the children and several relatives back and forth to school and to offices. Their suburban split-level home is dominated, in the living room, by a large TV set reminiscent of *Avalon's*.

CARMEN DEFELICE:

> The TV set is on ten hours a day, whether anyone is here or not. . . . The TV has always been on in our marriage, from the beginning. I talked to my brother about this. He tells me they used to play radio in the house in the same way in the 1930s. My father bought a TV very early, in 1950. I have known about the soaps for a long time.

MILDRED DEFELICE:

> My father worked for Emerson and designed cabinets, so we had one of the first television sets when I was a child. . . . I follow the soaps. I think of the characters as part of my family. I tape them when I can't watch them on broadcast. Usually I am here alone from 12:30 to 4:30 or 5. I watch the broadcasts until 2:30, then I play the tapes if I missed anything.

DANA SCHREINER:

> I often play TV when I'm working, as background. We have a TV in each room. But our viewing has definitely gone down at dinnertime. We don't watch it together anymore, as I have my three-year-old son, Quinn, at the table, and I don't want him exposed to TV too much. TV is bad for children. It makes them lazy. It kills their imagination because it does everything for them. If I am not going to be there, I don't want him watching.

BILL SCHREINER:

> I don't have the same reaction. When I watch TV with Quinn, we talk a lot, he asks questions, he's

quite involved. He often asks why the camera is switching off or moving. He doesn't zone out like other kids. Every other day for half an hour he watches one of his movies—he already owns a Disney library.

2. "THE PERSON RECOGNIZES THAT SUBSTANCE USE IS EXCESSIVE AND HAS ATTEMPTED TO REDUCE OR CONTROL IT BUT HAS BEEN UNABLE TO DO SO (AS LONG AS THE SUBSTANCE IS AVAILABLE)."

> *TV can warp your mind, yes. It doesn't warp mine because I keep thinking about other things when I am watching. I get lots of ideas watching TV just as I do when I am driving the truck.*
>
> —Carmen DeFelice, interview with author, February 1992

Almost every investigator of TV viewers, even the most committed, bordering on substance addiction, has noted this contradiction: over and over the investigator is told that excessive viewing is bad for *others*. Those who admit to "watching" for massive amounts of time—fifty hours per week, or more—nearly always maintain they are otherwise engaged while the set hums. It is this hyperactivity that guards against the pernicious effects of electronic transmission, they tell us. Of course this position reflects the persistent double-coded view of the medium adopted by the audience, including even those who manage, direct, and create network TV. In my own "sample" I heard the echo of the "double" persistently. Even if it is untrue—if the respondent is in fact a vegetable—the persistence of this claim is remarkable. It confirms that even among its most devoted, chained audience, TV hardly commands respect. Virtually everyone resists the *idea*, if not the fact, of passivity.

HARVEY GONICK:

TV is background for me. I cannot work in dead silence. When there is no one in the house and I can't hear anything, I can't work. TV helps me focus on my work. It gives me a background, a hum. It gives me what I need to get something built up in my mind, to get going. I've always needed something like this, ever since I was in college. I used music when I was a student; I even went out to visit friends in neighboring rooms as a distraction until I could harness my energies to focus on my studies. TV is the best. It can't just be anything that is on the air, though, because I *do* listen. I like detective stories because I can follow them easily while I concentrate at the same time on my writing or research. I check back and forth with TV. I don't watch or listen all the time. News programs are disturbing: when they come on, I switch to something else. Romance and comedy are good, along with mysteries. If I finish what I want to do, then I watch the news. But not C-SPAN because it is just too boring.

CARMEN DEFELICE:

No, I don't just watch TV. I read. I play with my three-year-old grandson. I read books about building, about cameras. I like PBS and often opera, symphony, documentaries. Early in the evening I watch the news. Since I get up early to drive the truck, I listen to all-news radio, so I know what is going on in the world even before TV, or the newspapers. We talk about a lot of things while the TV is on that have nothing to do with the program.

MILDRED DEFELICE:

> I think we are talking more with TV, not less.
> In the early years, we would watch TV only,
> completely involved, not speaking. I remember we
> would tell each other to keep quiet during
> dinner, so we could hear the program. Now we
> talk all the time, all of us, and pay no attention to
> the sound. Except when a news bulletin comes on,
> suddenly.

3. "IMPORTANT SOCIAL, OCCUPATIONAL, OR RECREATIONAL ACTIVITIES ARE GIVEN UP OR REDUCED BECAUSE OF SUBSTANCE USE. PERSONS MAY WITHDRAW FROM FAMILY ACTIVITIES AND HOBBIES . . . OR USE THE SUBSTANCE IN PRIVATE."

> *My aim (in suspending all references to the
> speaking subject) was to show what the dif-
> ferences consisted of, how it was possible for
> me, within the same discursive practice, to
> speak of different objects, to have contrary
> opinions, to make contradictory choices.*
> —Michel Foucault, *The Archaeol-
> ogy of Knowledge,* 1972

Myth Four depends on an inherent libido for docility. If we
are in fact truly happy only when overwhelmed by an external source, shutting down mind, heart, and body, then
it is at least possible that TV's ubiquity has reduced an entire
population to somnolence. But if there is some itch to speak,
move, or think, native to the animal (as well as the soul),
then Myth Four is in trouble. Indeed, the very vapidity of
most TV programming may act—in some cases—as a mne-
monic device. Boredom or at the very least predictability

may drive viewers to *act*, if not actually leave the house. The odds are that prolonged acquaintance with an image or sound may render it less, rather than more, powerful, as the repeated anti-capitalist messages beamed at audiences in Eastern Europe finally provoked a widespread call for the "free market" in the late 1980s.

BILL SCHREINER:

> During the Super Bowl this year, I remember that we talked about everything, from the personal lives of all the family members to the recent sex scandals—Clarence Thomas, William Kennedy Smith, Mike Tyson, Governor Bill Clinton. It was fascinating and surprising to see how various members of the family fell out on these issues, and who they believed. Though my mother is not a TV viewer, she was glued to the set during the Thomas-Hill hearings. To my surprise, she decided that Anita Hill was lying, even though she was against Thomas. As for the Clinton affair, almost everyone believed the media was wrong to sensationalize it. Over and over shows like *Nightline* would solemnly proclaim the tabloid press vulgar, then report on everything printed there. Did we zap during the Super Bowl? No. But we kept on talking all the time. We talk more when the set is on than when it's off. That's why I say TV has added a ritual—increased talking—to the family. We never talked like this before.

Maggie Murray, Los Angeles, sixty-nine, is a consultant to the fashion industry who lives in an elegant house nestled near the bottom of Overlook Drive in the Hollywood Hills. Encircled by a concrete wall, fronted by a curvaceous, Mexican-tiled swimming pool, Ms. Murray's home symbolizes the Arcadia that L.A. has become in the American mind. But inside, her fourteen-room house is laced throughout with television, a supposed alien in Arcadia. All but two rooms, upstairs and downstairs, feature a set, always playing, sometimes with sound, sometimes not. In one of the rooms there is a large desk drawer crammed with three tiny TVs, in case one elsewhere in the house goes out, for a round total of fifteen sets.

MAGGIE MURRAY:

I am often alone in my house. At night when I don't have guests or family, I turn all the sets on in every room. But even when the house is filled, I turn the screen on, leaving the sound down. No one pays it any attention, though they all know TV is here, everywhere. An exception is a big event, say the Oscar night, the Tony awards, or the Winter Olympics. Then I invite people here and turn the sound up. Sometimes they actually listen. They're too busy. I suppose I have fifteen TV sets, ranging in size from my little one-inch Sony to Hitachis to extremely large twenty-seven- and twenty-nine-inch RCAs. One of them, the small red Hitachi, I keep here just because it's pretty. Often, when people come here for the first time they say I'm an addict. But I don't care what is on the TV screen itself. It is movement, color, light, that's all. I care about the *set*.

GLORIA GONICK:

I am writing a book on Japanese textiles. I teach. I consult with museums. I manage this house, built in 1928, in frequent need of repair. I have an aged mother who is ill. I am the trustee of her estate and body. I am in frequent touch with four different children, each in a different place or situation. In graduate school, I collaborated on the making of an interactive videodisc for an exhibi-

tion I designed. I have a video camera. When I
go to Japan I use my camera to document what I
see there. I cannot look at television anymore without thinking of how it is edited, where the camera
is placed, all that. I am involved in what I see.

4. "WITH HEAVY AND PROLONGED USE, A VARIETY OF SOCIAL, PSYCHOLOGICAL, AND PHYSICAL PROBLEMS CAN OCCUR AND ARE EXACERBATED BY CONTINUED USE OF THE SUBSTANCE."

*What one ought to say is: I am not wherever
I am the plaything of my thought.*
—Jacques Lacan, *Ecrits*, 1977

Perhaps the surest proof of TV's present inability to hold
its audience is the general elation voiced by those who turn
away from it, either in whole or in part. Many studies of
quantum TV viewing conclude that the more people watch
the set, the less warmed or relaxed they become.[9] Similar
findings are reported for almost any mood-affective drug,
from amphetamines, or "speed," to sedatives, or tranquil-
ilzers. The first moment we turn on TV after settling into
an empty house or room after a long day is a kind or rush,
or high. We suddenly hear from another world. The sound,
the image breaks us into another reality, driving out the
tired background behind us. But the last moment, one or
several hours later, is fully as tired, if not more, than the
reality we first deserted. TV pales with the ebbing of time.
Almost any alternative, indulged for its own sake or to break
the habit, is bracing, at first. In most surveys Americans rate
TV significantly below other "leisurely" pursuits, like reading, swimming, attending the theater. Of all our daily pursuits TV is by far the least demanding, or consequential:
we turn it on almost as effortlessly as we breathe. Are we
rewarded? "Human beings are not designed to enjoy many

hours of passivity," says Professor Robert Kubey of Rutgers University, who collaborated on several exhaustive studies of TV "addiction."[10] Certainly he makes here a crucial, rarely attended point: neither brain nor heart nor legs are designed for any other purpose than movement, intellectual and spiritual, as well as physical.

KERRY OLSEN
(NINETEEN-YEAR-OLD NIECE OF THE DEFELICES,
IN FARMINGDALE, LONG ISLAND):

> My mother and father complain about my watching too much TV, so I have gotten a job just to get away from it, at a nearby clothing store. I didn't realize I was watching so much. It was just something to turn to, so I did. When I didn't have a job, I was forced to clean by my mother, so I would watch TV while I cleaned. Once you watch an episode [of a show you like] you watch again, if it continues. I didn't stay home in order to watch TV. It was just something to turn to, whatever's on. Nobody seemed to care, for a while. Then they complained. And now I'm out away from TV.

Ann Halverson, Chicago, age thirty-five, is a Ph.D. in chemistry who spends much of her free time renovating old houses—painting, plastering, building with her own hands. Born in Iowa, she grew up in rural America and recalls her childhood as a time of heavy TV watching. But with the approach of college and of graduate study (in the East, at Brandeis), she virtually deserted the medium, only returning for quite limited doses of viewing when she moved to Chicago to work for a large chemical firm. Now, living mostly alone while she finishes up a wood frame house on North Paulina Street in Chicago, she finds TV performing an entirely different role in her life.

ANN HALVERSON:

I began to watch *Star Trek* when I moved to Chicago, and the news. It was my first TV watching in years. Slowly, surely I got involved in the theme and the plot. Now as I work on the houses, I turn on *Star Trek*. In Chicago you can see an episode, often a rerun, every evening between 6 and 7 P.M. It is the only television I really want to watch, mainly because I have been following the content for a long time. Occasionally I watch the news and PBS. Some of the PBS documentaries are terrific—the Civil War series, for example. But television is still a minor event in my life, very minor. Though *Star Trek* has me hooked. I switch it on every night, while I am painting or plastering. That is my excuse—that I have work to do that goes well with *listening* to TV sound (I hardly ever watch it; I just glance at the screen). Once I finish this work, I will face the real test: can I get myself to leave the house and go to the health club for a workout between 6 and 7? I hope so.

GLORIA GONICK:

We raised four children, two of his from a former marriage, and two of mine from another marriage. They watched TV all the time when they were growing up. It worried us to death. What are they doing now? My oldest daughter is a botanist and the director of a new plant ecology program in the state of California. My youngest is a lawyer, a U.S. Attorney in Los Angeles. His son designs computer programs. His daughter is teaching at an international elementary school in Japan. They are all doing quite well. I don't know whether they are still watching lots of TV but I'd guess they don't have much time.

5. "WITH CONTINUED USE, CHARACTERISTIC WITHDRAWAL SYMPTOMS DEVELOP WHEN THE PERSON STOPS OR REDUCES INTAKE OF THE SUBSTANCE. SYMPTOMS VARY GREATLY."

> *Addicts lose a sense of time passing. Television provides meaning and purpose in their lives. . . . Their time is structured around the TV set. . . . They feel they watch too much TV. . . . They feel angry with themselves for giving in to its effects.*
>
> —Robin Smith, "Television Addiction," 1986

Though diverting, it seems finally that the drive to find analogies between the use of serious mind- and mood-altering drugs and watching television is fundamentally flawed, by the testimony I found as well as common sense. Though television is a daily presence in our lives, it is no more valid to see it as an equivalent to amphetamines than the presence of electricity or of running water. By the end of the century, TV has become as inexpensive and readily available as any utility. There is common testimony to its ease of use. Users habitually identify it as the "leisure" activity requiring the least attention, or commitment. The Global Village prophecies dating back to Marshall McLuhan, based on the flawed assumption that the gleaming screen exerts a persuasive effect, are nonetheless "good copy" for the critics. Professor Robin Smith's early studies of TV addiction, conducted in 1981 and 1986, were based on viewing traits described in the "popular press," which were, of course, lurid.[11]

Professor Smith's operational definition of this malaise even included the portentous statement that "Television provides meaning and purpose in their [the heavy viewers'] lives." In a sense, this claim could be fairly made for print or for central heating as well, though no one has lately convicted either of hypnotic powers. In any case, Smith's eighteen-item questionnaire mailed to residents of Massachusetts, based on these supposedly confirmed traits, drew 984 responses. From this fairly biased sample (only committed viewers would take the time to fill out the long questionnaire), only *eleven* people identified themselves as "TV addicts." Five of the contenders were male, six female, with an average age of forty-six years. But there was no discernible pattern uniting them, in terms of occupation, income, or marital status. Professor Smith's study surely does not support Myth Four.

It is not only the McLuhanites who believe in the Myth, however, and its implicit denigration of the audience. The intermittent attempts made by high-minded groups of parents and preachers to "turn off" television are equally misguided. The entire school system of the town of Farmington, Connecticut, instructed its students—with their parents—to turn off TV in the evening for one month, beginning on January 1, 1984. For thirty days the town basked in an unexpected gleam of international attention. The superintendent of schools found himself giving hundreds of radio interviews alone. He was called by satellite from city officials across the world, eager to learn "how" to do it. The librarian who plotted the turnoff, Nancy DiSalvo, was similarly targeted. "Our switchboard was jammed for two weeks," she recalls. "The foreign press was especially interested in sex. They wanted to know if turning off TV means going to bed earlier."[12] Hyped by all this publicity, the students of course performed better in the schools, leading teachers to report at the end of the month an overall improvement, in both attentiveness and in literacy. But on February 1, as later lamented by nearly all participants, TV viewing began gradually to return to normal levels, a pattern common to nearly all "turnoff" attempts.

Does this "return" document "addiction"? Only when the definition of this term is expanded to the point where it is meaningless. The turnoff was doomed because it focused on quantitative value rather than qualitative issues. Seen in isolation, simply as a withering numerical statement of "hours" when the set is switched on, when eyes and minds are allegedly fused to the screen, TV viewing does take on ominous overtones. Seen in a larger context, however, as one activity indulged among many others, at the end of a century when the very proliferation of TV sound and imagery renders the set virtually invisible, like the switch for the electric light, TV becomes a far more casual affair. Increasingly, we see TV literally on the run, between events in decidedly active and aggressive lifestyles. Further, TV-as-we-have-known-it, in its primordial, soundbite guise, progressively pales beside competing forms of information and entertainment. The continued rise in the percentages of viewers who claim they are watching "too much" TV (up 11 percent from the late 1970s, according to the 1990 Gallup-Newport poll) is not as often claimed a sign that Myth Four rules the day. Rather, it is a sign of mounting skepticism. The more we rue the time spent watching television the more we evidence a determination to find something better.

CARMEN DEFELICE:

> My aunt was into the daytime soap serials so much that you couldn't call her on the phone because she just wouldn't answer while she was watching. She hardly ever left the house. Then, finally, her husband died after a long marriage. He used to be companionship for her while she was watching, though he didn't watch. After a while of living alone, she began to leave the house during the day and take long walks. Now she walks more than she watches the soaps. The doctors are delighted. At eighty, her heart is strong. It is kind of odd. She is going out into the world because she is lonely, not keeping company with the soaps, like she used to do when she had her husband.

Irene Siegel of Chicago   is, at the age of forty-five, becoming known as a painter, in midcareer. Earlier, when she lived with her husband, Arthur, a widely respected photographer, she kept her career in second place while raising children. At the time I interviewed her, she was about to move to a new, larger home to live with a man, a doctor, who had come into her life, sharing her small studio, in the past year. Like the Schreiners, she is another model of the TV viewer who departs so sharply from the "norm," at least in profession, that is rarely accounted for in analyses of the audience.

IRENE SIEGEL:

> Television has played almost no significant role in my life, except for the news and occasional PBS documentaries. I only watch it, when I do, late at night to fall asleep. Occasionally when I am dining alone I will turn it on for company, watching the news if it is on. I remember that my children used to watch a lot in their early years but then stopped later. I never paid it much attention. There is one exception. When my husband was terminally ill, I used to watch it with him. We both became quite involved in a PBS serial adaptation of *I, Claudius* [a novel by Robert Graves about classical Rome]. It had five or six episodes. I remember thinking when it started that Arthur might not live to see the end of a serial in which he was quite interested, as was I. He didn't. This may have been the only time in his life or mine that television really mattered.

MAGGIE MURRAY:

> I think I see television in my house and everywhere else as a kind of portable art. I am conscious of it but I don't concentrate on it. Partly my use of it has to do with the scale of my house. If I lived in a one-room apartment I'd only need one

TV set. When people are here they don't pay much attention to all the sets either. They are aware of something moving, perhaps, of color, of light, that's all. I see TV as disposable. It is not set in concrete. I don't plan my rooms around it. It doesn't dominate me. It's just there. If I am going to buy a blouse, I can buy a TV for about the same price and discard it when I am finished with it, too. If I decide I don't like it, I just get another.

Anonymous, Evanston, Illinois, is an old friend who moved to Chicago long ago to write for a magazine. Now he lives in the country writing books and raising a large family. He was always outspoken about affairs of the heart and of the body but I believe he simply speaks more bluntly about a "use" of television than many of us who share his experience.

ANONYMOUS:

I have always found TV to be a great aphrodisiac. Whenever I want to turn my wife on, I bring her a glass of wine and turn on Johnny Carson or David Letterman without sound. She likes them both and I like the actresses they display with short skirts. It has become a kind of signal and after a while we usually make love. This began in college for me. If you got into a bed with a girl in those days late at night, they were used to watching *Tonight,* maybe for the same reason (think of what Johnny Carson has done for us all). But my experience can't be that unusual. Most couples make love late at night, particularly if they have jobs during the day or children. And most of them probably turn on TV if only to fall asleep, thanks to its boredom. So television and sex may be mutually reinforcing, rather than the reverse.

THE NEW MARKET: POTATOES, ARISE!

Where innovation is continuous and products are ever more tailored to customers' particular needs, the distinction between goods and services begins to blur.
—Robert Reich, *Tales of a New America*, 1987

The times demand that . . . flexibility and love of change replace our long-standing penchant for mass production and mass markets, based as it is upon a relatively predictable environment, now vanished.
—Tom Peters, *Thriving on Chaos: Handbook for a Management Revolution*, 1987

HONDA READY TO SHOW A CAR THAT GETS 100 MILES A GALLON
—*New York Times* headline, February 1992

The difference between products for peasants and aristocrats was symbolic, not technical.
—Jay Doblin, 1984

At some unmarked moment in the departing year, a milestone was passed. The 50 millionth VCR had been sold in the U.S. This means that videotape recorders were in more than half of all American households.
—Hans Fantel, "The Year the VCR Became Ubiquitous," *New York Times*, January 1991

In retrospect, it was inevitable that in the 1970s the Japanese would commit their resources to the perfection of the videocassette recorder, though it was pioneered in the United States by companies like Ampex and RCA. In its commitment to personal choice, the VCR denies the very ethic of a *mass* medium, programmed from above, accepted by the homogeneous and obedient market below. Though the VCR itself is a mass-produced object, what matters for the user is the choice of software, which can be as unlimited and unpredictable as the identity of the user, not the hardware that plays it. And this libido for choice signifies activism rather than pacifism, an audience up on its hands and feet, not on its back.

The captains of American industry, not to say their analysts and specialists, never adapted to the shattering VCR dynamic. The personal recorder after all appears to encourage disorder, much as did print, according to McLuhan and his disciples. The personal recorder attends to many disparate voices at once. It frames an ideal later called "pluralism" by media theorists never entirely comfortable with the concept. The late Jay Doblin, an atypical American management consultant, called it more accurately *de-massification*. Along with another American postindustrial prophet, W. Edwards Deming, Doblin came to be revered and followed by the Japanese, whose commitment to miniaturizing and personalizing electronic tools, providing an array of options to the user, inexorably crushed at least one American industry—consumer electronics—and threatened our dominance in several others, including automobiles and personal computers.

This author well recalls being present in New York in 1970 when RCA unveiled Selectavision, the first American VCR aimed at the mass market. Compact, streamlined, inexpensive, programmed to replay a series of preselected video movies, it wasn't yet able to allow the user to record his own TV programs off the air or produce his own tapes with his own portable camera. When I asked whether RCA was planning to add this feature, already available on Sony's early VCRs, the answer came back to me with an ominous, definitive flatness: "Not yet."

Before Selectavision could completely de-massify, it was out of business. In retrospect, "not yet" might well stand as a form of *sayonara* for the managerial elite of an entire culture. By opting out of the VCR, American industry signaled an indifference if not blindness to the evolution of its own culture, away from dependence on brawn to the brain, and the refinement of living "style." Doblin, who persuaded the Japanese early on, as an advisor to its Ministry of International Trade, that qualitative issues—design, responsiveness to individual needs, service—would matter more to this market than price, saw mass production as a dead end. Efficiency and low cost no longer counted to a postindustrial white-collar class that increasingly saw itself as classless. The symbols that used to separate the elite from the "workers"—a Cadillac Seville, say, versus a Ford—were now available to an entirely professional army. "Mass is shrinking," he said, and network TV, certain it could keep on feeding the bourgeoisie its old symbols, in the service of Myth Four, was shrinking, too.

Another American voice ignored in this period was W. Edwards Deming's, of course, though he had been hired by General Douglas MacArthur to reform the methods of Japan's business leaders in the 1950s, following the wartime destruction visited on the nation in World War II. The young man Deming contradicted much of the prevailing wisdom in the United States. He urged Japan to think long-range, to value the intelligence of the consumer, to change methods and products *constantly*. He urged them not to depend on consumer "loyalty" to the same cars and refrigerators mindlessly reproduced year after year once they obtained market acceptance. Before Robert Reich, he insisted on the virtue of constant innovation.[13] Given this premise, the mounting strength of Japanese exports to a nation whose industry depended on couch potato "loyalty" is wholly understandable. In his meticulous account of the American automobile's steady decline, *The Reckoning*, David Halberstam recounts how assiduously the Japanese carmakers studied and courted the American consumer, aided by Detroit's indifference, analogous to network TV's conviction that its viewers loved whatever they did, or programmed.[14] The Japanese research convinced them that the post–Vietnam War generation of Americans were a breed apart from the past, in education, training, and critical awareness. The new Americans resented the Big Three's inattention to repairs, their stolid refusal to change or re-form gas-guzzling engines, and their blatantly misleading advertising.

The rapidity with which Toyota, Nissan, Honda, etc., ex-ploited these errors is now history. But there is even a subtler distinction to be made, which applies directly to Myth Four. In their quicksilver inventions, the Japanese on all fronts refused to stand still once they had successfully marketed a new car, video camera, or Sony Walkman (followed almost immediately by a Sony Watchman TV). This instantaneous innovation, evidenced in the rise of patents obtained in the United States by foreign inventors and companies, which now include the Europeans, the Koreans, and the Chinese, plays directly to the libido of the new class.[15] In a time when both producers and designers can generate three-dimen-sional models directly from a computer terminal in a matter of weeks (whereas in the past they took a minimum of six months, if not a year), it is indeed true that "innovation is continuous." In certain markets like those for fuel-efficient automobiles and computer software, the next step is always, apparently, unpredictable. As the last decade of the century dawned, we saw functional models of new electric cars and combustion engines introduced that were capable of tripling past fuel efficiency. We saw "virtual reality" in computer software, hand-held translators, and Quicktime software ap-plied to Macintosh computers, enabling students to "illus-trate" their term papers with live film or video imagery.

The consumer now is therefore inordinately judicious, if not demanding, compared to his predecessors. Whereas two or three refrigerator, car, and TV manufacturers domi-nated the world that attended network television at its birth in the 1950s, there are now dozens of competitors. Sur-rounded by choices, the consumer, like the viewer, clearly prizes his freedom to pick precisely what he wants. Late in his life, Jay Doblin finally persuaded one American firm—Xerox—to play to this sophistication. In the late 1980s, Xerox began to offer its customers not *one* copier, but a range of flexible modules, which allowed each user to purchase precisely the services he needed. It is obvious, then, that the new market is molded by a generation of buyers that has left the trancelike subjugation to mass-produced products (as well as TV programming similarly motivated) far behind.

It is no wonder that once-sober management consultants like Tom Peters now speak openly about "chaos" as a proper model for aspiring corporations and entrepreneurs to follow. Assume nothing, hold fast to no principle, be prepared to contradict yourself—and your company's last success— every year, if not every month. He and others view the "market" now as a moving, writhing, animal presence. It can't be safely blocked and charted anymore on a graph or chart. Why? Because straight lines ignore the unpredictability of free, unhampered choice.

But one evening before any VCR, reexamining a film or serious work of television art—say CBS's *Lonesome Dove*, a one-time miniseries whose success surprised press and industry alike in the spring of 1989, brings many of these abstractions to life. A mordant and moving Western based on a novel by Larry McMurtry, *Lonesome Dove* garnered high ratings almost immediately after the epic serial form was pronounced dead in the press, after its halcyon years earlier in the decade. Originally shown in four two-hour episodes, *Dove* was almost impossible to track as broadcast. Not only did I miss parts of several episodes, but the conclusion as well, in which the tragic hero, played by Robert Duvall, dies; his partner, acted by Tommy Lee Jones, was excoriated by the woman between them, played by Anjelica Huston, or so I had learned, from the press and from friends. Like others, I was troubled by a difficult sound track during the broadcast, which made many of the lines almost impossible to hear, particularly when the orchestra swelled in moments of crisis in the accepted Hollywood fashion.

Had I been mesmerized by McLuhan's godlike light inside the screen, I probably would have accepted what was granted me by CBS in prime time. But in company with thousands of others, I rented *Dove* at my nearby video store for later viewing. I needed to "read" it, in effect, again. If the prime-time broadcast required rigid attendance, as if sitting in a pew in the church, the VCR allowed something else, the hedonism of picking my own time and viewing at my own leisure, cutting out what I didn't care to see again. Immediately I went to the fast-forward button and rushed through virtually the entire first hour of the final installment, landing at last on the moment when Ms. Huston confronts Tommy Lee Jones, the man bringing her lover, the dead Duvall, back home to Texas for burial. At last I heard her words, by playing the tape back twice: "I wasn't going to fight you for him every day," she says, snarling. "I despised you for what you did then. I despise you now."

Thus had I learned, in brief, what I missed before—that the heroine had lost her hero to another man, a neat and unexpected twist. I watched the rest of *Lonesome Dove* with less attention, having recalled it better from past viewing. As it unfolded, I enlivened the time by eating, reading a newspaper, and answering the phone. As I did so I realized I had demonstrated the same divided but entirely natural attention evidenced by the subjects of my tiny survey—and surely by the readers of this book. We are all free to see, think, and read at once. We owe no fealty to the Great God TV, or his profligate father/mother, Print.

THE CERTAINTY OF THE UNCERTAIN

> *President Johnson probably hopes and forecasts that his administration would be the "Era of Good Feeling" . . . "a new consensus on national purpose and policy." . . . But he is likely to be disappointed. We are about to enter an era of unprecedented conflict between our government and an entirely new electorate dominated by the young.*
>
> Peter F. Drucker, "American Directions: A Forecast," *Harper's*, February 1965

> *It's bad for the culture. People are retreating
> from the public world. VCRs are making the
> public realm into a sponge that sucks the pub-
> lic into movies.*
>
> —Todd Gitlin, quoted in *Time*,
> October 1986

> *"What would it have looked like," he said, "if
> this TV set projected all channels onto the
> cathode ray screen at the same time? . . .
> Think of the possibilities, if our brain could
> handle twenty images at once.*
>
> —Philip K. Dick, *The Electric Ant*,
> 1965

When we err on a grand scale, the consequences are similarly grand. In 1965, Lyndon Johnson, landslide victor over
a weak Republican opponent, concluded that the body politic was in the palm of his hand, waiting to be guided and
molded. This assumption surely reinforced his determination to intervene with military force in Vietnam, leading to
massive opposition at home, political defeat, and the loss,
albeit temporarily, of American influence in Southeast Asia.
Our collective assumptions about another body politic—the
consumers of television—are similarly fateful. In this country, for decades, goaded by Myth Four, we have assumed,
like Lyndon Johnson, that yet another huge body of voters
was without the intelligence or the will to resist whatever
the networks fed them, the assumption also shared by RCA
long ago and, until recently, by GM, Chrysler, and Ford.

We can already sense the quantitative damage caused by
these assumptions. Turning away from the individuating
potential of the VCR has cost us the receipts already earned
from the sales of a tool now found in the majority of American homes, slowly rising to the same level of ubiquity as
the TV set itself, or the newspaper. Nor is there any sign
that the desire of an immense educated class to form its
own flexible video library is diminishing: in the first week
of January 1992, more than 1.6 million video rentals oc-

curred, setting a new record in a new year. This is the same class that has already discomfited its elders by deserting churches, political parties, and labor unions, as well as the networks. Its lust for free choice could have been predicted.

Further. There is no sign that the trend can be turned off, or deflected. The command of and lust for information is rising, not declining. Everything depends upon the premise adopted by the rulers and shakers of our media and our society, as we survey the same events. Between the horror voiced by Todd Gitlin for the loss of the false "community" supposedly engendered by viewing broadcast television and the delight expressed by Philip Dick's hero over the intellectual command of twenty disparate channels there is a void as broad as the ocean, as Thomas Carlyle once told Ralph Waldo Emerson in a debate, as deep as the earth. On one side lies the destiny implied by knowledge at all times, however easily available, on the other the benefits of the single, focused voice, that is, one channel against twenty.

If we hold for the latter, we will view the arrival of an intensified verbal-visual literacy, informed by the divided or all-encompassing view of life evidenced in our sample, as irrelevant or inadequate. The assumption that TV inevitably drugs the viewer is an assumption beloved by both the friends and the enemies of the medium. In his provocative studies of preschool children in the late 1970s, John L. Debes, visual learning coordinator for Eastman Kodak, argued the reverse, that most American children under the age of five and one half "know more" than their peers of twenty years before. Informed at once by sophisticated parents—as well as by exposure to TV—these children evidence in standard IQ tests higher scores than in the past.[16] Dr. Robert Thorndike, president of American Educational Research Associates, supported Debes's contention: "We should recognize that with television the world of the child has changed and that the beneficial aspects are experienced primarily, even exclusively, in the preschool years."[17]

When educators and schools fail to respond to this unique

sophistication, they shut off the expansion of the achieve-
ment detected by Debes and others. Later, enmeshed in
traditional schools that ignore TV's capacity to inform as
well as seduce the child, their IQs and test scores decline,
according to Debes, feeding the monster that is Myth Four.
In this way, our schools may well enhance the obdurate
American refusal to recognize the upgrading of mind and
spirit that characterizes its citizenry, and its market.

Finally, in the 1980s, many American corporations began
to follow the lead of their foreign competitors and de-massify their concept of the customer. *Demographics*—the study
of *who* the customer is, where he lives, what he likes and
dislikes—became the magic method for making decisions
about where to advertise. Instead of simply buying numbers,
Chevrolet and Almaden wine sought sympathetic listeners,
readers, and viewers, which meant, in turn, radio, print, or
television commanding the specific attention of its audience.
The Claritas Corporation, utilizing the reams of information made available by the Census Bureau, developed a
highly praised breakdown of the variegated tastes and values of American citizens into forty "clusters." Each one is
based on zeal for varying kinds of housing, food, cars, books,
magazines, and social values.[18] Claritas found that Americans no longer see themselves as primarily ethnic or religious or regional entities. They identify self, family, and
friends as *related* individuals, pursuing specific but similar
needs and interests. At each stage of their lives, Americans
tend to join peers in neighborhoods wherever they might
move. "They can go to sleep in Fairfield, Connecticut,"
claims Claritas, in effect, "and wake up in Pasadena, California, where, except for the palm trees, they are in fundamentally the same place."

Fairfield and Pasadena attract what Claritas calls a *Pools
and Patios* lifestyle, affluent, conservative, cleaving to the
Wall Street Journal and *The New Yorker*. Among the other
critical clusters, each highly desirable, each totally different
from the other, at least in habit and income, are *Urban Gold
Coast*, spread from San Francisco to Manhattan, preferring

New York magazine, fresh chicken, and *Late Night with David Letterman,* while *Bohemian Mix* is addicted to *Harper's, The Atlantic Monthly,* Mitsubishi Mirages, and liberal Democrats.

But even the "cluster" model, though it is a welcome relief from past assumptions (that nearly all men and women think, believe, and ingest the same), though it begins for the first time to entertain qualitative issues on the same level as quantitative, is too simple. What is emerging from the set of forces that has de-massified television, if not its analysts, is entirely different. In this chapter we have gotten a sense of an audience at once indifferent to the seductive, mind-numbing "power" of television yet exquisitely sensitive to the infinite ways in which the medium can provoke, inform, entertain, or simply pass time, in the distant background. For these completely unpredictable "viewers," TV will often simply perform the function known as "Doing Nothing." Here it acts on the nihilistic level of cigarette smoking or staring out the window. Rarely acknowledged in media literature or management, Doing Nothing may well be the widespread contemporary equal to the traditional Zen master listening to leaves of grass move in the wind. Doing Nothing defies Myth Four almost as completely as the activism inherent in the viewers' turn to CNN's spontaneous coverage of the Gulf War, which they clearly preferred to the major networks', and their unexpected responses to Clarence Thomas, Anita Hill, and, at least in Evanston, Illinois, to Johnny Carson.

Certainly in the latter cases, in the aggressive use of the VCR, the home camera, and the remote control wand, we know there are qualities of mind and emotion still developing in the body politic that cannot be easily measured on the basis of age, sex, or even lifestyle, clustered or not. Larry Keeley, colleague of the late Jay Doblin, has spoken of something he calls "psychographics," as opposed to "demographics." If he is correct, and I think he is, we are best advised to sit back in awe of this evolving audience. The only certainty is: don't underestimate it. Myth Four not only blights our pocketbook and our soul: it robs us of the joy of anticipating the unexpected. Any TV producer, politician, or manufacturer who believes in the closed and comfortable destiny envisioned in the conclusion to *Avalon* does so at his peril. Almost no one reading these lines would remain there, prostrate before a humming set. What would you do? No one can say. But something.

MYTH FIVE

WE <u>LOVE</u> TV

In a major new poll you find out just how much you love your TV. When it comes to television, most Americans agree with the Pepsi slogan: "Gotta have it." We asked whether they would agree to "give up watching absolutely . . . for the rest of their lives in exchange for $25,000"—and found that fewer than one in four Americans would take up the offer. Almost half . . . say they would refuse to give up . . . for anything under a million dollars. One in four (25%) . . . would refuse *[emphasis added] to stop watching TV even for $1 million.*
> —TV Guide, October 10, 1992

We track daily viewing: 4 hours and 40 minutes for adults, 3 hours and 20 minutes for kids, 3 hours and 14 minutes for teenagers. That means the average TV set in America is on a total of 7 hours, 26 minutes every day.
> —A. C. Nielsen Company employee, interview with author, March, 1992

A show-business atmosphere apparently insures ecstatic winners, happy runners-up . . . smiling losers. An audience of more than 70 million viewers.
> —Thomas A. DeLong, Quiz Craze: America's Infatuation with Game Shows, 1991

*Love: 1 That disposition or state of feeling
with regard to a person which (arising from
recognition of attractive qualities, from instincts of natural relationship, or from sympathy) manifests itself in solicitude for the
welfare of the object, and usually also in delight in his presence and desire for his approval; warm affection; attachment. . . .
1812 Coleridge 7 Lect (1856) 70 Love is a
desire of the whole being to be united to some
thing, or some being, felt necessary to its com-
pleteness.*

—Oxford English Dictionary on
Historical Principles, 1983

Let me count the ways, sings the lady to her object of
desire in the memorable nineteenth-century lyric. If we
grant that the heart has always expressed itself in at least
as many forms as our hero enumerates, matching singular
method to singular content (that is, the beloved), then it's
just possible that the illogic of our final Myth, the fifth, can
be granted, if not its premise. Perhaps late at night, when
brain and senses are dimmed, you, that is, we might feel
warm affection for the TV that has performed before us for
hours. But *attachment*, no. Samuel Coleridge's notion that
"love" signals a desire for the two opposites to reunite, echoing the ancient Greek belief that men and women were once
joined in a single body (until an angry Zeus split them apart),
would barely occur to any of us now. We cannot imagine
ourselves *inside* the nightly local news, normally a parade of
rapes and muggings, or at one with the seamy *L.A. Law* or
ludicrously satiric *Batman*. Yes, we occasionally imagine ourselves striding the bases as Reggie Jackson in an Oakland As
uniform or foxing the boys as the streamlined Maddie in
Moonlighting. But these are primordial daydreams, based in
our lust for glory, not in the medium that presents them.

Why, then, do certain sociologists, advertisers, and random spokespersons here and abroad claim that we Amer-

icans (as well as Europeans, Africans, and Asians) adore
television? The statement, whether made in sobriety or jest,
is normally quite specific. Worse, it is pervasive in the popular—as well as some of the specialized—literature surrounding our subject. It is applied to the medium itself, to
the set that dwells in our living space, never to the content,
to the image or event watched. *Americans sleep with their TVs,
not each other,* said a friend of mine, visiting from Japan.
When I pointed out that his countrymen owned more TVs
per capita than Americans, he replied, "Yes, but we never
turn them on."

When I described my activist friend in Evanston, cohab-
iting before Johnny Carson, a decisive rebuff to his claim,
he argued that every society, like every rule, has exceptions.
In refutation, he pointed to an article in the day's paper
about an unusual exhibition of prime-time TV tapes at the
staid Los Angeles County Museum of Art. The producers,
directors, and casts of exemplary dramatic serials like *Hill
Street Blues, L.A. Law,* and *Beverly Hills 90210* embellished
the event by joining in lofty panel discussions on the "art"
of television. But it all collapsed on the last night, when the
leads from *Beverly Hills,* which narrates the sociosexual trav-
ails of upscale high school life in California, appeared,
bringing sobriety to an end in the audience. The late arrival
of Luke Perry, who plays Dylan, the troubled "older" teen
in *Beverly Hills,* trailing his colleagues, prompted hysterical
squeals from the museum faithful, young and old.[1] "I am
not surprised," trumped the Japanese visitor, "that you
Americans spend *seven years* of your lifespan watching TV."

So Myth Five is not only solid: it packs an international
wallop. The confidence with which my friend quoted the
number—*seven years*—confirms this solidity. Every apostle
of Myth Five is adept at such figures, including 7 hours 26
minutes, and following the skillful trap set in the path of
their subjects in the fall of 1992, *TV Guide's* conclusion that
$1 million couldn't wean millions of Americans away from
the screen. But none of these claims—not even *TV Guide's*—
can withstand the seriocomic examination they deserve. As

for the subjective animus—the strategic motive, conscious or not, lurking within those who supply the Numbers—this, too, ought to be laid out in the sun, to bleach. Virtually any sophisticated observer with a sense for the "art" of quoting figures, commissioning polls, or juggling statistics can refute or at least modify the sweeping arithmetic. So can almost anyone inside the TV industry conversant with the politics, not to say the fortunes at stake in the game of reference/cross-reference. As for *love,* or *romance,* would any self-respecting suitor or seductress equate the covert act of viewing TV in prime time, between eight and eleven in the evening, with the delicious pleasure/pain most of us associate with the fatal attraction . . . between animate beings . . . of varying minds and sexes? Let us see.

Covert viewing. Yes, prime time, the central arena of Myth Five, is forbidden territory for most of educated America. Yet here is the "wasteland" once lamented by Newton Minow, commissioner of the Federal Communications Commission in the 1960s. Here, in the center of the evening, is the content that supposedly stops entire nations dead in their tracks. The press regularly tells us that *Dallas,* syndicated in ninety countries, brings cabinet meetings to a halt in far-off Timor, if not Iceland. Surely these are the magic hours, if any, when suitors and their beloved object, the TV screen, consummate. Yet it is dinner party convention in the United States for adult professionals to claim they "never" look at TV except for the news and first-run films or sports, normally seen on the margins of prime time.

Perhaps the "love" mentioned in Myth Five needs definition, or at the least discussion. In one of his last books, the exceptional French semiotician, Roland Barthes, compiled a portable lexicography of crucial phrases and tropes used by lovers through the centuries, repeated over and over, beginning with *I-love-you* itself, spoken, as Barthes said, billions of times each week, always for entirely different reasons.[2] But the passion signified in Barthes's book, and in human life, is raw, even bleeding. When his lovers complain of "Absence," writhe in "Jealousy," or exalt "Ravishment," they do so with a positive urgency. Prime-time TV, however, at least in its network profile, exhibits a different libido, for easy familiarity, for the playing out of plots and characters designed gently to please the viewer, to extend his low-key involvement, not fire his loins or heat his heart. More even than in its early and late hours, network TV seems convinced that its audience desires nothing so much as a cheerful sedative, spiced with titillation, blood, and occasional controversy, yes, but all resolved, all intended to induce tuning in again, next week.

When *Dallas* ended, in fact, in 1991, it went out with a whimper, not a bang: guest star Joel Grey took J. R. Ewing, the black-hearted hero played by Larry Hagman, on an imaginary retelling of the "story" formed by the entire series, decidedly tamed down to ignore his many vicious acts. Violence, to be sure, is a staple of prime time. Statisticians tell us TV characters are murdered at a prolific rate, one thousand times higher than in the real life of an already brutal society.[3] Now murder is not likely to invoke that desire for intimacy implied in *love*, though the word, as well as its social formulae, occupy a sizable slice of those sacred hours. In the beginning, sitcoms like *Leave It to Beaver* and *Make Room for Daddy* celebrated a comfortable but hardly impassioned lifestyle. With the coming of various decisive changes in the divorce rate, extramarital sex later became— by the advent of *Murphy Brown* on CBS in the 1980s—as frequent, as comfortable as marriage twenty years before.[4] In the 1990s, gay coupling, if not marriage, was beginning to inch down a similar track.

Prime-time TV, closely viewed, then considered in terms of its implications (as it almost never is), has an almost unbroken track record of commodifying every subject deemed by its programmers relevant for the mainstream audience, no matter how initially polemical, or unsettling. The long, corrosive list includes extramarital sex, of course, gay sex, drugs, political corruption, violence (a continuing staple), race hatred, street gangs, militant feminism, abortion, and even, at the very moment it featured in weighty court trials in the early 1990s, rape. Seen in this way, prime-time 1970s hits like *All in the Family*, featuring its oafish spokesman for racism and ethnocentrism, Archie Bunker, are agents for compliance to a mildy reformist agenda. The same of course could be said for the activist, inevitably feminist heroines who starred in similar successes one decade later, like *Roseanne* (Roseanne Barr), *Cagney & Lacey* (Sharon Gless and Tyne Daley), and even Maddie, the flirtatious and irritable detective played by Cybill Shepherd on *Moonlighting*. The slow, steady turn of conservative opinion *against* prime time is almost proof in point of this conversion. As the mores of the sitcoms and soaps changed to match its audience, commentators like Reverend Jerry Falwell, columnist William Buckley, Jr., and Vice-President Quayle began to accuse the decidedly profit-making networks of supporting a subversive agenda. "Prime-time television," said critic Ben Stein in *The View from Sunset Boulevard*, echoing this viewpoint, "presents a unified picture of life . . . that is an alternate reality."[5] Needless to say, that "alternate," for traditionalists like Stein, is filled with antipathetic characters that appear to defame the old order.

But do these "characters," even the pro-choice Murphy Brown, the redneck Archie Bunker, or the svelte teenagers in *Beverly Hills 90210* merit our passion? our rage? In *Civilization and Its Discontents*, Sigmund Freud spoke approvingly in behalf of the "restorative role" of an art or literature that gives voice to our subliminal urges, our attraction to violence, lust, and power. Even the unvarnished fairy tale domesticates the child, in effect, or so certain Freudians, certain acolytes of the late Bruno Bettelheim believe, as these enchanting-terrifying tales allow the subconscious a measure of expression, or relief.

Yet network television, seen at a mature remove, seems neither restorative nor threatening. Despite Ben Stein's reservations, prime-time TV drama nearly always splices lust and terror to smooth conciliation. Its goal is not to seduce or move but to charm us. No structural political changes resulted from the reformist zeal Stein warned against in a period when Americans were consistently voting for conservative presidents, nor did our propensity to rob, divorce, or violate defenseless women (or young men) subside, despite the attention given psychosexual themes by the top-rated shows in the Nielsen and Arbitron surveys. In short, if we "count the ways" in which prime time seeks the intimate commitment of its audience, we'll quickly come to the end.

Examine, for example, *Beverly Hills 90210* at its peak, taking on no less a cutting-edge issue than rape in an episode syndicated by Fox-TV both in the lead and the wake of the William Kennedy Smith trial, not to say the angry feminist rhetoric that trailed the confirmation of Clarence Thomas for the Supreme Court. This episode focused primarily on Brenda Walsh, played by Shannen Doherty, the heroine daughter of the Minnesota family that just moved to elite Beverly Hills, secondarily on Brandon, her brother (Jason Priestly). Bored by friends who do nothing but "shop for clothes," Brenda volunteers to answer calls on the school's rap line, largely jammed by younger female students worried about the subjects that allegedly earned the show a high Nielsen—pregnancy, AIDS, divorced parents, drugs, the perils of wealth, etc. But Brenda immediately gets involved with a female caller who always rings her near the closing hour, in tears about a boy pressing her—sometimes with a male ally—to commit sex against her will. "Am I being raped?" she asks at one point, in tears, bringing down an immediate flood of commercials, the signal, on commercial TV, of hot action about to break loose.

While Brenda juggles the subtle art of crisis intervention with her caller, her brother fields two women at once, an older woman flirting dangerously with him at the coffee shop where he works, and a younger girl, no more than fourteen, trailing after him every day, stars in her eyes. While the plot is consumed with these two crises, one charged with an urgency lent it by the world beyond (not by the wooden professionalism of the acting), the other etched in easy charm, no more, there is no doubt in the minds of steady *Hills* viewers that the resolution will be perfect. Finally, as Brenda's caller faces the two young brutes beside her pay telephone booth on the street, the police arrive, catching them in the act of attempted rape. Our Brenda has saved the day by alerting the police to the exact site and time of the daily phone call. Next day, right on time, Brandon, definitively rejected by the older woman, decides to return the smile of his fourteen-year-old fan, who turns out—of course, we knew it all the time—to be a virtual role model for the rap line victim saved by his sister.

Is "love" the proper word for our cuddly response to shows like this, in which searing, intractable emotions and diseases are cured by a smile or a telephone call? By quiz shows in which now and then we will imagine ourselves in the place of the contestant, on the lip of riches? The same questions might be put to long-running spectacles like *Dallas, Dynasty, Little House on the Prairie, Hill Street Blues, L.A. Law,* and, perhaps most of all, *Star Trek* and *Star Trek: The Next Generation.* In each of these occasions, I believe, we regard the characters, the Brendas, Brandons, and J.R.s, as neighbors, not intimates. They are comforting presences even when they are easy to hate, returning always to the same time and hour with precisely the same problems, usually resolved without a hitch. They do not horrify us, either, as does the wicked wolf playing grandmother in *Little Red Riding Hood* or the vengeful giant stalking the little boy in *Jack and the Beanstalk.*

Even the prime-time epics that border by their own admission on Shakespearean plotting complexity, like *Hill Street, L.A. Law,* or *Civil Wars* (each the creation of one multiple-track writer, Steve Bochco), or the vintage *Star Trek,* primarily recommend themselves as comfortable uncles or aunts. They do not tear at our heartstrings in the manner of a film like *Annie Hall* (in which a unique woman darts in and out of our lives just once, never again) or prompt lust, save in the sense that the dashing man or woman next door might, by fleeting eye or word contact. Not even *Hill Street* or *L.A. Law,* richly infested with violent thugs barely warded off by ineffectual cops or lawyers, ever frightens us on the level of *Hansel and Gretel,* if only because the very regularity of their appearance in the home cushions our expectations. If *Civil Wars* brings us the searing words of divorce in the opening moments ("That's right, I'm reneging" . . . "Would you like to know just how much I hate you at this moment"), the pomp and polish of its far too sleek lawyer-heroine, Mariel Hemingway, promises redemption each week, whether she brings the warring couples back together or not.

Prime Time is too smooth and too certain to merit either anguish or commitment. The very intensity implied by these terms defies the reasons most often voiced by viewers for turning to the medium in the first place (that is, to relax, at least after dinner). Yes, it could be fairly said that various atypical intrusions in these hours tremble on the edge of intensity. The TV show at the top of all the ratings, CBS's *60 Minutes*, often offers incisive revelations about people and events that inspire attention almost as close as two lovers whispering across a crowded restaurant table. So, now and then, do long-running marathon specials like *The Civil War,* which briefly brought to PBS in 1990 audience "numbers" that at least neared Nielsen respectability. More importantly, it inspired a rash of books, films, and student attention to the 1861–1865 conflict, as well as a reconsideration of the old notion that TV viewers wouldn't sit still for a dense account of *any* historical subject. PBS's *Civil War* refused to "re-create" the past, to cast Robert Redford as Lincoln or Debra Winger as his wife. Indeed, it stressed old, weathered photographs of long-dead generals, soldiers, slaves. When viewers spoke then or speak now of *The Civil War,* they do so in a clearly moved state, as if fresh from a close embrace or at least a heart-to-heart talk.

But not even *Civil War* partisans confirm our last myth. They are rarely charged with either tear-streaked desire or deep-seated revulsion. Roland Barthes, always conscious that "Love" in the fullest dictionary meaning casts us in a role dictated by well-known models, identifies "Crying" and "Suicide," neither prompted by TV-viewing-as-we-have-known-it, as central to the script. *"I make myself cry,"* says the lover, always, according to Barthes, *"in order to prove to myself*

that my grief is not an illusion: tears are signs, not expressions."
Suicide, or its threat, rarely voiced by TV partisans, is the
same: *"The idea of suicide saves me,"* says the rejected lover,
"for I can speak it *(and do not fail to do so): I am reborn and
dye this idea with the colors of life."*

No, the figure inherent in the Myth, that we "love" TV
simply because we turn it on, is clearly absurd. The moment
we examine the Myth, as when the citizens examine the
Emperor Unclothed, we see at once that it/he/she is naked.
Why, then, is the claim, that is, the big lie, repeated, so
insistently, so confidently? Why do they tell us the big, whopping lie about "love"? Surely because it is driven by a smaller,
more practical set of lies, that is to say, the figures lurking
behind the metaphor. It is our assumption that statements
like *seven years out of every lifespan/7 hours 26 minutes viewing
per day/25 percent refuse to stop watching TV for $1 million* are
true that endows our myth. As for the ratings, the immense
percentages of devotees supposedly on hand between 8 and
11 P.M., these, too, certify the lie. But are any of these figures
solid, as a rock in the real world is solid? as our own experience of life itself . . . is credible? Once again, let us see.

PLEASURE BY THE SHALLOWS?

> *In a recent national survey it was found that
> more Americans reported getting pleasure
> from television than from sex, food, hobbies,
> religion, money, or sports.*
> —Robert Kubey and Mihaly
> Csikszentmihalyi, *Television and the Quality
> of Life,* 1990

> *I find my love fishing
> His feet are in the shallows
> We have breakfast together
> And drink beer
> I offer him the magic of my thighs
> He is caught in the spell.*
> —Love poem, Ancient Egypt

The apparent confidence with which scholars like Robert Kubey of Rutgers University and Mihaly Csikszentmihalyi of the University of Chicago accept the astonishing proposition that Americans prefer TV to sex, not to say God, proves yet again the divinity, in our time, of Numbers. In matters ultimately requiring a vote or decision based on faith, many of us clearly prefer to reach beyond this inconvenient trap for any evidence that appears to be "scientific" or, at least, quantitative, whether logically true or false. Those of us occasionally trapped in the corridors of network power when the "overnight" ratings supplied by the A. C. Nielsen Company arrive, offering equally astonishing conclusions extrapolated by computers from small viewing "samples," can cite similar evidence. In the presence of this silent awe, many of us surely want to roar question after question: *"Which* survey says Americans get more pleasure from TV than sex? *Who* was asked? *How* was the quesiton phrased? *What* do you mean, what do they mean by "pleasure"? *Why* are you so certain that the "overnight" percentages are correct? Again, whose viewing habits did you monitor? How? Whom did you leave out?"

When polls are rigorously questioned in this manner, their results can indeed guide us toward enlightenment, as well as merriment, if they are supplemented by other sources, as well as by the normal quota of skepticism that is proof of postindustrial sanity. *TV Guide's* merry calls and interviews in the fall of 1992, dangling an obvious jape before its surely bemused audience, is a succulent example: imagine being asked, in effect, "Would you give up watching television for $1 million?" Unless you are shown a certified check, there is only one possible riposte . . . for this riposte.

But, the supreme authority of the oft-cited Nielsen Numbers and the enormous extrapolations they inspire, including assertions that every day so many million Americans, or indeed so many billions of earthlings (3.5 billion people is a favored figure), "watch" television, is particularly fragile. For decades, enormous holes have been punched in the facade of Nielsen's methodology by a stream of conscientious sociologists and statisticians. More than one naysayer has pointed out that the company's Numbers, based on a robotic "audimeter" mounted on TV sets in the homes of its small sample (four thousand homes allegedly representing the entire nation), tell us almost nothing about the activity on the other end, that is, in the viewer's life and mind. For two decades, the audimeter simply told us whether the Nielsen "subscriber" had his TV *off, on,* and if so, *which channel.* Lately, thanks to the use of a second spy box called, ironically, the "People Meter," Nielsen now tells us *who* turns on the set, information provided in years past only by "audilogs" filled out by hand once a week, for a $1 reward. The audimeter could not, did not tell us whether the set duly counted as "on" was actually being watched.

Despite these imperfections, the power of the ratings compiled by Nielsen, a private, profit-making company, joined for a time in the 1980s by Arbitron, Inc., which used similar methods, grew, rivaling the income of several basic industries that feed, clothe, and house us. So did the sums demanded by networks from advertisers who wanted to reach these rusting if not leaky Numbers. In 1986, for example (one of the last of the network's glory years), the big three, ABC, CBS, NBC, grossed $8.6 billion, considerably more than earned or spent by certain basic industries. Yet this glittering reward depended on a standard of authority that in fact lacked authority. Suspended above the abyss of disbelief by a slender reed, the networks began to totter, in terms of profit and loss, when competition (CATV mostly) waxed and when the more efficient "People Meter" replaced the old audimeter-diary system, thanks to pressure from the clients, that is, the advertising agencies, all in the late 1980s. The fateful Numbers—particularly the sum total of viewers watching in prime time—began immediately to decline. Then we witnessed a painful crash in these mystic figures as the new decade dawned, in January of 1990.

Now it was never surprising that those who stood to benefit from the Numbers, that is, network managers, tended to treat them as holy writ. What is surprising to this day is the reverence accorded the abstract "25.7" or "18.6" credited to *Murphy Brown* or *Civil Wars* by TV critics, journalists, serious viewers, and professionals. This author has never once found a midlevel media professional who believed in the integrity of the Numbers. Some shake their heads in mirth, or disgust. But to almost a man or woman they end by accepting the Nielsen ratings because they provide a "standard," a measure of judgment in an otherwise supposedly chaotic field. Those professionals who are slighted by the Nielsen system end by supporting it as well, to my continuing surprise. They include producers of public television programming aimed at children and the elderly (neither, by common consent, well represented in the Nielsen "sample"), or creators of serious, demanding programming anywhere. "Of course I believe in the Numbers," Shad Northshield, the founding spirit of CBS's richly praised *Sunday Morning* news, once told me. "I have to. I believe them like I believe in Relativity."

The plight of Todd Gitlin, a respected reformist critic of the networks, is another poignant example of this illogic, a function of the fifth myth, which requires quantitative "proof" as a condition of survival. In a searing chapter in his book *Inside Prime Time* (1983), Gitlin lashes into the Nielsen methodology on many counts, from its biased sample (anyone willing to accept the surveillance of an audimeter is likely to be a "heavy user") to its failure to aggressively recruit black, Hispanic, and poor citizens into its sample. Gitlin even dares to doubt the premise of virtually all polling—that we can objectively select an accurate microcosm of the entire society on which to base stupendous conclusions. How can each Nielsen subscriber represent tens of thousands of other viewers, Gitlin asks, including the lame, the blind, the halt, and most of all those too proud or independent to allow the monitoring of his/her behavior?[6]

Despite all this, Gitlin in the end joins his enemy by buying into the spurious notion that we need at all cost accept an "objective" rating standard, no matter how overstated or inaccurate. "Plainly the Nielsen system has had its short-comings," he concludes, "but in the end there are strong pressures to keep it honest," that is, from sponsors who will demand assurances about audience count. In support of this shaky assumption Gitlin cites the determination of advertisers to learn the "truth" about audience count, ignoring equivalent network pressure to overstate that count. Since he wrote his book before the advent of the People Meter, Gitlin was certain that the growing interest in demographics, in *who* is watching, as opposed to simple Numbers, would produce finer, more precise methods of audience measurement. But his final trump is the industry's high regard for the Nielsen method: "I think it's among the finest research done in the social sciences," one network executive says, quoted by Gitlin. "And to the degree that they are somewhat imprecise . . . they [the ratings] are not imprecise in terms of ranking what is most popular to least popular. And that's all that matters."[7]

Though the "facts" are in error, in brief, the order of shows in the ratings is not. Now this assumption, also widely accepted in media analysis, has nothing to do with the scientific method, strictly defined. As Gitlin himself concedes elsewhere, the tiniest error, no more than a few percentage points (well within the range assumed by most statisticians for any "poll"), could have reversed the placement of shows as disparate in content as *Dynasty* and *Hill Street Blues*, escalating the latter over the former.[8] None but a careless doctor would base a solution to a patient's illness on incorrect "numbers" (about body temperature, say), nor would a microbiologist prescribe soil treatment in the face of incorrect mineral counts, no matter how slight. As the later crisis caused by the People Meter confirmed, the Nielsen ratings were *not* valid in terms of "popular" to "least popular," to say nothing of overall audience size.

Then and now, the Numbers are *an act of faith*. Not only do they rigorously simplify the highly diverse responses of an exceedingly complicated postindustrial society to a medium of communication that is more diverse and complicated than ever, following the advent of cable TV and VCRs: the primordial Numbers demand a range of outrageously subjective interpretations. How, to take one example alone, do we judge the relative "popularity" of any late-night program, Johnny Carson's beloved, long-running *Tonight* show, say, which landed in its late lifetime Nielsen numbers like "12" or "13," representing the percentage of TV homes tuned in, against an uproven newcomer like *Civil Wars*, which occasionally rose in the early 1990s into "20"-something numbers? Since a "20" is far easier to achieve in primetime hours when more viewers are awake and watching than near midnight, *Tonight*'s time zone, how are we to judge the "popularity" of one over the other, save by instinct, hunch, hearsay?

The early Nielsen-Arbitron dependence on handwritten diaries produced exquisite evidence of the role played by whim and opinion in this supposedly neutral, white-coated system. In "True Confessions of a Nielsen Family," Robert Woodward enlivened the *New York Times* in 1991 with a spicy account of his deviltry ten years before, when he and a girlfriend ("picked at random" by Nielsen) conspired to "tilt" her diary in what seemed a morally correct direction:

> *My friend and I stayed up late one night to fill out the pamphlet. Seldom at home long enough to watch anything, she felt obliged to support a few names that she had heard were worthwhile—Phil Donahue, MacNeil/Lehrer, Jacques Cousteau; and together we pretended to have seen nearly every mature documentary and news analysis on the air.*[9]

Needless to say, Woodward's account, which does not markedly differ from similar public and private "confessions" made by the keepers of the diaries throughout the 1970s and 1980s, does not sound like a lover's memoir. Had his lady friend stumbled upon a TV program as desirable as the fisherman in the ancient Egyptian poem, she might have served Myth Five, but it seems unlikely. Surely the busy, two-career lifestyle he describes in his account is widely shared in the 1990s, as women join men in the work force in escalating numbers. Lovemaking, whether human or electronic, requires free time that's increasingly hard to find.

Gitlin's prediction that Nielsen and Arbitron would adopt more precise counting methods proved correct, in a sense. The People Meter in all its permutations slowly took over the monitoring function once performed by diaries. Each night, indeed, sophisticated systems like Arbitron's aborted "Scan America" box, mounted in selected households, can feed a range of data into a central computer over the phone line that is printed out in neat rows the next morning. But the need to press an array of buttons means that the "sample" is now more biased than ever. To join this cadre of subjects, you and I must now do much more than simply turn a TV on or off. We are required to press a series of buttons. In the case of the once-proud "Scan America" system, questions flash on the screen when we are slow, lazy, or indifferent, demanding information about who we are and who is sitting nearby: *Enter Relatives/Guests*, for example, or *Age and Sex of Guest*. This is hardly like stumbling upon *Tonight* or *MacNeil/Lehrer* with the ease of the lady chancing on her lover at poolside. If we can "measure" more precisely than before, what—or whom—are we measuring? It is perhaps the most critical question we can now ask.

THE NEW DECADE: THE BIG CRASH

> *I don't think that any of the new technologies can recruit an honest sample. The elderly will say no to the buttons. The kids won't press them. The intellectuals would be totally offended by the surveillance. If you're a poor person living in the ghetto you wouldn't trust it. I know I personally wouldn't want to do it.*
>
> —Audience analyst for PBS, interview with author, 1992

*The blinking questions are a pain. Some peo-
ple resist. All market research is plagued by
the problem of how to get people to participate.
We go door to door. . . . You can make up to
$350 a year by joining our panel.*

—Arbitron spokesperson, interview with author, 1991

*Suddenly in January 1990, the HUT
[Houses Using TV] dropped like a rock. It
was inexplicable. Nobody could figure out why
the numbers dropped so far in one year . . . six
to eight percent. . . . The networks went crazy.
The news came just before the Up Front Market, when the networks traditionally earn most
of their revenue by preselling time for the rest
of the year. They screamed at us. They said
people were getting tired of pressing the People
Meter buttons. We said we were also reporting
a decline in the total number of hours the TV
is turned on, just as before, through the old
auditmeter system. They still didn't buy it. . . .*

*There was blood all over the floor here. In
the end the networks announced they wouldn't
accept the Nielsen ratings. They said they
would set their guarantees to the agencies
based on the average of Nielsens going back
two or three years. . . . Each network announced this separately, so they couldn't be
accused of collusion. . . . But the agencies
said they wouldn't buy time based on this plan.
We'll never know what actually happened or
who paid what to whom in 1990 and 1991.
But certainly we know that there was never
universal acceptance of this adjusted guarantee. We are back to reality, such as it is.*

—A. C.Nielsen employee interview with author, 1992

*Dream of total union. Everyone says this
dream is impossible, and yet it persists. . . . I
am no longer myself, without you.*

—Roland Barthes, A Lover's Discourse, 1978

Whatever claim the Numbers had to scientific objectivity destructed, for those who cared to notice, the moment the new, supposedly more "scientific," People Meter was installed in the homes of A. C. Nielsen's viewing samples in the fall of 1987. The tiny meter boxes, perched on top of the TV set, simply required the user to press a few buttons—not keep a diary. They also identified the viewer doing the pressing, unlike the old Nielsen meter, which simply recorded "on" and "off." Of course the new ratings—and particularly the revision downward of the total number of viewers supposedly watching TV at all—prompted complaints throughout the industry. The networks argued that many viewers, bored by the task of button-pressing, simply weren't pressing. The big three were irritated by People-Meterized changes in the rankings of shows like *The CBS Evening News with Dan Rather* (up) and *The Bill Cosby Show* (down). They were angered by the drop in the total number watching in prime time, sometimes reported as 10 percent off the old, comfortable figures.

The 1989–1990 nosedive demanded and received a furious response. When the networks demanded a recount, in effect, despite mounting evidence that the new, lower numbers, representing millions of lost viewers, were accurate, they opened themselves to the charge that the Numbers were hardly "the finest research done in the social sciences," but a convenient tool to maximize profits. While researching this event in 1991–1992, long after the networks had announced their abandonment of their "adjusted audience" totals, I was often pressed not to name names. At first I resisted, but I began to see that the request was not only justifiable but confirmed again that our august TV numbers are as malleable, as politicized as are all "numbers" based on calling, polling, interviewing, pressing buttons, ad infinitum, as many of those who "count" the results, including Nielsen itself, often confess in various ways—conceding, for example, that their results can be subjected to varying "interpretations."

In any case, the networks, battered by recession, apparently lost out in the end: agencies and clients simply refused to pay for millions of viewers that apparently *weren't* copulating at home with their TV sets. But this compromise hardly proves the contention that market pressures guarantee honesty. Who says the figures finally accepted by the buyer (the agencies) and the seller (the nets) are *Real*, either? More to the point, what did the old audiometer off-on total prove in those vintage Nielsen reports that fused the immense HUT numbers into our brains and our mythologies? In a moving passage in *Television and the Quality of Life*, Professors Kubey and Csikszentmihalyi critique *all* methods of measuring the audience that alter what they call the "normative viewing experience," which is unmonitored and uninterrupted. "What is needed," they conclude, "is evidence taken in the real conditions in which people watch television, in the complex context of their daily life, with all its attendant vicissitudes."[10]

But the recent answers provided by Kubey and Csikszentmihalyi, along with countless others, each making use of extraordinary new methods of measurement, are in the end no more satisfying than the humble Nielsen diaries, which at least openly flaunted their handmade subjectivity. As the People Meters grow in complexity, they demand active attention from their users that seriously distorts the profile of the user. The Scan America system deluged its viewers with reminders on their TV screens; further, it provided a portable scanner in the kitchen that registered products purchased at nearby stores, when they were held before the scanner, like totems from the hunt. In a series of laboratory studies during the 1980s, zealous researchers managed to outfit batteries of subjects with electroencephalograph (EEG) electrodes, seeking to discover whether TV viewing provokes changes in internal brain wave activity. They concluded, surprise, surprise, that TV does *appear* to induce low cortical energy states, closer to daydreaming or idling ("doing nothing") than reading.[11] But it is difficult to imagine any electroded viewer seated before a TV in a laboratory, flanked by associates similarly strapped, focusing on TV content with the same intensity possible at home, or even in a saloon. The totally "passive" systems surely in our future, already tested in Europe, require a similar indifference, if not distraction. The "Motivac" black box, tested by Arbitron, was installed in a small sample of French homes in 1991. Using a photo sensor that hides behind the surface of the TV screen, Motivac detects movement in a 120 degree arc beyond the set, carefully distinguishing between adults, children, pets, and "reflections." The exceedingly special family ready to live with Motivac—men and women remarkably indifferent to Big Brother, if not Sister—does nothing. His or her every movement is surveiled, then stored in computers for later analysis.

The well-intentioned "Experience Sampling Method" (ESM) devised by Professors Kubey and Csikszentmihalyi exceeded even Motivac in its ingenuity, as well as the restrictions it imposes on the "sample." Collaborating with five Chicago firms ("selected by joint agreement between company executives and staff researchers"), they outfitted 107 subjects ages 18 to 63 with pocket-sized electronic pagers and booklets of "self-report forms" over a period of one week. When they were "beeped" at random, the respondents wrote out answers to forty questions that attempted to determine how they felt and what they were doing when watching television, as well as performing other tasks, from reading to walking.[12]

Designed to tell us what the actual "experience" of television viewing is like, in its "natural context," the Kubey-Csikszentmihalyi ESM is as Rube Goldbergian as any of its less high-minded competitors. Once again we are faced with the inherent bias of the sample: those willing to allow interference in their daily lives are clearly preselected. As test after test tells us, "cooperators" tend to view more television than noncooperators. As common sense tells us, the subject willing to respond to other-directed beepers tends to be less private, less alienated, and certainly less busy than hard-pressed executives, working mothers, and "intellectuals," as our nameless PBS analyst puts it. By working only with employees of Chicago-based companies, the ESM study is further discriminating, if not discriminatory.

In its admirable determination to assess how people *feel* when watching TV, to discover when, if ever, they are "happy" before the set, *Television and the Quality of Life* asks all the questions rarely asked by Myth Five advocates, but answers none of them. Locked into the responses of its tiny, selected 107-person model, the book finally endorses nearly all of the specious platitudes perpetrated by less conscientious studies. Kubey and Co. appear to believe that Americans prefer TV over almost every other working or leisure activity, save when reading, eating, or walking, by whopping margins. Curiously, they also concede, with admirable academic humility, that their beloved ESM studies cannot begin to tell us how viewers actually *interpret* what they watch. The "self-report forms" do not explain the role of *narrative* in gaining the deep-focus attention of the audience. "Nor have we spent a great deal of time," finally, "analyzing television content."[13]

Surely this is why none of the methods and machines from the Nielsen audimeter to Motivac's Big Brother to the ESM explain now or prepared us in the past for the massive changes already noted in this book in the medium and its audience. Radical departures in lifestyle, in behavior, and in technology have raced on beyond our lumbering insistence on quantifying what cannot be quantified. Virtually every broadcaster or advertiser I spoke to in 1991–1992 conceded that neither zapping nor VCR usage, for example, can be codified, or predicted. We have no Number to account for the hordes of children now interacting with computerized TV programming in schools and day-care centers, where they have been deposited far from the Great God Passive TV by working mothers and bachelor fathers. As the population ages, the viewing habits of reclusive senior citizens go unrecorded as well. There is no reliable Number for the class variously known as "Know-a-Lots" to hardworking pollsters, or "Class X," by Paul Fussell, in his acerbic

"Notes on Class," perhaps the only assessment of American life that takes affectionate account of the decisive role now played by "artists, writers . . . rock stars, celebrities . . . and the shrewder sorts of spies" in the changing "content" of prime-time television.[14] Yet certainly Class X has provided the skills and brains that developed programs like *Hill Street Blues* and *Murphy Brown*. It was surely the Know-a-Lots who further invented entire cable TV phenomena like C-SPAN and Court TV, none of which could have been sighted ten years ago through the cobwebs stretched across our eyes by the methodologies of "scientific" measurement. In the 1970s and early 1980s, substantive change in the grooved patterns of TV was widely deemed as impossible as the *perfect union* of man, woman, or more.

THE IMPROBABLE PROBABLE

1607 . . . We are the greater pole. . . . They gave us our demands.
    —Oxford English Dictionary on Historical Principles, 1983

Probability theory: *that branch of mathematics which treats of probability. Probability theory is based on certain assumptions regarding the uniformity of nature, laws of change, equality of opportunity, of occurrence of certain events, and complementary errors cancelling each other out if sufficient observations occur.* **Probability error (PE):** *the probable error is equal to .6745 of the standard error.*
    —J. E. Chaplin, *Dictionary of Psychology*, new rev. ed., 1975

Disorder depicts dishonour.
    —S. M. Salim, *Marsh Dwellers of the Euphrates Delta*, 1962

*Who is the other? I wear myself out. I shall
never know.*
                        —Roland   Barthes,   "Unknow-
able," *A Lover's Discourse*, 1978

Often the lover contends, like the Nielsen and Arbitron
overnight charts, that he/she *knows* his/her beloved. But at
other times the lover, at least, knows better. He/she relishes
both knowing and not knowing. Those who measure and
manage TV are anguished before this mystery. When their
counting fails, when they are forced to admit, usually in
private, that they do not know why the viewer prefers this
program or that, or worse, does not even tune in, blood
spills, as my informant tells us. This belief in the ability of
certain empirical methods to observe/record/predict everything, down to the last detail, which began to firm in our
minds in the Renaissance, is shared by those who poll voters
during political campaigns.

The "poll" and the Numbers are symptoms of the same
malaise. In the beginning, the word "pole" or "poll" simply
meant a count of votes, clearly rewarding the "demands" of
those won. It was only later, as the eighteenth and nineteenth centuries unfolded, as confident scientists and math-
ematicians like Blaise Pascal, Jacques Bernouilli, and Pierre
Simon de Laplace purified what became known as "the *science* of probability," that the *count* took on magical prop-
erties. Men and women became confident that a partial
count—of some voters, stars, or marbles—could be assumed
to "represent" many more, that is, a "probable" truth. With
the coming of the grand universal measurements inspired
by relativity theory, we came to think that love itself, as well
as the entire universe, answered to *uniformity*. Now scientists
are no longer so certain. Various absurd discoveries—that
space is dotted with dense black holes reversing the laws of
gravity—summed up in what has been called quantum me-
chanics, have severely shaken what might be called the prob-
abilists. The past few decades have refuted one deductive
"law" after another. We are no longer sure we can predict

the course of sun storms or wind patterns. The new anti-science, called *Chaos* by James Gleick, the best-selling author who proclaimed it, is grounded in humility.[15]

It is only in the vulgar realms of TV Numbers and political polling that we still find a measure of the old, convinced arrogance. Yet these Numbers gird all of our myths, most of all the last, despite reversals that include the unforeseen flight and fragmentation of the viewing audience, inaccurate political polling and the mounting evidence that voters distrust and dislike the obsessive charting of elections.

Surely it is time to consider why counting and predicting err so often, beginning with the debatable assumption that subjective phenomena like viewing or voting can easily be quantified or projected. If we move further, to the belief that small subsets of larger wholes, say Nielsen's four thousand homes or a pollster's eight thousand telephone calls, can stand for everyone else . . . if we finally and vainly cloak our projections in the mantle of science by admitting on a tiny "probability of error" nearing 5 percent . . . we are doomed to either short- or long-run failure, depending on the complexity of the subject or problem being defined.

And here is the critical answer to our critical question: when the subject is the cranky human spirit, the rater-pollster must cover his tracks with extraordinary care. For years Nielsen was protected by a multibillion-dollar industry desperately eager to guard the integrity of the Numbers because they provided the rationale for the stratospheric pricing of TV time. Worse, the primitive on-off function of the audimeter went unchallenged, as long as no embarrassingly qualitative questions were asked (is anyone watching? if yes, does anyone like what is there?). But social and technological changes finally defrocked the Nielsens. When channels proliferated, when the irreverent, difficult-to-measure VCRs brought personal choice to the home, when zapping ruined the simple on-off equation, the entire world seemed finally to understand that the mystical premise behind the Nielsens—and the polls—wasn't mystical enough.

What is this premise? Does it deserve a lover's revenge?

Listen carefully: *if we follow the correct procedures, the "prob-ability" is that our "sample" (four thousand homes, six hundred voters, etc.) will stand as a representative of every other home, or voter.* The textbooks love to bring this premise to life by calling on the proverbial can filled with two thousand red marbles and two thousand blue marbles. If we shake the can and pull out four hundred marbles, one by one, blind-folded, the odds are we will end up with a red-blue per-centage close to 50-50. Whether the raters or pollsters choose their marbles, viewers, or voters at random or by demographics, the theory tells us the result is always the same—accurate within a few percentage points (no worse than .6745).

But of course no human action is either as random or as regular as a rolling marble. If anything, the true lover, that is, the human animal, is as whimsical, as changeable, as guarded as the wind patterns we no longer claim we can chart. Whether we narrow our sample disastrously, recruiting heavy, uncritical, or cooperative viewers in the manner of the paid Arbitron polls, the ominous Motivac tests, or the intrusive pager questions, whether we broaden our sample to include selective viewers, professional women, and day-care kids, we face the same risk: improbable human intel-ligence. Probability theory not only assumes a universe that obeys regular laws. It also assumes a subject, human or mineral, that cannot resist, outthink, defy, or surprise whoever or whatever attempts to track him. Yet we know that diaries can be falsified, that angry or confused voters can change their minds the next day, that Motivac's 120 degree arc can be ducked. Call one of these subjects "Brand X," if you are Paul Fussell, or a subversive "New Class" partisan if you are Ben Stein, Probability cannot possi-bly ingest their resistance. The moment we attempt to count the very higher intelligence that often initiates social change, we fail. This is why we were unprepared for the rush of doctors, lawyers, and teachers to the streets, cafes, and theaters in prime time, for the attractiveness of long-form cable television, for massive last-minute voting swings such as occurred on the eve of the 1980 election, when Ronald Reagan won with percentages well above any predicted by the Probabilist pollsters.

Does this mean we can't calibrate the fortunes of adventurous television programs or richly thematic political campaigns? Yes, this is exactly what it means. No, we cannot predict the unpredictable. In the hard empirical sense we only know for sure what can be verified by sources that support our Numbers. We can tabulate for example how many television sets have been sold in the United States, in Europe, in Asia, beyond. We can know how many hours the audimeters and scanners tell us they are on. We know the habits, the movements, perhaps, in time, even the eye movements of a totally unrepresentative sample of viewers, on the day and hour they are recorded. From time to time even the opinions of this tiny collective can be counted. Similar careful, qualified statements can be made about other samples. But no more.

Beyond that, for everything that matters in media, politics, and life, we must rely upon our wits, our talent, on what has been called "common sense," inevitably based in trial and error. None of these strategies guarantees that our decisions will be inevitably correct. We must be prepared for "polls" and "surveys" to constantly contradict each other, as they did in instances of overwhelming political sobriety, witness 1973–1974, when the numbers told us both that the average American didn't want to see Nixon impeached and that they did,[16] or in lighter instances, as when Professors Kubey and Csikszentmihalyi find that TV viewers prefer TV to love vs. *TV Guide*'s fall 1992 verdict that "viewers" prefer the reverse, when left alone on a desert island, and hang the $1 million, useless there, anyway.[17]

Yes, trial, error, imagination are collectively an untidy process, without the spurious comfort offered by neat numbers, laws, customs. Among the marsh-dwellers of the Euphrates, memorably described by S. M. Salim, the mere acceptance or refusal of a cup of coffee at the wrong time by a confused guest can lead to angry rejection. As in the case of the small Azande boy who stumbled before E. E. Evans-Pritchard, his chronicler, it is always simpler to refer to a "standard," however abstract, than attempt to confront natural causes, which are inevitably disquieting. Evans-Pritchard goes on to confess that the link between what we call "common sense" (in the Azande's case, the possibility that he didn't see the stump that made him trip) and mystical beliefs is "complicated."

But when we turn away from this complexity to order the meaning of an evolving medium like television, we commit a greater error. Worse, this error deprives us of delight. It keeps us from exploration and invention. Our mythic awe robs us of the power to influence our own fate. When we similarly cast our audience in this role, akin to a bit part, we ignore its libido for change and reversal. No manner of external witchcraft can compare with the surprises inherent in a society as diverse as this one. Now, we also know that "love" itself dies when forced into a straitjacket of fixed expectation. The testimony of the ages, not of Myth Five, is that love thrives on mystery, on the confession that we don't know, entirely, what to expect next.

LOVE, MYTHS, LIPS

Are you very happy? Are you fairly happy?
Or, are you not very happy?
  —Gallup Poll, 1985

Are you very happy? Are you pretty happy?
Or, are you not too happy?
  —National Opinion Research Center poll, 1985

TV is like masturbation. If you do it, you do it by yourself in a dark room. Theater is completely opposite. . . . I don't want to write for television
  —David Mamet, playwright, 1978

The first expansions of the human heart were the effects of a novel situation.
—Jean-Jacques Rousseau, *The Social Contract*, 1771

And when she parts her lips to kiss/My head is light, I am drunk without beer.
—Love poem, Ancient Egypt

I am considering whether I love television as I end this book. I am also considering whether I ought to reveal precisely how I use it on this last evening, reversing the manner adopted by those who dare written conclusions about a medium that is far from concluded. When I had once the good fortune to escort one of Marshall McLuhan's daughters to a dinner, she revealed that her father rarely watched TV for pleasure, preferring to relax and read while listening to classical music. This seemed to me worth knowing. So I confess that I finished this page on a Saturday night and Sunday morning in New York, interspersed with dinner and attendance at a late film, *Kafka*, starring Jeremy Irons, made in England and Czechoslovakia in 1990–1991.

By far the signal insight of Kubey and Csikszentmihalyi's book, *Television and the Quality of Life*, is that the vast majority of us watch television along with other activities. The pathetic Probabilist question asked by Gallup and others about "happiness" can only incidentally touch the medium so often declared the central organizing agent in contemporary life. Surely I share this larger prognosis, save on those rare occasions when professional need or riveting content demand total attention. On this last night while I edited these lines, my wife and daughter were locked into a series of mildly diverting NBC series: *Golden Girls*, *The Powers That Be*, and *Empty Nest*. Out of one ear I tracked the plots, as did my wife, who was also preparing a meal. As my nine-year-old daughter watched, she tossed a football up and down. Often she would look away, open up a comic book, or telephone a friend.

The plots demanded no more. The three women who

dominate *Golden Girls* were at odds over how to handle the
latest male brought home by the lubricious post-sixty character whose sexual activism is not lost on my frowning
daughter. In *The Powers That Be*, the wife married to the
presidential hero played by John Forsythe, clearly modeled,
viciously, on Nancy Reagan, battles with her daughter to
get an invitation to lunch with Princess Diana from England.
Empty Nest was ending as our meal began, with the widowed
father, Richard Mulligan, being browbeaten by a nurse who
"guards" him from the rapacious demands visited upon him
by his two grown daughters, living at home with vengeance.
Once again I needed to pay nothing but incidental attention
to the abortive drama, which was soon replaced by the vivid
testimony of an elderly woman defrauded by a health in-
surance salesman on *Real Life Heroes* (CBS), to which my
wife, a social worker, turned out of professional interest.
While the heroine accepted a $10,000 savings bond from
the glowing network hostess, we left.

At the theater, *Kafka* demanded and received unremitting
attention. On all such occasions, most of us go "out" to a
film theater, pay for a ticket, and join a society of committed
supplicants far from bouncing footballs and sizzling steaks.
On this occasion, *Kafka,* etched in deep black-and-white
hues (occasionally relieved by by stretches of brilliant color),
seemed by surprise a paradigm for this book. The hero,
modeled on the life of the great Czech author, finds himself
about to be imprisoned if not tortured in the imperious
"Castle," where layers of fiendish bureaucracies are laced
with equally fiendish cells. Inside the cells, prisoners are
strapped down by ruthless scientists who use futuristic electrodes and ray guns to study and torture them. "You are
modern," says the chief tormentor to Kafka, "but you don't
accept it. I do." In the end, Kafka defies the madman, es-
capes, and returns, chastened, to his former life, as a humble
clerk. No, he does not destroy the Castle. Rather, he simply
ignores it, appears to play its game, and later, or so the film's
finale implies, writes his brilliant book, *The Castle*, parrying
his tormentor.

By similar means we have parried TV, in its monolithic, early network phase, until finally the medium begins, painfully, to change. Following my return home that evening, I switched on cable TV late at night and found myself watching the resignation of Senator Paul Tsongas from the Democratic primary race for President, on C-SPAN. At a certain point in his halting speech, his wife planted a wet kiss on his cheek. Tsongas never noticed the imprint of her parted lips on the side of his face during the following hour, but the camera—and the rest of us—did. This chance event added an edge of Kafkaesque absurdity to the proceedings. It also, with equal inevitability, softened Tsongas's character. Taken together with the depth of feeling shown by his friends and co-workers, the imprinted kiss underlined the force of his words. The kiss became the medium for the message, which might otherwise have gone ignored. Without the camera, without the unedited spontaneity of the moment, without the relaxed, unmetered, unedited pace of C-SPAN, we would never have learned quite so much about this candidate, however lost, for the moment.

In Rousseau's memorable phrase, the twenty-four-hour C-SPAN channel is a novel situation, a new means of embellishing and delivering ideas. We are permitted a certain closeness at moments like this, a certain lack of guard or preparation not allowed in the past, in print or on network TV. It made me think at once of David Mamet and McLuhan, Mander & Co. Mamet refused to work in television for a time because it gave him only a lone viewer, away from the committed cadre assembled by theater, or a film like *Kafka*. But the lonely viewer is as critical to theater, and to the race, as the lonely reader. Even when isolated in libraries and living rooms, informed or inspired by what he or she learns, the reader, be he Jefferson, Lenin, or Kafka, has a long record of activism, of reaching out later to write books, decide elections, and change events, if not the world. If we regarded him or her with the same reverence lately given to four thousand homes or *an audience of 70 million*, we might begin to sense a similar benefit, implicit in a medium whose

negative power over us is primarily imagined. And this benefit is not implicit in the medium itself but in those who
have access to its marginal moments, sending or receiving.
Let the exuberant McLuhan, the enraged Mander, let
countless others assume that TV will drive us toward its own
irrational ends. As I turned off both the set and the light
on that final night, I thought, rather of other ends, not often
cited or programmed, of that imprinted kiss and of Kafka,
who did, after all, expose the Castle.

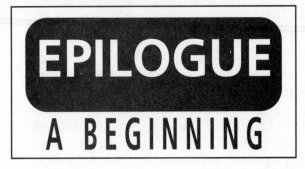

EPILOGUE
A BEGINNING

The world today is a world in which generality, objectivity, and universality are in crisis. This world presents a great challenge to the practice of politics, which, it seems to me, has a technocratic, utilitarian approach to Being. . . . Sooner or later politics will be faced with the task of finding a new postmodern face. A politician must become a person again.
— Vaclav Havel, Speech, "The End of the Modern Era," 1992

We have been told over and over in this century that our crisis is the crisis of man depraved. Certainly the incredible destruction that accompanied the great world wars, the continuing erosion of nature, and the seemingly inexorable spread of mind-numbing telecommunications media make these warnings appear both fit and proper. But Vaclav Havel's speech to the World Economic Forum in Switzerland in 1992 raises an equally valid warning, perhaps more relevant to the end of the century. We may in fact underestimate men, women, ourselves. And this may explain why we have been surprised by events in the world, and its media, at the end of the century.

It is likely that we have misappropriated blame. Instead of sensing the infinite capacity in all men and women to grow and change in response to unprecedented cultural, economic, and technological conditions, we continue to provide them with less than their expanding body of knowledge deserves. Our perception of the world does not begin to match its reality, or direction. When the people rise above the conditions engendered by those conceptions, as they did throughout Eastern Europe and Russia near the dawn of the century's last decade, we are at first shocked, then confused, and finally locked in place, unable to move, certain that our past habits of mind failed us but afraid to revise them.

In part the fall of Communism caught us short because we underestimated the capacity of moral an intellectual resistance in both the individual and the collective soul. In this book, I have tried to explain how and why we were caught short as well by the fall of network television—or rather, the conviction that the audience deserved nothing better than mass-production programming, sans thought, passion, or invention. These two massive errors in judgment and planning are so close, in their fundamental illogic, that they are virtually the same. For sure no one expected the "masses" in Eastern Europe to ignore the lessons preached insistently on state-controlled TV. We forget now how many Western leaders warned us that the citizens of Russia, shorn of a democratic past, would never oppose their army, police, or government. Nor did their brethren predict, or expect, the recent rise in activism, avoidance, and selectivity by the "masses" who attend television.

Perhaps the very term "mass" is now irrelevant, in an age when education and information levels those who command or send with those who "receive." Perhaps Havel and his colleagues are right to call for an end to the politics of determinism, to the peculiarly modern assumption that "the world—and Being as such—is a wholly knowable system governed by a finite number of universal laws." But the call must be expanded, to the culture, to the media, to the logic of psychology itself. Freudian analysis, like network programming, returns us to the psychic wounds of the past, to the essence of man, not to his Being, his capacity, in fine, to act. The times demand precisely that existential psychoanalysis no one yet practices. Without it, we will continue to prepare ourselves for a fixed future based on a presumably fixed past.

The issue is not whether man is guilty, depraved, or steeped in sin (any one of which insures the extinction of the race). The issue is whether he/she can change, whether, given our recent display of independence, given the inexorable growth of an unexpected telecommunication system (in which picture, text, and interactivity are fused), we can find new ways to think, love, and live rather than die. If this condition is met, the chance that the improbable world and its media will continue to elude our mechanistic predictions is at least even.

CONTRARIAN STATS: AN ADDENDUM

IN WHICH CERTAIN LINE-ITEM RESULTS RARELY STRESSED ARE FURTHER NOTED [WITHOUT PRETENSE TO FINAL TRUTH]

I. THE NETWORKS DECLINE

A. ESTIMATED PERCENTAGE OF THE PRIME-TIME AUDIENCE FOR ABC, CBS, NBC

> 1981—87%
> 1985—77%
> 1992—63%

B. AUDIENCE FOR THE THREE NETWORKS' EVENING NEWS

> The percentage of those tuning in during the newscasts shrank between 15% and 20% in the 1980s. Some statisticians predict a similar decline in the 1990s, which will reduce the network audience approximately 40% off the 1980 base.

C. NETWORK NEWS VS. ALTERNATIVES

Almost one-half of viewers surveyed by *TV Guide* in 1992 stated that it would be "acceptable" to them if the networks discontinued their national news programs, meaning that national news would be primarily available to them on cable TV through CNN and C-SPAN.

D. DECLINING MINIMUM FOR SURVIVAL OF PRIME-TIME NETWORK SERIES

The 30% share generally accepted in the early 1980s fell to 26% to 27% by the end of the decade, then into the lower 20s and upper teens in the 1990s.

In April 1992, CBS was declared the "winner" in the ratings "race" for the season, scoring an average of 21% for TV sets turned on, only 12.3% of all TV sets in the U.S.

E. SHRINKING NETWORK NUMBERS VS. RISING TV SET NUMBERS

In 1992, three in four American homes possess more than one television set; 15% possess more than *three* TVs. Yet the major network's share of this expanded audience has shrunk to 66%, off a base of 90% several decades ago in 1977.

II. ZAPPING CHANNELS TO CHANGE PROGRAMS, AVOID COMMERCIALS, OR TURN OFF TV ENTIRELY

A. Homes Using Remote-Control Zappers

1983—21%
1988—43%
1991—nearly 90%

B. Zappers and Zapping

Presence of remote-control zapper increases the zapping rate—that is, changing channels, turning off sound—by nearly 60%.

C. Zapping Commercials

Almost two-thirds of all TV viewers in the U.S., about 58 million people, flip channels during commercials or programs.

III. VIEWER ATTITUDES TOWARD NETWORK TV PROGRAM "QUALITY" PLUS THEIR OWN SENSE OF "SATISFACTION" AND/OR "GUILT"

A. National Association of Broadcasters Survey

	1977	1983
TV is of high importance in your life	41%	32%
TV is in tune with modern times	86%	78%
TV is lively and realistic	72%	59%
TV is varied and has better programs	65%	52%

B. Satisfaction Level: The Gap

In 1991, only 62% of viewers surveyed reported getting "satisfaction" from viewing television, lower than many other leisure-time activities.

C. Satisfaction Level vs. Income

In a 1991 survey by the Roper Organization for the Television Information Office, a little more than one-third of the respondents (35%) reported that viewing TV is "very satisfying." But this figure, already modest, drops even further among college graduates and/or those reporting incomes higher than $50,000 per year, to 23%.*

D. Viewing Guilt

12% of those surveyed in 1992 by Peter Hart Associates reported "guilt" when watching TV.

E. Discontent over Viewing

In a 1990 Gallup-Newport poll, 42% of 1,241 adults reported they spent *too much time watching TV*," an increase of 11% in the same complaint made in the 1970s.

F. Familiar Gripes About TV and CATV

"Our [1991] survey . . . turned up echoes of the familiar gripe about TV—*there's nothing to watch* [author's italic]. One-third of the readers with cable complained about insufficient variety—too many of the channels look alike. At the same time, readers want more. One-third want specific channels that their system doesn't offer. One-sixth complained that the system they're stuck with doesn't have enough channels. . . . They [our readers] were lukewarm about the four big pay-movie channels, and they put the three big broadcast networks at the lower half of our ratings."

IV. LESS TIME SPENT VIEWING NETWORK TV AND/OR CABLE TV PROGRAMMING, AS OPPOSED TO PERSONAL VCR LIBRARY, ETC.

A. LESS PROGRAM WATCHING

In the 1992 Hart survey, a little less than *one-half* of all viewers reported watching *less* programming now than in their past. Only 18% reporting watching *more*. A little more than one-third (38%) reporting watching about the same.

An earlier survey, for the National Association of Broadcasters (1983), reported similar results:
Watching more TV—21%
Watching the same—30%
Watching less—49%

B. CLAIMS TO LESS VIEWING

12% of respondents to the 1992 Hart survey reported spending *less than 7 hours per week watching television.* This contradicts most of the published assumptions about quantum TV viewing in America, as *TV Guide* points out. The magazine also reminds us that people tend to report *less* viewing than they actually do. But this is hardly a recommendation for the act of viewing TV. Other figures in the survey:
7 to 14 hours viewing per week—29%
15 to 21 hours—22%
22 to 28 hours—12%

29 to 35 hours—9%
36 to 49 hours—4%
50 to 70 hours—3%
More than 71 hours per week—1%
Nonetheless, 44% of those interviewed said they were watching less TV than "a couple of years ago."

C. Non-Network Favorites

In the Hart survey, fewer than one-third of the respondents reported that their "favorite" stations were affiliated with the major commercial broadcasting networks, "an incredible turnaround in viewer preference," says *TV Guide*. Among the new favorites: CNN (12%), ESPN (11%), Discovery Channel (9%), Turner stations (7%), Arts & Entertainment Channel (4%).

V. DOES TV DOMINATE US OR MERELY DISTRACT US?

In 1992, the following activities occurred among the viewers while the TV set was on:
Eating dinner—63%
Engaging in another activity (i.e., TV as "background noise")—36%
Falling asleep—29%

VI. ALTERNATIVES TO NETWORK TV VIEWING AND TO THE VIEWING OF ALL TV, INCLUDING CABLE TV AND MORE

A. More VCR Usage

1988—Videocassette recorders were in 53% of American homes.

1992—More than 1.5 million videos were rented in January of this year.

B. PUBLIC TV

Since the 1977–78 season the audience for public television has grown 47%. From that first date, 57% of American households with television sets watched each week (up 38% from the previous decade). Viewing public television in prime time expanded from 20% to 44% by the 1990s.

C. INDEPENDENT STATIONS

The number of independent stations in the U.S. grew from 62 in 1970 to 550 in 1992.

D. HIGH CULTURE

Bravo, the national satellite-delivered cable television channel devoted entirely to arts programming and serious films, grew from 48,000 nationwide subscribers at the close of 1981 to 9 million in 1992.

E. ALTERNATIVE LEISURE

Swimming is America's favorite leisure activity.
92% of Americans prefer listening to music rather than any of the following leisure activities:
Watching movies at home—89%
Watching television—85%
Reading books—82%
Reading magazines—81%
Using personal computers—69%
Playing video games—50%
In 1991, the Roper Organization reported, "When it comes to meeting the needs of families,

TV shows and video games score well below the average among a list of a dozen products and services asked about."*

Books rated the highest in terms of overall product/service satisfaction: 94%

Videotapes scored an 80% satisfaction rate, while TV shows rated only a 62% satisfaction rate.

VII. ALONE ON A DESERT ISLAND

If you were restricted to a TV set or a telephone, which?
   Telephone—61%
   Television—34%
If you were restricted to significant other or a TV set?
   Significant other—93%
   TV set—5%

VIII. WHAT HAPPENS WHEN TV SET OWNERS COME HOME AFTER WORK

Two in five Americans say they generally turn the TV set on, while half (51%) say they usually leave it off [Author's underlining].

CONTRARIAN SOURCES

Anonymous. Ad agency memo, NBC, April 7, 1984. (IIb)
Bedell, Sally. "Study for TV Industry Says Viewers Are Watching Less." *New York Times*, April 10, 1983.(Ia)
BRAVO. Telephone Interview, 1992 (VID)
Calaum, Myles. "What Viewers Love/Hate About Television." *TV Guide* (May 12, 1979). (IIa, IVa)
Carter, Bill. "CBS in First Place of Ratings Race for Year." *New York Times*, April 15, 1992. (Ib)
Consumer Reports, "Television." September 1991 (IIIF).
Diamond, Edwin. "The Big Chill." *New York* (August 11, 1986). (Ib)
Fantel, Hans. "Satellite Dish Views With Cable." *New York Times*, August 9, 1984.
Gallup, George, Jr., and Dr. Frank Newport. "Swimming Still Americans' Favorite Recreation." *Gallup Poll News Service*, vol. 54, no. 47 (April 18, 1990) (IIIe) (VI E)

*See footnote at bottom of p. 229.

Peter D. Hart Associates. Washington, D.C. National telephone survey for *TV Guide.* "Would You Take $1,000,000 to Give Up TV Forever? In a Major New Poll, You Find Out Just How Much You Love Your TV." (October 10–16, 1992). Ic, IIa, IIId, IVa-b-c, Va, VII, VIII)

Harmetz, Aljean. "Home Video Industry Feeling Middle Age." *New York Times,* February 2, 1988 (VIa).

Kleinfeld, N.A. "As Viewers Wander, the Networks Scurry After." *New York Times,* February 26, 1989. (Ia)

National Association of Broadcasters. Telephone interview, 1992. (Ia, VIc)

Nichols, Pete M. "Rentals Set a Record in January, but Some People Are Hoping for a Broader Base than Just the Top 10 or 20 Films." *New York Times,* February 6, 1982. (VIa)

O'Connor, John J. "Cable Flexes Its Options." *New York Times,* December 27, 1987. (If).

Patterson, Thomas E. *The Mass Media Election.* New York: Praeger, 1980.

Public Broadcasting Service. Telephone conversation with author, 1980; Executive Summaries, January –March 1992.

The Roper Organization. *America's Watching: Public Attitudes Toward Television,* 1991. (IIIc*)

The Roper Organization. *Give Us More: A 1991 Study of America's Attitudes Toward Electronic Home Entertainment and Compact Disc Interactive, 1991.* (IIIb), (VI E).

Schwartz, Tony. "The Major TV Networks' Dwindling Audiences." *New York Times,* January 14, 1982. (Id)

Unger, Arthur. "Studies Show TV Viewers 'Tuning Out.' " *Christian Science Monitor,* April 25, 1983 (IIIa).

Weller, Barbara. "Don't Let Channel Switching Flip You Out." *USA Today,* January 29, 1987. (IIc)

*Fairness as well as wonder obliges me to report that the two Roper reports, published in the same year, tend to cancel each other out on the issue of American satisfaction with the viewing of broadcast television. *America's Watching,* commissioned primarily by the networks, reports significantly higher viewing pleasure. *Consumer Reports,* "Television." September 1991 (III F).

Notes

Thesis: The Medium As Myth

1 E. E. Evans-Pritchard, "For Example, Witchcraft," in *Witchcraft, Oracles, and Magic Among the Azande* (Oxford, 1937), pp. 64–67.

2 Cf. Bill Carter, "TV Industry Unfazed by Rise in Zapping," *New York Times*, March 2, 1992.

3 Network Television Association, *Network Television: The Gold Standard* (New York, Spring 1991.

4 As quoted in Douglas Davis, "Zapping the Myth of TV Power," *New York Times*, Op Ed, May 20, 1988.

5 Marie Winn, *The Plug-In Drug: Television, Children, and the Family* (New York, 1977).

6 Cf. Irving Howe, ed., *1984 Revisited: Totalitarianism in Our Century* (New York, Harper and Row, 1983).

7 The Roper Organization, "Give Us More: A 1991 Study of America's Attitudes Toward Electronic Home Entertainment and Compact Disc Interactive"; and Peter D. Hart Associates (Washington, D.C.), National Telephone Survey for *TV Guide*, "Would You Take $1,000,000 to Give Up TV Forever? In a Major New Poll You Find Out Just How Much You Love Your TV" (October 10–16, 1992).

8 Denis McQuail, ed., "Introduction," in *Sociology of Mass Communication* (New York, 1972), p. 15.

9 George Gilder, *Life After Television: The Coming Transformation of Media and American Life* (Knoxville, 1990); Kathleen Hall Jamieson, *Dirty Politics: Deception, Distraction, and Democracy* (New York, 1992); Jerry Mander, *Four Arguments for the Elimination of Television* (New York, 1975); and Neil Postman, *Amusing Ourselves to Death: Public Discourse in the Age of Show Business* (New York, 1986).

Myth One: TV Controls Our Voting

1 Cf. Elizabeth Kolbert, "Political Ads May Wound, but Not Win Races," *New York Times,* April 10, 1992.

2 Cf. Davis, "Zapping the Myth of TV Power, *New York Times,* Op Ed, May 20, 1988; Curtis Gans, "Is TV Turning Off the American Voter: The Fall-Off at the Polls," *New York Times,* Op Ed, July 3, 1988; and Joseph Vitale, "Chasing the Political Ad Dollar on TV," *Channels,* vol. 8, no. 1 (February 1988), pp. 91–93.

3 Joe McGinniss, *The Selling of the President 1968* (New York, 1969).

4 Jamieson, *Dirty Politics* (New York, 1992), p. 175.

5 Lawrence K. Grossman, "Reflections on Television's Role in American Presidential Elections," Discussion paper, D-3, Joan Shorenstein Barone Center, John F. Kennedy School of Government, Harvard University (January 1990), p. 1.

6 Marvin Kalb, "Campaign TV Coverage Has Gone Downhill Fast," *USA Today,* April 23, 1992.

7 Dayton Duncan, "Press Polls, and the 1980 Campaign: An Insider's Critique," Discussion paper, D-1, Joan Shorenstein Barone Center, John F. Kennedy School of Government, Harvard University (August 1989).

8 Doris Graber, *Processing the News: How People Tame the Information Tide* (New York, 1988), p. 17.

9 Charles Guggenheim, "For Accountability in Political Ads," *New York Times,* Op Ed, August 21, 1990.

10 Cf. Thomas E. Patterson and Robert D. McClure, *The Unseeing Eye: The Myth of Television Power in National Elections* (New York, 1976), pp. 74–90.

11 Kiku Adatto, "Soundbite Democracy: Network Evening News Presidential Campaign Coverage," Research paper, R-2, Joan Shorenstein Barone Center, John F. Kennedy School of Government, Harvard University (June 1990), p. 5.

12 Peter D. Hart and Doug Bailey, "People versus Politics: Citizens Discuss Politicians, Campaigns, and Political Reform," Report for the Centel Corporation, Washington, D.C., 1991.

13 Cf. Brian Lamb, *America's Town Hall* (Washington, D.C., 1988).

14 *No Sense of Place: The Impact of Electronic Media on Social Behavior* (New York, 1985), pp. 276–277.

15 Cf. "Washington *Post–ABC* News Poll," *Washington Times,* October 10, 1991; Maureen Dowd, "Image More Than Reality Became Image, Losers Say," *New York Times,* October 16, 1991; and Felicity Barringer, "Hill's Case Is Divisive to Women," *New York Times,* October 18, 1991.

16 Thomas Ferguson and Joel Rogers, "The Myth of America's Turn to the Right," *The Atlantic* (May 1986), pp. 43–63; and Kevin Phillips, *The Politics of Wealth and Poverty* (New York, 1991).

17 Walter Karp, "The Lie of TV's Political Power," *Channels* (May–June 1989), p. 40.

18 Hart and Bailey, "People versus Politics."

19 Thomas E. Patterson, *The Mass Media Election: How Americans Choose Their President* (New York, 1980).

20 Patterson and McClure, *The Unseeing Eye*, p. 134.

21 Graber, *Processing the News*, p. 90

22 Michael A. Lipton, "Exclusive TV Guide Poll: Campaign '88 and TV," *TV Guide* (January 23, 1988), pp. 2–7.

23 Times–Mirror Poll, "Bush vs. Dukakis vs. You," advertisement in *New York Times*, October 26, 1988.

24 Peter D. Hart Research Associates, *A Post-Election Survey Among Voters Conducted for AFSCME* (Washington, D.C., December 1988).

25 Richard L. Berke, "Cooking Up Some Ideas for Negative Campaigns," *New York Times*, September 27, 1992.

26 Lars-Erik Nelson, "Bush Jabs Giving Bill Momentum," *New York Daily News*, October 11, 1992.

27 Elizabeth Kolbert, "What Worked in 1988 Is No Aid to Bush Now," *New York Times*, October 6, 1992.

28 Douglas Davis, "Presidential Debates—My Way," *New York Times*, Op Ed, August 28, 1992.

29 Cf. Sandra Ball-Rokeach and Kathleen Reardon, "Monologue, Dialogue, and Telelog," *Advancing Communication Science*, eds. Robert Hawkins, John Kliemann, and Suzanne Pingree (Newbury Park, Calif., 1988), pp. 135–36.

Myth Two: TV Has Destroyed Our Students

1 John Holt, *The Underachieving School* (New York, 1969), pp. 16–17.

2 Wilbur Schramm, Jack Lyle, and Edwin B. Parker, *Television in the Lives of Our Children* (Stanford, 1961), pp. 178–188.

3 Winn, *The Plug-In Drug*, pp. 82–83.

4 Bob Hodge and David Tripp, *Children and Television: A Semiotic Approach* (Stanford, 1986), p. 49.

5 Harvey Graff, *The Literacy Myth, Literacy and Social Structure in the Nineteenth Century City* (New York, 1979).

6 Jonathan Kozol, *Savage Inequalities: Children in America's Schools* (New York, 1991), p. 236.

7 Hodge and Tripp, *Children and Television*, pp. 133, 138, 175–178.

8 Neil Hickey, "Is TV Violence Battering Our Kids?," *TV Guide* (August 22, 1992), pp. 8–22; based on an earlier study, published separately, *Violence on Television: A Symposium and Study Sponsored by the Editors of TV Guide* (1992).

9 Hodge and Tripp, *Children and Television*, p. 175.

10   Kathleen Teltsch, "To Teach Distant Pupils, Educators in Kentucky Turn On Interactive TV," *New York Times*, October 30, 1991.

Myth Three: TV Is (Our) Reality

1   Martin Mayer, *Whatever Happened to Madison Avenue? Advertising in the '90's* (Boston, 1991), p. 35.

2   Hal Himmelstein, *Television and the American Mind* (New York, 1984), pp. 77–119.

3   Christopher Lasch, *The Culture of Narcissism: American Life in an Age of Diminishing Expectations* (New York, 1978), p. 4.

4   Robert S. Lichter, Linda S. Lichter, and Stanley Rothman (with the assistance of Daniel Amundsen), *Watching America: What Television Tells Us about Our Lives* (New York, 1991), p. 49.

5   Helen E. Fisher, *The Sex Contract: The Evolution of Human Behavior* (New York, 1982); See also *Anatomy of Love: The Natural History of Monogamy, Adultery, and Divorce* (New York, 1992).

6   Paul Hollander, *Anti-Americanism: Critiques at Home and Abroad, 1965–1990* (New York, 1992).

7   As quoted in Elaine Pagels, *Adam, Eve, and the Serpent* (New York, 1988) p. 132.

8   Lichter et al., *Watching America*, p. 26.

9   Irv Letovsky, "And for the Bleep Word," *Los Angeles Times*, September 10, 1991.

10   Cf. Sar A. Levitan, Richard S. Belous, and Frank Gallo, *What's Happening to the American Family: Tensions, Hopes, Realities*, rev. ed. (Baltimore, 1988).

11   Arlene Skolnick, *Embattled Paradise: The American Family in an Age of Uncertainty* (New York, 1991), pp. 4–5.

12   Lichter et al., *Watching America*, p. 48.

13   Ibid., p. 119.

14   Cf. Ferguson and Rogers, "The Myth of America's Turn to the Right," pp. 43–53; Marc Cooper and Lawrence C. Sole, "All the Right Sources," *Mother Jones* (February–March 1990), pp. 1–12; FAIR (Fairness and Accuracy in Reporting), "Are You on the Nightline Guest List?" (January 1989), report.

15   As quoted in Bill Carter, "News Events Become Biggest Television Hits," *New York Times*, December 20, 1991.

16   Cf. "Professor Catharine A. MacKinnon: Defining Law on the Feminist Frontier," *New York Times Magazine* (October 6, 1991), pp. 28–31, 52–56; and Andrea Dworkin, *Our Blood: Prophecies and Discourses on Sexual Politics* (New York, 1976, 1981).

17   Erving Goffman, *Frame Analysis: An Essay on the Organization of Experience* (New York, 1974), p. 508.

18   Ibid., pp. 14–15.

19 Courtroom Television Network, *Viewer Comments*, Thomas confirmation hearings (transcribed October 14, 15, 1991); see also Elizabeth Kolbert, "Most in National Survey Say Judge Is the More Believable," *New York Times*, October 15, 1991.

20 Courtroom Television Network, *Viewer Comments*, Thomas confirmation hearings.

21 Courtroom Television Network, *Viewer Comments*, Smith trial (transcribed December 4, 5, 6, 8, 10, 1991).

22 Barringer, "Hill's Case Is Divisive to Women"; see also Kolbert, "Most in National Survey"; and Sen. Nancy L. Kassebaum, quoted in "Women in Senate Have Their Say Before the Vote Confirming Thomas," *New York Times*, October 19, 1992.

23 Levitan et al., *What's Happening to the American Family?*

24 Conrad Lodziak, *The Power of Television: A Critical Appraisal* (New York, 1986).

Myth Four: TV Pacifies Us

1 Bob Sipchen, "Tuning In to the Spirit: Like a Garrulous Patriarch, Television Now Presides at Most Holiday Gatherings," *Los Angeles Times*, November 22, 1991.

2 George Gallup, Jr., and Dr. Frank Newport, "Swimming Still America's Favorite Recreation," The Gallup Poll News Service, vol. 54, no. 47 (April 18, 1990).

3 Bureau of Labor Statistics, *Consumer Expenditures Index* (Washington, D.C., 1991).

4 Cf. Daniel Coleman, "How Viewers Grow Addicted to Television," *New York Times*, October 16, 1990; See also Robert McIlwraith, Robin Smith Jacobvitz, Robert Kubey, and Allison Alexander, "Television Addiction: Theories and Data Behind the Ubiquitous Metaphor," *American Behavioral Scientist*, vol. 35, no. 2 (November–December 1991), pp. 104–21; and Robert Kubey, "A Body at Rest Tends to Remain Glued to the Tube," *New York Times*, August 5, 1990.

5 Robert Kubey and Mikhaly Csikszentmihalyi, "Charting a New Course: The Experience Sampling Method," in *Television and the Quality of Life: How Viewing Shapes Everyday Experience* (New York, 1990) pp. 42–68.

6 McIlwraith et al., "Television Addiction."

7 American Psychiatric Association, *Diagnostic and Statistical Manual of Mental Disorders*, 3rd rev. ed. (Washington, D.C., 1987).

8 Ibid. (for all subsequent citations employed as subject titles in this chapter).

9 George Gallup, Jr., and R. Newport, "Americans Love and Hate their TV's," *San Francisco Chronicle*, October, 10, 1990.

10 Kubey, "A Body at Rest."

11 Robin Smith, "Television Viewing: A Study of the Habits and Opinions of the Citizens of Springfield, Mass.," unpublished, 1981; See also "Television Addiction," in J. Bryant and D. Anderson, eds., *Perspectives on Media Effects* (Hillsdale, N.J., 1986) pp. 109–28; and Lodziak, *The Power of Television*, pp. 20–22, 92–95.
12 Interview with author, 1984.
13 Cf. David Halberstam, *The Reckoning* (New York, 1986), pp. 311–18; see also Ronald Yates, "Game Plan," *Chicago Tribune Magazine*, February 16, 1992.
14 Halberstam, *The Reckoning*.
15 Cf. Robert Reich, *Tales of a New America* (New York, 1987); see also Douglas Davis, "America Needs to Pour Its Soul into Its Products," *New York Newsday*, April 6, 1989.
16 Frank Mankiewicz and Joel Swerdlow, "Reading, Learning, and Behavior," in *Remote Control: Television and the Manipulation of American Life* (New York, 1978), pp. 208–13.
17 Ibid., p. 209.
18 Michael J. Weiss, *The Clustering of America* (New York), 1988.

Myth Five: We *Love* TV

1 Bernard Weinraub, "Paying Respects to TV," *New York Times*, March 10, 1992.
2 Roland Barthes, *A Lover's Discourse: Fragments*, trans., Richard Howard (New York, 1978).
3 Lichter et al., *Watching America*, pp. 205–39.
4 Ibid., p. 26.
5 Ben Stein, *The View from Sunset Boulevard* (Garden City, N.Y., 1980), p. 87.
6 Todd Gitlin, *Inside Prime Time* (New York, 1983), p. 49.
7 Ibid., p. 53.
8 Ibid.
9 Robert Woodward, "True Confessions of a Nielsen Family," *New York Times*, July 13, 1991.
10 Kubey and Csikszentmihalyi, *Television and the Quality of Life*, p. 39.
11 Ibid., p. 101.
12 Ibid., pp. 42–68.
13 Ibid., p. xv.
14 Paul Fussell, "Notes on Class," *The Boy Scout Handbook and Other Observations* (New York, 1982), pp. 46–60.
15 James Gleick, *Chaos: Making a New Science* (New York, 1987).
16 Michael R. Kagay with Janet Elder, "Numbers Are No Problem for Pollsters. Words Are," *New York Times*, August 9, 1992.
17 Kubey and Csikszentmihalyi, *Television and the Quality of Life;* and *TV Guide* (October 10, 1992)

BIBLIOGRAPHY

Adatto, Kiku. "Soundbite Democracy." Research paper R–2. Joan Shorenstein Barone Center, John F. Kennedy School of Government, Harvard University (June 1990).

Arbitron Company. *Redefining the Television Audience.* Advertising bro-
chure. New York: 1990.

Auletta, Ken. *Three Blind Mice: How the Networks Lost Their Way.* New
York: Random House, 1991.

Ball-Rokeach, Sandra, and Kathleen Reardon, "Monologue, Dialogue,
and Telelog: Comparing an Emergent Form of Communication with
Traditional Forms," ed. Robert P. Hawkins, John M. Kliemann, and
Suzanne Pingree, *Advancing Communication Science: Merging Mass and
Interpersonal Processes.* Newbury Park, Calif.: Sage Publications, 1988.

Barringer, Felicity. "Hill's Case Is Divisive to Women." *New York Times,*
October 18, 1991.

Barthes, Roland. *A Lover's Discourse: Fragments.* Translated by Richard
Howard. New York, Farrar, Straus, 1978.

Bartlett, Donald L., and James B. Steele. *America: What Went Wrong.*
Kansas City: Andrews and McMeel, 1992.

Baumann, Zygmunt. "A Note on Mass Culture: On Infrastructure." In
The Sociology of Mass Communications, edited by Denis McQuail. New
York: Penguin, 1972.

Beck, Kirsten. *Cultivating the Wasteland: Can Cable Put the Vision Back in
TV?* New York: American Council for the Arts, 1983.

Berk, Richard L. "Cooking up Some Ideas for Negative Campaigns."
New York Times, September 27, 1992.

Bryant, J., and D. Anderson, eds. *Perspectives on Media Effects.* Hillsdale,
N.J., 1986.

Carter, Bill. "News Events Became Biggest Television Hits." *New York
Times,* December 20, 1991.

———. "Industry Unfazed by Rise in Zapping." *New York Times,* March
2, 1992.

Cavell, Stanley. *The World Viewed: Reflections on the Ontology of Film.* Cambridge: Harvard University Press, 1979.

Chaplin, J. P. *Dictionary of Psychology.* Rev. ed. New York: Dell, 1975.

Chiba, Susan. "Report Card on Educational Goals: At This Rate, the Nation Is Flunking." *New York Times,* October 2, 1991.

Coleman, Daniel. "How Viewers Grow Addicted to Television." *New York Times,* October 16, 1990.

Cook, Philip S., Douglas Gomery, and Lawrence W. Lichty, eds. *The Wilson Quarterly Reader: American Media.* Washington, D.C.: The Wilson Center Press, 1989.

Cooper, Marc, and Lawrence L. Sole. "All the Right Sources." *Mother Jones* (February–March 1990).

Davis, Douglas. "America Needs to Pour Its Soul into Its Products." *New York Newsday,* April 6, 1989.

———."Presidential Debates—My Way." *New York Times,* Op Ed, August 28, 1992.

———. "Zapping the Myth of TV Power." *New York Times,* Op Ed, May 20, 1988.

Davis, Stanley M. *Future Perfect.* New York: Addison-Wesley, 1987.

Dayan, Daniel, and Elihu Katz. *Media Events: The Live Broadcasting of History.* Cambridge: Harvard University Press, 1992.

Diamond, Edwin. "The Big Chill." *New York,* August 11, 1986.

Di Biaso, J. Richard. "The Revolution Will Be Televised." *Video Times* (Winter 1990).

Dionne, E. S., Jr. *Why Americans Hate Politics.* New York: Simon & Schuster, 1991.

Doherty, William. "Private Lives, Public Values: The New Pluralism—a Report from the Heartland." *Psychology Today* (May–June 1992).

Donovan, Robert J., and Ray Scherer. *Television News and American Public Life.* New York: Cambridge University Press, 1992.

Douglas, Mary, ed. *Rules and Meanings: The Anthropology of Everyday Knowledge.* New York: Penguin, 1973.

Dowd, Maureen. "Images More than Reality Become Image, Losers Say." *New York Times,* October 16, 1991.

Drucker, Peter F. "American Directions: A Forecast," *Harper's* (February 1965).

———. *The New Realities in Government and Politics/In Economics and Business/In Society and World View.* New York: Harper and Row, 1989.

Duncan, Dayton. "Press Polls, and the 1980 Campaign: An Insider's Critique." Discussion paper. Joan Shorenstein Barone Center, John F. Kennedy School of Government, Harvard University (August 1989).

Dworkin, Andrea. *Our Blood: Prophecies and Discourses on Sexual Politics.* New York, G. P. Putnam, 1976, 1981.

Enkelaar, Carol. *Behind the Screen: The Greatest TV Stories Never Told.* Naarden, The Netherlands: Hilversum, 1979.

Evans-Pritchard, E. E. "For Example, Witchcraft." In *Witchcraft, Oracles, and Magic Among the Azande*. London: Clarendon Press, 1937.

Eyler, David, and Andrea Bsaridon. "Far More Than Friendship: The New Rules for Reckoning with Sexual Attraction in the Workplace." *Psychology Today* (May–June 1992).

FAIR (Fairness and Accuracy in Reporting). "Are You on the Nightline Guest List?" (January 1989).

Ferguson, Thomas, and Joel Rogers. "The Myth of America's Turn to the Right." *The Atlantic* (May 1986).

Finn, Chester E., Jr. *We Must Take Charge: Our Schools and Our Future*. New York: The Free Press, 1991.

Fisher, Helen E. *The Sex Contract: The Evolution of Human Behavior*, New York: William Morrow, 1982.

Frazer, Sir James. *The New Golden Bough*, edited by Theodor H. Gaster. New York: Mentor Books and S. Y. Philips, 1959.

Fussell, Paul. *The Boy Scout Handbook and Other Observations*. New York: Oxford University Press, 1982.

Gallup, George, Jr., and R. Newport. "Americans Love and Hate Their TV's." *San Francisco Chronicle*, October 10, 1990.

Gallup, George, Jr., and Dr. Frank Newport. "Swimming Still Americans' Favorite Recreation." *Gallup Poll News Service*, vol. 54, no. 47, April 18, 1990.

Gans, Curtis. "Turning Off the American Voter," *New York Times*, Op Ed., July 3, 1988.

Gardner, Howard. *The Unschooled Mind: How Children Think and How Schools Should Teach*. New York: Basic Books, 1991.

Gerbner, George. "Mass Media and Human Communication Theory." *The Sociology of Mass Communications*, edited by Denis McQuail. New York: Penguin, 1972.

Gilder, George. *Life After Television: The Coming Transformation of Media and American Life*. Knoxville: Whittle Direct Books, 1990.

Gitlin, Todd. *Inside Prime Time*. New York: Pantheon, 1983.

———. *The Whole World Is Watching: Mass Media in the Making and the Unmaking of the Left*. Berkeley: University of California Press, 1988.

Gleick, James. *Chaos: Making a New Science*. New York: Penguin, 1987.

Goffman, Erving. *Frame Analysis: An Essay on the Organization of Experience*. New York: Harper Colophon, 1974.

Goodman, Cynthia. *Digital Visions: Computers and Art*. New York: Abrams, 1987.

Gouldner, Alvin W. *The Future of Intellectuals and the Rise of the New Class*. New York: The Seabury Press, 1979.

Graber, Doris. *Processing the News: How People Tame the Information Tide*. New York: Longman, 1984.

Graff, Harvey. *The Literacy Myth: Literacy and Social Structure in the Nineteenth-Century City*. New York: Academic Press, 1979.

Graubard, Stephen R. *Generations*. New York: W. W. Norton, 1979.

Greenfield, Patricia Marks. *Mind and Media: The Effects of Television, Video Games, and Computers*. Cambridge: Harvard University Press, 1984.

Gross, David M., and Sophronia Scott. "Twentysomething: Laid Back, Late Blooming or Just Lost? Overshadowed by the Baby Boomers, America's Next Generation Has a Hard Act to Follow." *Time* (July 16, 1990).

Grossman, Lawrence K. "Reflections on Television's Role in American Presidential Elections." Discussion paper D–3. Joan Shorenstein Barone Center, John F. Kennedy School of Government, Harvard University (January 1990).

Guggenheim, Charles. "The Accountability in Political Ads." *New York Times*, Op Ed, August 21, 1990.

Halberstam, David. *The Reckoning*. New York. William Morrow, 1986.

Harris, Louis. *Inside America: Who We Are, What We Think, Where We're Heading*. New York: Vintage, 1987.

Peter D. Hart Research Associates. "A Post-Election Survey Among Voters Conducted for A.F.S.C.M.E." Washington, D.C., December 1988.

Hart, Peter D., and Doug Bailey. "People versus Politics: Citizens Discuss Politicians, Campaigns, and Political Reform." Report for the Centel Corporation. Washington, D.C., 1991.

Havel, Vaclav. "The End of the Modern Era." *New York Times*, Op Ed, March 2, 1992.

Hickey, Neil. "Is TV Violence Battering Our Kids?" *TV Guide* (August 22, 1992).

Himmelstein, Hal. *Television, Myth, and the American Mind*. New York: Praeger, 1984.

Hodge, Bob, and David Tripp. *Children and Television: A Semiotic Approach*. Stanford: Stanford University Press, 1986.

Hollander, Paul. *Anti-Americanism: Critiques at Home and Abroad, 1965– 1990*. New York: Oxford University Press, 1992.

Holt, John. *The Underachieving School*. New York: Pitman Publishing, 1969.

Howe, Irving, ed. *1984 Revisited: Totalitarianism in Our Century*. New York: Harper and Row, 1983.

Illich, Ivan. *Tools for Conviviality*. New York: Harper and Row, 1973.

Jakobson, Linda. "Lies in Ink, Truth in Blood: The Role and Impact of the Chinese Media during the Beijing Spring of 1989." Discussion paper D–6, Joan Shorenstein Barone Center, John F. Kennedy School of Government, Harvard University (August 1990).

Jamieson, Kathleen Hall. *Dirty Politics: Deception, Distraction and Democracy*. New York: Oxford University Press, 1992.

Johnson, Nicholas. "TV: What Do We Do About It?" *Saturday Review* (July 11, 1970).

Kalb, Marvin. "Campaign TV Coverage Has Gone Downhill Fast." *USA Today*, April 23, 1992.

Karp, Walter. "The Lie of TV's Political Power." *Channels* (May–June 1989).

Kassebaum, Nancy L., and Barbara Mikulski. "Women in Senate Have their Say Before the Vote Confirming Thomas." *New York Times*, October 19, 1992.

Kirkpatrick, Jeane. "Dictatorships and Double Standards." *Commentary* magazine, vol. 68, pp. 34—45 (November 1979).

Kolbert, Elizabeth. "Most in National Survey Say Judge Is the More Believable." *New York Times*, October 15, 1991.

———"Political Ads May Wound, but Not Win Races." *New York Times*, April 10, 1992.

———"What Worked in 1988 Is No Aid to Bush Now." *New York Times*, October 6, 1992.

Kozol, Jonathan. *Prisoners of Silence: Breaking the Bonds of Adult Illiteracy in the United States*. New York: Continuum, 1980.

———. *Savage Inequalities: Children in America's Schools*. New York: Crown, 1991.

Kubey, Robert. "A Body at Rest Tends to Remain Glued to the Tube." *New York Times*, August 5, 1990.

Kubey, Robert, and Mikhaly Csikszentmihalyi. *Television and the Quality of Life: How Viewing Shapes Everyday Experience*. Hillsdale, N.J.: Lawrence Erlbaum Associates, 1990.

Lakoff, George, and Mark Johnson. *Metaphors We Live By*. Chicago: University of Chicago Press, 1980.

Lamb, Bryan (with the staff of C-SPAN). *America's Town Hall*. Washington, D.C.: Acropolis Books, 1988

Lasch, Christopher. *The Culture of Narcissism: American Life in an Age of Diminishing Expectations*. New York: Norton, 1979.

Letovsky, Irv. "And for the Bleep Word." *Los Angeles Times*, September 10, 1991.

Levitan, Sar A., Richard S. Belous, and Frank Gallo. *What's Happening to the American Family. Tensions, Hopes, Realities*. Rev. ed. Baltimore: Johns Hopkins University Press, 1991.

Lichter, Robert S., Linda Lichter, and Stanley Rothman (with Daniel Amundsen). *Watching America: What Television Tells Us about Our Lives*. New York: Prentice-Hall, 1991.

Lichty, Lawrence W. "Television in America: Success Story." In *American Media: The Wilson Quarterly Reader*, edited by Philip S. Cook, Douglas Gomery, and Lawrence W. Lichty. Washington, D.C.: The Wilson Center Press, 1989.

Lipton, Michael A. "Exclusive TV Guide Poll: Campaign '88 and TV." *TV Guide* (January 23, 1988).

Locke, John. "On Civil Government." In *Man and the State: The Political Philosophers*, edited by Saxe Cummins and Robert H. Linscott. New York: Random House, 1947.

Lodziak, Conrad. *The Power of Television: A Critical Appraisal.* New York: St. Martin's, 1986.

Mander, Jerry. *Four Arguments for the Elimination of Television*, New York: Morrow Quill, 1978.

Mankiewicz, Frank, and Joel Swerdlow. *Remote Control: Television and the Manipulation of American Life.* New York: Times Books, 1978.

Marc, David. *Comic Visions: Television Comedy and American Culture.* Boston: Unwin Hyman, 1989.

————. *Demographic Vistas: Television in American Culture.* Philadelphia: University of Pennsylvania Press, 1984.

Mayer, Martin. *Whatever Happened to Madison Avenue? Advertising in the 90's.* Boston: Little, Brown, 1991.

McGinniss, Joe. *The Selling of the President 1968.* New York: Trident Press, 1969.

McIlwraith, Robert, Robin Smith Jacobvitz, Robert Kubey, and Alison Alexander. "Television Addiction: Theories and Data Behind the Ubiquitous Metaphor." *American Behavioral Scientist*, vol. 35, no. 2 (November–December 1972).

McKibben, Bill. *The Age of Missing Information.* New York: Random House, 1992.

McQuail, Denis, ed. *The Sociology of Mass Communications: Selected Readings.* New York: Penguin, 1972.

Meyrowitz, Joshua. *No Sense of Place: The Impact of Electronic Media on Social Behavior.* New York: Oxford University Press, 1985.

Morito, Akio (with Edwin M. Reinfeld and Mitsuko Shimomura). *Made in Japan.* New York: Dutton, 1986.

Myers, Jack. *In Search of Value: Behind the Scenes in the War for the Consumer's Mind.* Parsippany, N.J.: Worldwide Marketing Leadership Panel, 1990.

Naisbitt, John. *Megatrends: Ten New Directions Transforming Our Lives.* New York: Warner, 1982.

Nelson, Lars-Erik. "Bush Jabs Giving Bill Momentum." *New York Daily News*, October 11, 1992.

Network Television Association. *Network Television: The Gold Standard.* New York: Network Television Associates, 1991.

Newcomb, Horace, and Robert Ally. *The Producer's Medium: Conversations with Creators of American TV.* New York: Oxford University Press, 1983.

Noelle-Neumann, Elizabeth. *The Spiral of Silence: Public Opinion, Our Second Skin.* Chicago: University of Chicago Press, 1984.

Otten, Charlotte M., *Anthropology and Art: Readings in Cross-cultural Aesthetics.* Garden City, N.Y.: The Natural History Press, 1977.

Pagels, Elaine. *Adam, Eve, and the Serpent.* New York: Random House, 1988.

Paglia, Camille, and Neil Postman. "She Wants Her TV! He Wants His Book!" *Harper's* (March 1991).

Patterson, Thomas E. *The Mass Media Election: How Americans Choose Their President.* New York: Praeger, 1980.

Patterson, Thomas E., and Robert D. McClure. *The Unseeing Eye: The Myth of Television Power in National Politics.* New York: Putnam, 1976.

Peters, Thomas J., and Robert H. Waterman. *In Search of Excellence: Lessons from America's Best-Run Companies.* New York: Harper and Row, 1982.

Peters, Tom. *Thriving on Chaos: Handbook for a Management Revolution.* New York: Knopf, 1987.

Phillips, Kevin. "The Pendulum of Politics." *Los Angeles Times,* July 16, 1989.

Poltrack, David. "Managing Market Diversity." Lecture for Insights and Opportunities '90, New York, June 1990.

Pool, Ithiel De Sola. *Technologies of Freedom.* Cambridge: Belknap Press of Harvard University Press, 1980.

Postman, Neil. *Amusing Ourselves to Death: Public Discourse in the Age of Show Business.* New York: Viking, 1986.

Price, Monroe, and John Wicklein. *Cable Television: A Guide for Citizen Action.* Philadelphia: Pilgrim Press, 1972.

Reich, Robert B. *Tales of a New America.* New York: Times Books, 1987.

Rosenberg, Bernard, and David Manning White, eds. *Mass Culture: The Popular Arts in America.* New York: The Free Press, 1957.

Sacks, Sheldon, *On Metaphor.* Chicago: University of Chicago Press, 1978.

Schramm, Wilbur, Jack Lyle, and Edwin B. Parker. *Television in the Lives of Our Children.* Stanford: Stanford University Press, 1961.

Shanker, Albert. "U.S. Expenditures on Education." In "Where We Stand," newspaper advertisement for the United Federation of Teachers. *New York Times,* May 5, 1991.

Sipchen, Bob. "Tuning in to the Spirit: Like a Garrulous Patriarch, Television Now Presides at Most Holiday Gatherings." *Los Angeles Times,* November 22, 1991.

Skolnick, Arlene. *Embattled Paradise: The American Family in an Age of Uncertainty.* New York: Basic Books, 1991.

Sloan Commission on Cable Communications. *On the Cable: The Television of Abundance.* New York: McGraw-Hill, 1971.

Smith, Robin. "Television Viewing: A Study of the Habits and Opinions of the Citizens of Springfield, Mass." Unpublished study, 1981.

Smythe, Dallas W. "Some Observations on Communications." *Audio-Visual Communication Review,* vol. 2 (1954).

Stein, Ben. *The View from Sunset Boulevard.* Garden City, N.Y.: Basic, 1980.

Strebeigh, Fred. "Prof. Catharine A. MacKinnon: Defining Law on the Feminist Frontier." *New York Times Magazine* (October 6, 1991).

Swerdlow, Joel. "A Question of Impact." *American Media: The Wilson Quarterly Reader*. Washington, D.C.: The Wilson Center Press, 1989.

U.S. News and World Report. "Television's Blinding Power: How It Shapes Our Views." Cover story. July 27, 1987.

Teltsch, Kathleen. "To Teach Distant Pupils, Educators in Kentucky Turn on Interactive TV." *New York Times*, October 30, 1991.

Times-Mirror Poll. "Bush vs. Dukakis vs. You." Advertisement in *New York Times*, October 26, 1988.

Toll, Robert C. *The Entertainment Machine: American Show Business in the Twentieth Century*. New York: Oxford University Press, 1982.

Vance, Carole S., ed. *Pleasure and Danger: Exploring Female Sexuality*. Boston: Routledge and Kegan Paul, 1984.

Vitale, Joseph. "Chasing the Political Dollar on TV." *Channels*, vol. 8, no. 2 (February 1988).

"Washington Post U.S. News Poll." *Washington Times*, October 10, 1991.

Weinraub, Bernard. "Paying Respects to TV." *New York Times*, March 10, 1992.

Weiss, Michael J. *The Clustering of America*. New York: Harper and Row, 1988.

White, Theodore H. *America in Search of Itself: The Making of the President 1956–80*. New York: Harper and Row, 1982.

Winn, Marie. *The Plug-In Drug: Television, Children and the Family*. New York: Penguin, 1977.

Wood, Elizabeth J., and Floris W. Wood. *She Said, He Said: What Men and Women Really Think About Money, Sex, Politics, and Other Issues*. New York: Poseidon Press, 1991.

Woodward, Richard B. "True Confessions of a Nielsen Family." *New York Times*, July 13, 1991.

Yates, Ronald. "Game Plan." *Chicago Tribune Magazine*, February 16, 1992.

INDEX

ABOUT THE AUTHOR

DOUGLAS DAVIS, critic, artist, educator, has taught media theory at several universities. A consultant in media for the Rockefeller Foundation in 1990–91, he has also created innovative video programs for TV networks in the United States and Europe. He has written about culture and politics for *The New York Times, Newsweek, The Los Angeles Times, Vanity Fair,* and *Esquire.* He lives in New York City.